VIRTUE
and
PSYCHOLOGY

VIRTUE
and
PSYCHOLOGY

Pursuing Excellence
in Ordinary Practices

BLAINE J. FOWERS

American Psychological Association
Washington, DC

Published by
American Psychological Association
750 First Street, NE
Washington, DC 20002
www.apa.org

To order
APA Order Department
P.O. Box 92984
Washington, DC 20090-2984
Tel: (800) 374-2721
Direct: (202) 336-5510
Fax: (202) 336-5502
TDD/TTY: (202) 336-6123
Online: www.apa.org/books/
E-mail: order@apa.org

In the U.K., Europe, Africa, and the Middle
East, copies may be ordered from
American Psychological Association
3 Henrietta Street
Covent Garden, London
WC2E 8LU England

Typeset in Goudy by World Composition Services, Inc., Sterling, VA

Printer: United Book Press, Inc., Baltimore, MD
Cover Designer: Cassandra Chu Design, San Francisco, CA
Technical/Production Editor: Genevieve Gill

The opinions and statements published are the responsibility of the authors, and such opinions and statements do not necessarily represent the policies of the American Psychological Association.

Library of Congress Cataloging-in-Publication Data

Fowers, Blaine J., 1956-
    Virtue and psychology : pursuing excellence in ordinary practices / Blaine J. Fowers.
        p. cm.
    Includes bibliographical references and index.
    ISBN 1-59147-251-2
    1. Psychology—Moral and ethical aspects. 2. Virtue—Psychological aspects.
3. Ethics—Psychological aspects.   I. Title.

    BF76.4.F69 2005
    174'.915—dc22   2005002126

British Library Cataloguing-in-Publication Data
A CIP record is available from the British Library.

Printed in the United States of America
First Edition

To Jeremy and Alyssa,
whose innate trust and dear spirits
have inspired me to learn what I can of virtue.

CONTENTS

PREFACE

I trust that it is acceptable to admit joy in scholarship, for writing this book has been one of the most joyous experiences of my academic life. It is the outgrowth of many years of avid study of virtue ethics, which I have found deeply rewarding both personally and professionally. Virtue ethics has been enormously personally inspiring to me even though when I first began to investigate it, I did not have any particular scholarly destination in mind. As I read further, I found that virtue ethics had a great deal to say about why many features of my professional activities seem indispensable and central, even though psychological theory and professional training are either silent about or depreciatory toward them. These features include the importance of character strengths such as courage, honesty, and justice and the ability to recognize what is central in our circumstances. Virtue ethics highlights the concept that excellence is more about the kind of person one is than the number of possessions or honors one accumulates. This perspective reminds us of the deep and inextricable dependence we have on each other for living well. Virtue ethics calls these and other vital concepts out of the dim shadows of forgetfulness into the light of comprehensibility. I hope that some of the joy I experienced in this work of reclamation comes through to you, the reader.

To some degree, excellent psychologists already understand and practice in ways that reflect the concepts of virtue ethics, but whatever degree of understanding exists, it is largely implicit, for we do not have an adequate language to articulate, evaluate, and teach this manner of activity. I find it enormously useful to have a framework and a vocabulary for understanding, discussing, and teaching these concepts and practices. I wrote this book to share that framework and vocabulary with my fellow psychologists. The book is my expression of cautious optimism that we can find ways to better recognize, conceptualize, and practice these essential elements of our profession.

I have tried to set out a coherent framework that can indicate what is required for a virtue-based account of psychological matters. One of the chief difficulties attendant on the increasing popularity of virtue in psychology is the belief that we all already know what virtue and character are. I am convinced that it is essential to move beyond commonsense notions of virtue and to reflect carefully on what we mean by the term. In the absence of thoughtful consideration, we are likely to incorporate the modern preoccupation with individualism and fascination with means–ends reasoning without even recognizing how incompatible these convictions are with virtue ethics.

Even an entire book on the relevance of virtue for psychology can barely scratch the surface. No single book can capture all of what needs to be said about the place of virtue ethics in psychology. I clearly have neither the first word nor the last word on this topic. One of the clearest signs of success for this book will be a vigorous conversation in the discipline about just what virtue is and what role it can play in our practices. I look forward to that conversation.

One of the major obstacles to exploring the worth of virtue ethics for psychology is our traditional attempt to separate fact and value. In spite of this disciplinary proclivity, psychology as a discipline has gradually, if very reluctantly, recognized that there is an ineluctable ethical dimension to all that we do. The positive psychology movement, with its emphasis on desirable, worthwhile, and praiseworthy actions and outcomes, is one outgrowth of this dawning realization. If we are promoting some goods as psychologists (and it is hard to deny this), then we may be best served by clarifying what these goods are and developing theoretical resources for understanding goodness. Although positive psychologists have done us the service of bringing us up to the boundaries of the goods with which psychologists occupy ourselves, they have stopped short of transcending conventional understandings of what is good. I sense a deep reluctance among the leaders of this effort to embrace fully and directly the fact that our professional practices are defined by the personal and social goods that we are seeking. This reluctance is an understandable, if questionable, concession to the canons that define contemporary scientific respectability. In contrast, one of the primary themes of this book is the conceptual exploration of what is good, drawing on the resources of ancient philosophers who were not chagrined by the topic.

Throughout this book, I challenge the deeply problematic and quixotic distinctions psychology has attempted to make between fact and value, empirical and ethical, objective and subjective by clarifying how these aspects of our lifeworld are inextricably intertwined. Ironically, the attempt to avoid moral concerns on the way to purely objective science and practice has distorted our attempts to study and improve that world. The science and practice of psychology are inherently ethical endeavors that we can pursue best if we are clear about the goods we seek and cultivate the character strengths that support that pursuit.

I came to write this book as I struggled over the years to articulate the everyday ways in which psychologists are engaged in irreducibly ethical activities. My efforts to illuminate our moral commitments and ideals have taken many forms, including empirical studies, hermeneutic analyses, and virtue-ethics-based descriptions of our professional practices. I have drawn on philosophical, historical, anthropological, and sociological sources over the years to make the case that we psychologists embody and express deeply held ethical views that animate and guide our scholarly and practical work. In particular, I have found hermeneutic philosophy and critical theory useful in throwing light on these commitments. I have used these resources freely in the project of highlighting the ethical dimension of psychology, but throughout I have endeavored to make the complex and subtle arguments of philosophers, the vastly detailed accounts of historians and anthropologists, and the broad sweep of sociologists and political theorists accessible to and practical for psychologists. I have redoubled my efforts in the service of accessibility and practicality in this book. I have endeavored to imbue this book with sufficient philosophical depth to be illuminating for psychologists, but to retain a straightforward presentation that will also be readable and useful.

My fascination with hermeneutic philosophy led me inexorably back to Aristotle, who was enormously influential for some of my philosophical heroes: Hans-Georg Gadamer, Alasdair MacIntyre, and Charles Taylor. As I delved into virtue ethics, it became clearer and clearer that it provided a uniquely valuable framework with which we can organize the many ways in which we seek important goods in psychology and the essential characteristics that make those pursuits possible. Virtue ethics has a clear focus on the pursuit of goodness, the character strengths that make that pursuit possible, and the practical wisdom that guides one in seeking what is good.

Although I hope it is unnecessary, I say at the outset that in writing this book I do not claim any moral superiority or special access to ethical truth. I credit the study of virtue ethics with much-needed personal growth and professional clarity, yet I remain a deeply flawed, frequently confused, and clearly limited mortal. I hope that no one will expect more of me in this book or in my everyday activities, for they are bound to be disappointed by the clay feet they will inevitably find.

I want to thank the many people who have helped me to bring this book into being, including many wonderfully supportive students and colleagues at the University of Miami. I am deeply indebted to the many friends and colleagues who have buttressed my efforts through their explicit encouragement, but perhaps more important, through embodying, in unmistakable form, the virtues I discuss in this book. My appreciation for this support goes particularly to David Fowers, Lynne Harkless, and Jean-Phillipe Laurenceau. I have been especially encouraged to pursue this topic by several people with whom I have had the privilege to learn about the joys of character friendship in our joint efforts to deepen psychological discourse. It has been wonderful to share this project, with deep affection, occasional hilarity, and long toil, with Frank Richardson, Philip Cushman, and Barbara Held. My thoughts and their expression have been wonderfully deepened and clarified by the thoughtful comments and insightful questions of my editor, Ed Meidenbauer, and three kind, encouraging, but firm readers of the manuscript, Alan Tjeltveit, Brent Slife, and Barry Schwartz. I am deeply moved and inspired by the generosity with which all of you, as friends and colleagues, have showered me. Foremost among those to whom I am grateful, for living a life of character, for sharing life goals, for undying support, and for endless patience, is my wife Susan. I have learned more about virtue from her quiet goodness than from a library of scholarly texts.

I

VIRTUE AND WHAT IS GOOD IN PSYCHOLOGY

1

THE VITAL ROLE OF VIRTUE
IN PSYCHOLOGY

Good, the more communicated, more abundant grows.
—John Milton, *Paradise Lost*

What kind of account of human being and behavior can we give without concepts such as generosity, loyalty, justice, honesty, and courage? How might psychology be distorted and impoverished by the startling absence of these aspects of our humanity from the predominant theories of our discipline? I suggest that our field of vision is drastically narrower and shallower as a result of our traditional exclusion of these and related virtue concepts. Without virtue concepts, the generosity and compassion of a Mother Teresa is reduced to an exchange of beneficence for the gratification of feeling saintly or at best reduced to "prosocial" behavior. The loyalty of devoted spouses and patriots is seen in terms of the self-interested pursuit of rewards. The courage of New York firefighters and police on September 11, 2001, may be portrayed as thrill seeking, machismo, or a form of mastery motivation. How can we understand the profound ties that individuals feel toward their country, their families, and their cultural groups without considering the virtue of loyalty? If we disqualify generosity, how can we conceptualize the joy in giving without expectation of recompense? If we do not recognize justice as a character strength, how can we understand the devotion to fairness that might actually be costly to the individual?

We live in a time when our economy has been shredded by widespread corporate fraud and our world has become dramatically more dangerous because of domestic and international terrorism. These events have made it clear that character strengths such as honesty and courage are indispensable to fashioning a strong, secure, and productive society. Can psychology contribute to such an important effort or must we remain on the sidelines of the quickening cultural conversation about character?

A growing number of psychologists are beginning to explore the relevance and importance of virtue as an explanatory model for improving our understanding of the full range of human action. For example, virtue figures very prominently in the burgeoning positive psychology movement, where it is given a large role in explaining more praiseworthy human actions and motivations (Baltes & Staudinger, 2000; Baumeister & Exline, 1999; McCullough & Snyder, 2000; Peterson & Seligman, 2004; Seligman & Csikszentmihalyi, 2000; Sheldon & King, 2001). Other authors have explored the place of character in existing theories and practices (Fowers, 2000, 2001, 2003; Kitchener, 2000; Meara & Day, 2003; Meara, Schmidt, & Day, 1996; Richardson, 2003; Sandage & Hill, 2001; Tjeltveit, 1999, 2003).

Our discipline desperately needs conceptual enrichment to account adequately for praiseworthy activity and the characteristics that allow humans to flourish by successfully pursuing their ideals. Although the initial explorations of how virtue ethics can contribute to psychology are promising, most have been too brief to allow a thorough exploration of this possibility. This book provides the systematic theoretical perspective that has been lacking in our efforts to use a virtue framework so far. In this book, I show how the incorporation of this framework will dramatically expand and deepen the discipline.

I define and discuss virtue much more thoroughly in chapter 2, but let me provide a working definition here to clarify what I mean by that term. The original Greek term for virtue was *aretē*, best translated as excellence. Virtues are, simply, human excellences, and I focus on excellences of character in this book. *Virtues are the character strengths that make it possible for individuals to pursue their goals and ideals and to flourish as human beings.* Character strengths play an integral role in the warp and woof of ordinary life because "an *excellence* or *virtue* . . . is nothing but a characteristic which makes the difference between functioning and functioning well" (Broadie, 1991, p. 37, italics in original). The capacity to act generously, loyally, courageously, honestly, and justly allows individuals to fulfill their potential as the rational social beings they are. These and other character strengths are just as necessary for psychologists to engage in the best psychological practices as they are for living well in our personal lives.

Virtues are multidimensional characteristics that have considerable overlap with standard psychological topics. Having virtue means having a cognitive understanding of the character strength and a spontaneous motivation to act in accordance with it. Acting in the best way creates a reliable disposition or habit of acting well, and this activity further strengthens the disposition to act well in pursuing worthwhile aims. The dispositional, cognitive, emotional, and behavioral aspects of character strengths are integrated seamlessly. This integration of knowledge and affect regarding how to act well is one of the most appealing aspects of virtue ethics. Individuals who have developed good character *want* to act ethically because they are attracted by what is good. The attraction to worthwhile goals elicits a desire to pursue them wholeheartedly rather than being conflicted between duty and desire. This internal motivation is a key feature of virtue ethics, as I discuss in chapters 2 and 3. The ability to make wise decisions about how best to pursue one's aims, which character strengths are relevant, and in what way is also central to a virtue framework. This capacity is known as practical wisdom, which is the focus of chapters 5 through 8.

THE PROMISE OF VIRTUE

The central thesis of this book is that virtue ethics provides a deeply integrative conceptual framework that ties many diverse aspects of psychology together and thereby offers a very rich account of the neglected areas of praiseworthy human activity and of excellence as a psychologist. One attractive feature of the virtue perspective is that it is equally applicable to professional and ordinary activity and does not force us to adopt a fragmenting dichotomy between these two domains. Virtue ethics begins with a focus on what is good for human beings as the particular creatures that we are. Thus, a virtuous life is a life lived well as a whole, with a coherent, integrated set of aims, the strengths of character necessary to pursue those ends, and the social bonds that give place and purpose to our activities. It is integrative in taking the agent's entire life as the domain of interest, not just some particular incidents or experiences. The concept of virtue encompasses essential features of individuals' psychological lives—dispositions, cognitions, affect, motivation, goals, behavior, relationships, communities, and society—and shows how these elements of life can be brought into an integrated whole. Virtue ethics also provides a way to bridge the frequently criticized separation of facts and values in psychology, as I discuss later in this chapter.

We can assess the value of a virtue ethics framework for psychology in several ways. Its merit, like that of any theoretical perspective, can be evaluated in its ability to organize, explain, and integrate research results that were not previously interrelated. Virtue ethics should have important things to say about central domains of human life such as work, relationships, social and political life, individual goals, and individual well-being. To be worthy of psychologists' consideration, virtue ethics must make contributions to our understanding of key aspects of human functioning, and these formulations should not be derivative of some other theoretical point of view. We can judge the contributory value of virtue ethics to psychology by the extent to which it allows us to see and understand aspects of human behavior that have been previously opaque. I focus particularly on the domains of human goals, motivation, and social bonds, and on how these domains can be harmonized conceptually in both personal and professional activities. I argue that virtue ethics provides an integrative framework that encompasses ordinary and professional activities, episodes of behavior and the individual's life as a whole, research and practice, personal and professional ethics, individual identity and cultural belonging, and private and social life.

Of course, the discipline of psychology has, for most of its history, actively eschewed examination of virtue as part of its effort to separate presumably objective facts about behavior and presumably subjective considerations about morality and values. If you are perusing or reading this book, I assume that you are willing to question the traditional attempt to separate facts and values in that way. It is important to recognize that the attempt to create a value-neutral science and practice, valiant as it has been, has failed us in many ways. One of its key failings is the unacknowledged infusion of individualism and instrumentalism, two key aspects of contemporary moral frameworks, into our theories, research, and practice, as I discuss later in the chapter. Another shortcoming of the attempt at value neutrality is that it distorts and obscures much of what we as psychologists do and why we do it. The submerging of questions of character is an important instance of how the ethical dimension of our profession has been obscured and driven "underground" to adopt an ostensibly value-neutral stance.

There are many ways in which we as psychologists already study, teach, and intervene that are not only consistent with aspects of character but directly involve or presuppose virtues for their success. Our professional predilection to see our work as free of moral color obscures the importance of character strengths in psychological research and practice. I argue that what is at issue is not so much whether we will pursue the general topic of virtue in psychology as whether we will recognize the extent to which we already do. There are two benefits to acknowledging the role of character in psychological practice, research, and teaching. The first is that we will understand and represent our work more accurately and comprehensively. The conceptual tools, practical applications, and training opportunities illuminated by a virtue framework can significantly deepen and enrich our professional work.

The second is that virtue ethics provides a perspective that allows us to see and explore vitally important ethical questions that are often neglected in psychology. Is all human behavior egoistically motivated, or are there goals and activities that are possible only if they are shared with others?

Are all human actions characterized in means–ends terms, or are there activities that are inseparably linked to the ends the actor is seeking? Are our professional activities and human action in general a matter of learning and applying techniques, or is there a deeper relationship between the characteristics, sensibilities, and judgment of the actor and the quality of the action? Are human lives a series of episodic goal pursuits, or are there features that unify and organize individual lives? Are all goals equally important, or are there some goals that have priority and serve to organize other aims? This book addresses these questions and shows how virtue ethics sheds light on many underdeveloped aspects of professional practice and ordinary activities.

Two brief examples indicate how the incorporation of a virtue framework can enhance our professional endeavors and our personal lives. First, we commonly expect researchers to report their findings accurately, and science is utterly dependent on this kind of honesty. From time to time, spectacular cases of scientific fraud remind us that we cannot take this honesty for granted. Moreover, there are enormously powerful incentives for fabricating results, misrepresenting findings, or "massaging" data, including academic tenure and promotion, grant funding, public recognition, and political influence. In the face of these inducements, what keeps scientists honest? One reason for honesty may be fear of being discovered in fraud. Another reason may be a simple predilection to follow the rules in a conventional manner. Although honesty based on these kinds of motives is better than dishonesty, these are not the most satisfactory or mature rationales for truth telling. A third reason for honesty that is more powerful and appealing is an enduring interest in truthfulness that grows out of a personal devotion to truth seeking. At its best, being a scientist involves one in a genuine search for the best ways to understand phenomena of interest. Anything less than this may not even count as science. Dishonesty about one's results is not merely an error. Rather, it is a kind of bad faith. Deception is intrinsically contradictory to science because it undermines the very possibility of pursuing the most accurate account of a phenomenon by distorting or fabricating one's findings. Scientists who willingly and consistently report procedures and findings accurately are enacting the virtue of honesty. Their honesty serves the good of expanding our knowledge, and the only way to pursue this good is to be truthful about one's results. It seems clear to me that we can enhance our science by emphasizing honesty based on a love of truth rather than being honest only for the purposes of following rules or avoiding consequences.

Obviously, I am not suggesting that every psychologist will conduct research motivated purely by the love of truth. This kind of excellence may never predominate. Nevertheless, a well-articulated account of scientific excellence can dramatically improve our discipline. Above all, it provides a clear aspirational standard by which we can measure our own activities and find guidance as we conduct our inquiries, serving as a necessary and inspiring alternative to the inducements of bald ambition, prestige, and material rewards. Recruiting students with a focus on attracting those who are drawn to truth adds an important dimension to our admissions efforts. Training students to love truth will enrich and sustain their professional efforts and the future of our discipline as well.

Virtues are also highly relevant to everyday life. Consider the kind of person most of us would want as a mate. It seems obvious that we want our closest companion to be honest, loyal, generous, and fair. We want our lifelong partner to have the virtue of friendship, which leads him or her to be genuinely devoted to our best interest and able to pursue valued goals with us. Moreover, we want our mate to demonstrate these qualities in a dependable way rather than according to mood or reinforcement contingencies. We also want our spouses to be honest, loyal, and generous gladly rather than reluctantly. It is difficult to conceive of a high-quality, long-term relationship in which the partners do not have characteristics like honesty, loyalty, and justice (Fowers, 2000). In short, character excellence is vital to our hopes and experiences in marriage and other long-term personal relationships.

The promise of a virtue ethics framework for psychology is that it highlights traits such as scientific honesty and loyalty in relationships in ways that standard psychological theory and training give short shrift. Our ability to recognize, investigate, and practice these admirable qualities is largely dependent on having a framework that directs our attention to them and helps us to make sense of them. Virtue ethics also shows how these character strengths can be cultivated and practiced.

STRUCTURE OF THE BOOK

Because terms like *virtue*, *character*, and *goodness* are part of our ordinary vocabulary, it is important for me to clarify how I use them here. It is also important for me to explain the structure of this book, because many readers will wonder why I have structured the book around the topics of human goods and practical wisdom rather than around a catalogue of specific virtues.

Initial Definitions

The commonsense approach to virtue is to list and describe specific virtues such as courage or loyalty. Such specific character strengths are concrete, relatively easy to grasp, and they have a place in our ordinary speech about praiseworthy actions. One of the purposes of this book is to deepen our understanding of virtue by taking us beyond commonsense ideas and showing how a systematic conceptual understanding of virtue can be illuminating for psychology. In spite of the common usage of virtue terms, the conceptual framework of virtue ethics will be unfamiliar to many readers, so clarifying the terminology I use is important. *Virtue ethics* is the term used to describe the contemporary study of virtue. Virtue ethicists distinguish between particular virtues (e.g., honesty, generosity) and virtue in general. I use the singular term *virtue* to refer to the overall constellation of particular virtues and the wisdom to enact them well. I refer to specific virtues from time to time as concrete examples of how virtue shows up. This book focuses primarily on the general conceptual structure of virtue rather than providing a catalogue of specific virtues. I have chosen to emphasize the more general concept of virtue because I believe that we must begin by understanding what we mean by the broader concept of virtue itself before we delve deeply into specific virtues. If our understanding of virtue in general is inadequate or erroneous, these shortcomings will lead us to misconceive all of the specific virtues.

The term *character* is central to virtue ethics because it refers to the overall state of an individual with regard to virtue. Character is extremely important, because the primary concern of virtue ethics is the kind of person one is, the way in which one's life shapes up as a whole. Character refers to the overall quality of a person's life and what it amounts to as a totality. From this perspective, it does not make sense to talk about virtues as distinct traits that may or may not have any relationship to one another or to the quality of an individual's overall life. An individual's character can be more or less virtuous, or more or less developed. A person with good character is a virtuous person, one whose actions embody the virtues. A person with bad character is one whose actions are characteristically cruel, exploitive, or self-indulgent. Most individuals fall somewhere between these extremes. I use the phrase *character strengths* synonymously with virtues—a specific virtue such as generosity is also a character strength.

Virtue and the Virtues

In a very ambitious and courageous book, Peterson and Seligman (2004) presented a *DSM*-style classification scheme of virtues that they hoped would foster empirical research through defining specific virtues and proposing measurement parameters. Their detailed definitions and empirical emphasis are valuable in supporting the careful study of virtues. These authors are passionate advocates for the positive psychology movement, and they designed an approach to virtues that they hoped would convince psychologists that positive psychology is scientifically respectable.

Unfortunately, Peterson and Seligman's (2004) strong focus on cata-loguing specific virtues led them to neglect the development of an adequate general concept of virtue. This creates two significant problems. First, the whole point of studying virtue is to understand how virtues contribute to human flourishing. This means that the central feature of a virtue framework must be a rich concept of what is good for humans.

Peterson and Seligman (2004) hoped to document the presence and effectiveness of virtues in fostering "the good life." Although they recognized that the good life has to be broader and richer than individual outcomes such as subjective well-being, creativity, productivity, and longevity, they had very little to say about transcending individual outcomes. In 644 pages of text, they devoted 2 pages to defining a criterion for their list of strengths, specifying, "A strength contributes to various fulfillments that constitute the good life, for oneself and for others" (p. 17). This criterion sounds promising, but these authors had very little to say about what fulfillment or the good life consist in. In their description of each character strength, they offered a short paragraph to discuss how the strength meets this criterion. Examples include "Creation feels good" (p. 96) and,

> Bravery is fulfilling. We feel good when we do the right thing. . . . The world is filled with things that produce fear. . . . But when we can act regardless of our fear, segregating our physiology from the rest of us, we are fulfilled. (p. 199)

On rare occasions, Peterson and Seligman (2004) referred to larger, richer, or more social goods, but this focus on individual fulfillment predominates.

In keeping with the prevailing objectivism in psychology, these authors described the good life primarily in terms of "positive subjective experience" (p. 5), even though they aspired to a richer concept of goodness. To give one short example of how a richer concept of goodness would show up, consider the goodness that bravery serves. The point of bravery is not so much that we feel good because we have been valiant (although this is perfectly acceptable). The point of acting against our fears is that we are pursuing some important goal or good (victory in battle, combating injustice, deepening a personal relationship through self-disclosure). The virtue of courage is inextricably tied to seeking such goals or goods in spite of our fear. Simply acting counter to fear without a worthwhile aim is mere bravado or thrill seeking. Taking risks is only praiseworthy when there is something important at stake. This helps us to differentiate between the courage of a firefighter and the thrill seeking of a bungee jumper. In contrast to Peterson and Seligman's (2004) approach, I emphasize the centrality of what is good by making human goods the primary theme of Part I of this book. In these chapters, I articulate a rich concept of what is good, a conception that I believe can be transformative for psychology.

The second general problem with Peterson and Seligman's (2004) approach is that their preference for empirical accessibility over theoretical elucidation led them to choose a measurement-driven approach to virtue that emphasized "subdividing it . . . and distinguishing various strengths from one another . . ." (p. 6). Subdividing virtues in this way is deeply incompatible with the "whole person" focus of virtue theory, as I argue in chapter 3. Virtues cannot be understood in a piecemeal fashion, because the full import of virtue is only evident in relation to the overall shape of one's life and the harmonious integration of character. Although these authors gestured at "seeing a virtue as a property of the whole person" (p. 87), their entire scheme is one of division into component parts (six virtues divided into 24 more or less independent components). They illustrated their piecemeal approach to virtue as follows: "We are comfortable saying that someone is of good character if he or she displays but 1 or 2 strengths within a virtue group" (p. 13).

To their credit, these authors recognized that their classification system lacks a rich, systematic theoretical framework. They modestly noted, "[I]t was beyond our ability to specify a reasonable theory . . ." (p. 6) and hoped that "yet-to-be-articulated theory [will] make sense of the classification entries, individually and collectively" (p. 9). This book provides such a theory, although it may not be the sort of theory Peterson and Seligman (2004) had in mind.

Virtue and Goodness

I focus especially on the pursuit of what is good as the heart of virtue, for virtues are the character strengths that make that pursuit possible. The theme of Part I of the book is an exploration of what is good, emphasizing goodness as the central concept of virtue (chap. 2). In chapter 3, I highlight the ways that pursuing what is good plays a role in integrating the way that one's life shapes up as a whole. In chapter 4, I clarify the importance of shared goods for virtue and a good life. Understanding virtue requires frank discussion of what is good, of what is praiseworthy, and of what is vicious, which psychologists often find uncomfortable. One reason for this discomfort is the fear of moral coercion. As I discuss throughout the book, goodness is an open-ended concept, because a historical community's concepts of goodness evolve over time, partly through contact with new circumstances and other cultural groups. I begin with quite ordinary conceptions of what is good, including objects, outcomes, states of affairs, or experiences that are seen as worthwhile by individuals and their historical communities.

Examples of goods include democracy, loving relationships, knowledge, and artistic excellence. Many virtue ethicists use the term *the good*, but I have chosen the alternative phrasing of *what is good* to emphasize that I do not have a predetermined, circumscribed idea of what is good.

In any viable cultural group, there is ongoing debate and flux in the understanding of what is good. From a classical point of view, all who believe that they can definitively specify *the* good are guilty of hubris, or excessive pride, because they are adopting a godlike posture. This means that ordinary finite human beings are unlikely to be able to pin down a definitive, once-and-for-all view of what is good. I certainly do not claim to be able to do so. For this reason, I present virtue ethics from a secular point of view that is neither allied with nor hostile to contemporary political or religious viewpoints. I rely on classical sources (primarily Aristotle's *Nicomachean Ethics*, 1998) rather than contemporary political or religious doctrines.

We can acknowledge the elusiveness of a conclusive statement about what is good without conceding that anything goes, however. It is all too easy to use terms like *virtue* and *goodness* to mask tyranny, self-righteousness, or even viciousness. Consider an extreme example such as Hitler and the Nazis. Hitler and his minions certainly could have claimed that they were acting virtuously and that they were seeking a great good for humankind in purifying the human race and setting the "master race" to rule all others. The Nazi vision of "goodness" portrays humans at our best as filled with hatred toward particular groups and willing to engage in mass murder in the service of eliminating some and dominating and exploiting others. Any such claims to virtue and goodness are not credible because they are a cover for hatred, bigotry, and injustice. Seen with open eyes, such a description of what is best in human beings is nothing short of appalling.

Most discussions about what is good for humans are not so clear-cut. There are many different ways to see what is good, and I suggest that the capacity to respectfully discuss such differences and learn from other perspectives is an important character strength (Fowers & Davidov, 2005). Within a given cultural perspective, such debates are common, and I discuss at length two such debates regarding the excesses of the predominant Western cultural ethics of individualism (chap. 3) and instrumentalism (chap. 4). In these two chapters, I argue that these cultural understandings have become exaggerated and thereby limit and distort important human goods. I also suggest correctives for the one-sidedness of these views.

Virtue ethics does not provide a set of rules to follow. Rather, it describes how to cultivate a good character and act in the best ways, using concepts of goodness and virtue to guide one's actions. Virtue ethicists recognize that the best way to act will vary across contexts and situations and cannot be formulated in a definitive way. For this reason, practical wisdom, the ability to make wise choices about flexibly pursuing what is good in the many concrete situations one encounters, is vital to virtue ethics. In virtue ethics parlance, practical wisdom is the capacity that helps one to choose the best course of action, and I give a brief introduction to it in the next section. Part II of the book (chaps. 5–8) explores practical wisdom in much greater depth, and it complements the first part by focusing on the wisdom necessary to recognize how to pursue what is good in the myriad situations of ordinary life.

The Indispensability of Practical Wisdom

Practical wisdom is one of the key features of good character and pursuing what is good. I want to highlight the relationship between virtue and practical wisdom here to clarify how essential and central a role practical wisdom plays in the best kind of personal and professional life. In a nutshell, practical wisdom is the ability to make wise decisions about how to act well in a specific situation. As I explain more fully in chapter 5, it is impossible to guide our personal or professional activities solely on the basis of following rules or guidelines. No set of procedural, methodological, or ethical rules can be sufficient to encompass the nearly infinite variety of situations we encounter. Any set of rules requires an extensive array of exceptions, caveats, and qualifications to make it flexible enough to be responsive to the endless variation of daily life. These qualifications would have to be qualified further, leading to an infinite regress. In short, there is no algorithm for life. We have to use our judgment continually to decide how best to act in a given state of affairs.

Acting well requires good judgment, because human beings always have to decide whether a circumstance calls for courage or modesty, generosity or justice. In addition, we have to decide *how* to be courageous or generous in each situation we face. For example, being honest in a relationship is never simply saying whatever crosses my mind. I have to decide what to express and how to express it in keeping with the kind of relationship I am in. Humans exercise judgment by identifying the important aspects of our situations and separating them from the trivial features, giving our attention primarily to what is central. Practical wisdom combines this attention to what is important here and now with an awareness of how we can pursue our overall goals in a particular situation. The capacity to make good decisions in view of these considerations is essential for both ordinary living and for professional activity. Practical wisdom provides flexibility in one's moral choices, sensitivity to the nuances of one's circumstances, an ability to address complexity, and the capacity to pursue multiple goals harmoniously (Dunne, 1993).

As I discuss more fully in chapter 6, practical wisdom is absolutely crucial to good therapeutic practice. The psychotherapist must be able to recognize and respond to what is central in clients' lives and avoid being distracted by what is peripheral. Psychotherapists must be honest, courageous, and fair with their clients, and they have to choose how to embody those character strengths in each situation. Psychotherapy theories and treatment manuals can be helpful in directing therapeutic activity, but applying the general guidance provided by these resources is useful only through the clinician's perceptiveness and judgment. Each professional is responsible for sensitively interpreting clinical situations and deciding which theoretical precepts apply in what particular way for a given state of affairs.

Similarly, choosing the most important questions for investigation is crucial to the researcher, as is the judgment necessary to match investigative methods to the research topic, as I discuss in chapter 7. There is no simple algorithm or cookbook that can show novice researchers how to productively identify and approach a research problem, which is among the most important and difficult aspects of research. Interpretation of results and discussions of applications also require judiciousness.

Perhaps the most important application of practical wisdom arises in our ethical decision making. The core of ethics is the ability to use good judgment. Ethical principles provide helpful guidelines, but these general statements are only beneficial if they are interpreted and applied wisely. Chapter 8 illuminates how practical wisdom makes it possible for therapists, researchers, and teachers to recognize the ethical dimension of their work, to clearly perceive what is central to the situation, and to respond in a way that is appropriate to the circumstances. The importance of cultivating practical wisdom in psychology trainees cannot be overstated, because the quality of their independent work will depend entirely on whether they can act wisely in their professional activities.

Generosity as an Example

Let me illustrate the points I have made so far with a brief example of how the virtue of generosity plays a role in ordinary living and is of significant heuristic value to understanding human flourishing. A person with the virtue of generosity understands the nature of giving to others, is motivated to give gladly, and does so regularly in appropriate situations. This generous activity follows naturally from the individual's understanding of the role of giving in the best kind of individual and social life. This character strength gives rise to many different actions, such as doing a kindness for a friend, forgiving a spouse's mistake, and donating money or time to those less fortunate. An individual with the virtue of generosity gives wisely, knowing when, how, and how much giving is appropriate in various circumstances.

The concept of generosity can help us to bring together many disparate areas of psychological research and practice and deepen our understanding of these phenomena. For example, there is a growing literature on the role that forgiveness plays in individual lives and in relationships that strongly suggests that it is a very important aspect of individual and relationship well-being (Finkel, Rusbult, Kumashiro, & Hannon, 2002; McCullough et al., 1998; McCullough & Worthington, 1995; McCullough, Worthington, & Rachal, 1997). I see acts of forgiveness as a form of generosity because it is a gift that we give to others—it cannot be coerced, only freely given, and it is valuable only when it is offered willingly. Researchers have also documented the importance of activities in romantic relationships that can be understood in terms of generosity, such as the willingness to sacrifice for a partner (Van Lange et al., 1997), accommodation to a partner (Rusbult, Verette, Whitney, Slovik, & Lipkus, 1991), concern for a partner's needs without regard to recompense (Clark, Mills, & Powell, 1986; Williamson & Clark, 1992; Williamson, Clark, Pegalis, & Behan, 1996), and giving partners and children more credit than seems justified to uninvolved others (Fowers, Lyons, & Montel, 1996; Fowers, Lyons, Montel, & Shaked, 2001; Murray, Holmes, & Griffin, 1996). Volunteer work (Clary et al., 1998; Omoto & Snyder, 1995) and helping behavior (Batson, 1998) also come under the rubric of generosity.

Generosity provides an overall trait description of these disparate activities that ties together disposition, emotion, motivation, cognition, and action. Moreover, it presents a promising alternative explanation of these actions that goes beyond the tired and simplistic distinction between self-interest and selflessness. As demonstrated in chapter 4, this sterile dichotomy generally results in portraying humans as primarily self-interested (see Batson, 1998, for an exception) and fails to account for the ways in which self-interest often coincides with and is enriched by social interest. Generous individuals accommodate, sacrifice for, and give to their loved ones because they love these people, want the best for them, and wholeheartedly seek to have good relationships. The benefits of generous activity are shared by the giver and the recipient, and they tend to be self-perpetuating in positive relationships (Fowers et al., 1996). When volunteers give time for political, social, or charitable purposes, they are promoting the overall well-being of the communities and nation in which they live. There is no neat dividing line between what is good for the individual and what is good for the group.

WHY HAVE WE NEGLECTED VIRTUE?

If I am right about the importance of virtue in our personal and professional lives, it raises the question of why we as psychologists have neglected character in the last century. Is it because psychologists have definitive evidence that virtues do not exist or are impossible to practice? No. Is it that we have evidence that other ways of describing human behavior and clinical skills are superior to a virtue conception? No. Is it that character cannot be studied in a systematic manner? Not at all. Is it that there is something bad or negative about virtue, that psychologists believe that courage, generosity, and justice are undesirable? Now we are getting closer. No one seriously or explicitly argues that there is something wrong with these character strengths, but there are reasons why these constructs have been excluded from the discipline in both its research and clinical domains.

Character and virtue were prominent topics in the early years of psychology, but they fell into disfavor as the discipline decisively moved to split scientific fact from moral value according to the reigning concept of the development of a social science (Nicholson, 1998; Ross & Nisbett, 1991). A coincident and likely related shift in emphasis from character to personality in understanding the individual was also occurring in the popular culture. The cultural historian Warren Susman (1984, p. 273) called the 19th century a *culture of character* whose preoccupations were with citizenship, duty, golden deeds, honor, reputation, and integrity. In the popular culture, this Victorian "vision of self-sacrifice began to yield to that of self-realization" found in the *culture of personality*. "From the beginning the adjectives most frequently associated with personality suggest a very different concept from that of character: *fascinating, stunning, attractive, magnetic, glowing, masterful, creative, dominant, forceful*" (pp. 276–277, italics in original). This emphasis on personality was designed to help the individual stand out in the crowd and was frequently touted as the best way to succeed in an increasingly competitive world. Thus, character lost favor in both scientific and popular domains during the same period.

The Devaluation of Character

Allport (1937) is frequently identified as a pivotal figure in the shift in scientific focus from character to personality, and his pointed couplet is often taken as emblematic for this move: "*Character is personality evaluated, and personality is character devaluated*" (p. 52, italics in original). This devaluation of character has been an important part of psychology's attempt to exclude evaluative and popular terms from personality psychology. To be sure, Allport did not concern himself with the popular fascination with personality as a way to stand out in a crowd. Yet his emphasis on personality cannot be seen in isolation from the cultural developments of his time. In accord with the popular theme of the time, he repeatedly stressed the uniqueness of the individual. Allport (1937, p. 3) began the book that brought personality research into the mainstream with "The outstanding characteristic of man [sic] is his individuality. He is a unique creation of the forces of nature."

In the service of a science of personality, Allport (1921; Allport & Vernon, 1930) frequently asserted the necessity of rigidly separating personality traits as scientific phenomena from character and virtue as normative elements of social ethics. As Nicholson (1998) pointed out, "Allport's goal was not to destroy the traditional ethical foundations of America but to revitalize them" through scientific rigor. He embarked on this endeavor because "he was convinced that the solution to America's ethical dilemmas lay not in history, culture, or religion, but in science, in particular, psychology" (p. 64). Allport was not able to fully effect this separation partly because he worried that psychologists would not do "justice to the *richness* and *dignity* of human personality" (Allport, 1937, p. vii, italics added). Allport's commitment to a morally informed understanding of living well is even clearer in his description of "the mature personality." The mature person is one who has a variety of autonomous interests; that is,

> he [sic] can lose himself in work, in contemplation, in recreation, and in loyalty to others. . . . Egocentricity is not the mark of a mature personality. Contrast the garrulous Bohemian, egotistical, self-pitying, and prating of self-expression, with the man of confident dignity who has identified himself with a cause that has won his devotion. . . . Unless directed outward toward socialized and culturally compatible ends, unless absorbed in causes and goals that outshine self-seeking and vanity, any life seems dwarfed and immature. . . . Whenever a definitive objective orientation has been attained, pleasures and pains of the moment, setbacks and defeats, and the impulse for self-justification fade into the background, so that they do not obscure the chosen goals. (p. 213)

Allport's theory of personality failed to devaluate character, for it retained substantial normative and evaluative terms. His contrasts clearly espouse commitments to an outlook on better and worse ways of life: devotion to socially compatible goals versus egocentricity, confident dignity versus self-seeking and vanity, ability to lose oneself in work and loyalty versus self-pity and prating self-expression, steadfastness in purpose versus self-justification. He clearly saw one set of traits as admirable and worthy and the other as base. Indeed, there is much to admire in the picture Allport recommended, but it is clear that his aspiration toward separating scientific fact and normative value was unsuccessful.

The extreme difficulty of separating moral ideals from objective descriptions of personality was not limited to Allport as an individual or to the undeveloped nature of psychology as a science in the early part of this century. As I show throughout this book, character is intertwined with psychological concepts in virtually every aspect of the discipline. One further example with personality theory and research is suggestive. Character remains evident in the most widely accepted and best documented contemporary understanding of personality: the five factor model of personality (Costa & McCrae, 1991). McCrae and John (1992) noted that the Five Factor Model contains two factors that are clearly related to traditional virtue terms: Agreeableness and Conscientiousness.

> Like A, C is a highly *evaluated* dimension: indeed, A and C are the classic dimensions of character describing "good" versus "evil" and "strong-willed" versus "weak-willed" individuals. Perhaps it was these moral overtones that often led scientific psychologists to ignore these factors, but in fact, both represent objectively observable dimensions of individual differences. (p. 197, italics added)

The evident difficulty of divesting character from accounts of personality suggests two possible courses of action. Psychologists can either relinquish the attempt and make character an integral part of our theories or redouble our efforts to expunge moral matters from our theories. With rare exceptions, such as the one previously cited, psychologists persist in our efforts to eliminate virtue from theory. Given the long history of failure in this endeavor, we might ask ourselves why the devaluation of character seems to be the automatic choice.

The Project to Eliminate Human Interpretation

The effort to separate facts and values has been pursued in the interest of enhancing the scientific status of the discipline by eliminating the moral and value coloring of earlier psychological theories. Psychology adopted the Enlightenment viewpoint that evolved over several centuries, through which science cast itself increasingly as the voice of reason in contrast to tradition and arbitrary authority on the one hand, and ungrounded personal preference on the other. This scientifically inspired "disenchantment" of the world was intended to open first the natural world and then the social realm to free and objective investigation. The scientific outlook grew in conjunction with the Enlightenment's emancipatory emphasis on human reason. Therefore, science has been fundamentally morally motivated as well, seeing itself as a liberating force, freeing not only modes of inquiry but also the human mind from the tyranny of inherited authority and error.

Science came to be defined as the activity of perceiving the world as a neutral domain of facts rather than as a locus of meanings through which one can understand oneself and one's place in the world (Taylor,

1985). This objectification of the cosmos was the essence of the 17th-century revolution in science led by Bacon, Descartes, and Newton. They produced an epoch-making polemic against the worldview of the Middle Ages and the High Renaissance, with its vision of the universe as a hierarchy of meaning. Bacon castigated this earlier vision as "Idols of the Mind" and pointedly stated that true knowledge brought power and freedom, in contrast to the bonds and darkness of this earlier illusory, interpretive view of things.

To free themselves from the constraints of tradition and unreason, natural scientists, from Galileo onward, attempted to carefully separate the realm of fact from personal experience, interpretation, and dogma. Facts were to be objectively established through intersubjectively verifiable procedures rather than founded on authority or subjective perception. The application of these procedures requires the investigator to take a step back from the phenomena of interest and adopt a disengaged, unbiased point of view. This freedom of inquiry is related closely to the Enlightenment ideal of self-responsibility. All knowledge is verifiable by anyone, at least in principle. Confidence in one's results is assured by carefully specified methods that allow critique and replication. Therefore, each knower can rely on his or her own judgment about what is true and, if necessary, heroically defend this empirically grounded account against the opinion of the age (Taylor, 1985).

This outlook provided the considerable advantage of being able to attain a greater and greater ability to predict and control the physical world by tracing the contingent correlations among and causal influences on phenomena. At the same time, this separation of the observer from a meaning-laden cosmos in which one had an intelligible and significant role was a dramatic loss, which opened the possibility for a profound sense of alienation and meaninglessness to us moderns. The comforting interpretation of the world as having a meaningful order was sacrificed to the aim of scientifically describing and explaining the world as it is, undistorted by dogma, personal desires, or, indeed, any human interpretation. We take this separation of the objective and subjective realms for granted today, but it is of relatively recent origin. The Enlightenment isolation of meaning within the subjective domain magnified unsettling existential questions that continue to be profound and open. The austere stance of the neutral observer is taken to be the only scientifically legitimate posture toward the world, even if it deepens our doubts about the meaning of our existence.

The Enlightenment thinkers' interest in the separation of the objective and subjective realms was not focused solely on freeing scientific inquiry but involved an intense concern with enhancing individual autonomy more generally. Separating "objective" and "subjective" domains was a powerful move toward opening up scientific observation of the world, but part of the allure of this separation has been that it makes personal feelings and preferences subjective affairs, unconstrained by either traditional dogma or scientific fact. The separation of truth (to be determined scientifically) from the good (to be defined in terms of personal preferences) was designed to liberate individuals to pursue their own freely chosen ends. In this developing worldview, we in the West increasingly see the world as neutral matter for individuals to shape according to their own purposes.

The project to separate objective fact and human value was doomed from the beginning, because the separation was itself a morally motivated enterprise that sought two interrelated goods: knowledge and freedom. Knowledge is valuable, both in its own right and in serving instrumental human interests by enhancing our ability to predict, control, and use material phenomena. The disenchantment of the cosmos also freed individuals from the constraints of a meaning-laden world so that they could pursue their chosen aims. Yet the process of seeking objective knowledge requires a particular stance toward the world, one in which scientists distance themselves from their own desires and personal aims. As discussed below, this stance embodies a character ideal for scientists that belies the separation of fact and value in the practice of science.

PSYCHOLOGY'S CHARACTER IDEALS

Standing apart from one's personal and cultural interpretations and goals in scientific inquiry demands a significant disengagement from the scientist's cherished beliefs and outlook. This austerity is, ironically, a central feature of a key character ideal. This character ideal also includes being genuinely curious, able to recognize significant scientific questions, honest in pursuing and reporting on one's research, courageous in presenting controversial findings, respectful of research participants' autonomy and rights, able to deal with funding sources and the media with integrity, and so forth.

The traits necessary for doing good science comprise a set of virtues that are cultivated to pursue the goods of attaining unbiased knowledge and improving the human condition. Although science is usually construed as a methodical set of procedures, carrying out these procedures faithfully in the face of ever-present temptations to corrupt them requires character strength and a genuine allegiance to the goods of science.

Psychologists and other mental health professionals have attempted to rule virtues out of the clinical domain as well. The founders of applied psychology feared that therapists would misuse the power that clients give to us by imposing our values, which may be contrary to the client's sense of what is good and proper. This attempt at value neutrality was undertaken as a way to promote the rights and dignity of clients as autonomous individuals who should be allowed to make their own unfettered decisions about how best to live. Ironically, the disciplinary stance of value neutrality was embraced in the service of the essential and widely endorsed social value of supporting client autonomy.

Clinicians are trained to maintain some distance from their own feelings, wishes, and aims so that they can serve their clients' interests. Successfully adopting this distance and other-regard requires a well-developed capacity for self-awareness and the management of one's own feelings and behavior that takes years to master. The best practitioners are those who are self-aware, focused on seeking beneficial outcomes for their clients, respectful of client autonomy, respectful of cultural differences, honest, sufficiently courageous to confront difficulties, and so forth. Various psychotherapy theories add to and subtract from this list and have particular interpretations of desirable therapist traits, but each psychotherapy perspective has a model of practitioner excellence. These essential capacities of the successful clinician also constitute a character ideal that is cultivated in the service of the good of helping clients to flourish as human beings. In other words, clinical skill and beneficence can be described as virtues as well.

It seems clear that we do have character ideals for our professional roles and that attempts to portray high-quality researchers and clinicians in terms that are more neutral only obscure the aspirations that we have and the personal strengths necessary to pursue them. One of the central themes of this book is that developing greater clarity about the character ideals we seek to embody and promote in our training can enhance our professional activities and the training we provide our students. It seems obvious that attaining a better grasp of our goals as professionals and our aims as educators will lead to greater clarity and focus in our efforts and increase the degree of our success in reaching these goals. I argue that the development of desirable character traits provides an excellent framework for these endeavors.

The repudiation of virtue in psychology obscures much as we try to explain ordinary behavior as well. Psychological theory, research, and practice have always been suffused with character ideals, even though we have attempted to distance ourselves from them with the paper-thin veil of our functionality discourse. Psychologists prefer to use terms that appear to be morally neutral such as *functional, healthy,* and *effective* to denote the characteristics that help individuals to live well. The value neutrality of these terms is more apparent than real, however, because the terms themselves are empty and require further specification. What do we mean by functional? What counts as healthy? These terms are proxies for desirable traits that promote the best kind of life. Our ability to identify what is abnormal and pathological depends on a concept of what is normal and healthy, and our views on good outcomes in psychotherapy rely on notions of optimal human functioning (Guignon, 2002). Indeed, one of the guiding principles of the American Psychological Association is to promote human welfare. We can only do this if we have some idea of what are better and worse ways to live. We can and do take refuge in the idea that choices about how to live should be left up to individuals, but this is hardly a value-neutral stance because the primacy of individual choice regarding values is a central premise of the moral perspective known as individualism.

In any case, our theories of human functioning do not stop short of describing better ways to live but give rather direct indications of characteristics that contribute to living well. In psychotherapy theories, these characteristics include the prudent rational control advocated by Freud, the capacity to delay gratification in favor of longer-term goals favored by behaviorists, the self-awareness and positive self-regard valued in humanistic approaches, and the rational capacity for empirically testing the truth value of beliefs promoted in cognitive therapy. Scientific theories also assume that certain characteristics are more healthy than others, such as the calculating self-interest of social exchange theory, the focus on instrumental control in a variety of cognitive theories, the evaluation of marital and life quality in terms of personal happiness, and so on. Numerous authors have identified these kinds of trait ideals as central to modern individualism, the predominant cultural ideal in North Atlantic societies, particularly America (Bellah, Madsen, Sullivan, Swidler, & Tipton, 1985; Cushman, 1990, 1995; Richardson, Fowers, & Guignon, 1999; Sampson, 1985; Sandel, 1998; Sarason, 1981, 1986; Spence, 1985).

I am suggesting that psychology is suffused with modern values. Psychology systematically promotes the moral perspective of individualism, as seen in its primary aims of increasing human freedom, control, and welfare. To the extent that psychology is already guided by moral motives, character ideals, and contemporary values, the adoption of a virtue framework would not represent a shift from a value-neutral discipline to a psychology that included a moral dimension. Rather, the incorporation of virtue in psychology represents a shift from an implicit and unsystematic approach to moral matters to an explicit and well-formulated framework, an openly articulated framework that can be questioned, debated, and evaluated. If the incorporation of values and ideals is unavoidable, as so many scholars have argued, then it is presumably better to come to terms with that situation with open eyes rather than blundering around blindly because we do not wish to see ourselves as morally engaged actors. The burden of this book is to show that the virtue ethics framework provides a superior perspective by illuminating previously obscure aspects of what we do and by helping us to do our work better.

WORRIES ABOUT VIRTUE AND PSYCHOLOGY

There are several concerns that many readers are likely to have about integrating virtue into psychology. This brief section provides an initial response to these worries, all of which are addressed more fully later in the book.

Can Character Be Studied Empirically?

One of the tests of the value of character as a guiding framework is whether it can be studied empirically. Even if we decide to dispense with the pretense of moral disengagement in our discipline, there is considerable value in empirical explorations of our theories. Theories about virtue are not exceptions.

Many have concluded that virtue cannot be studied and that its presence was disconfirmed by Hartshorne and May's celebrated studies of honesty among schoolchildren (Hartshorne & May, 1928; Hartshorne, May, & Maller, 1929; Hartshorne, May, & Shuttleworth, 1930). The canonical interpretation of their results (Doris, 2002; Emler, 1999; Ross & Nisbett, 1991) is that children generally lie when given the opportunity, even those students who were rated as honest by peers and teachers. Because many students took advantage of experimenter-contrived opportunities to be dishonest, these authors concluded that moral behavior is determined more by the situation than by character. This interpretation misunderstands virtue, however. Hartshorne et al. (1930) stated that about 60% of the children's honesty was situationally determined. Contrary to the canonical interpretation, these results are entirely consistent with a virtue perspective. No virtue ethicist would expect the majority of people to exhibit character excellence, much less the majority of *children*. In chapter 2, I stress that virtue is quite an achievement, one that takes many years to cultivate and significant maturity to master. Recognizing the maturity necessary for character development severely undermines any general conclusions about the existence of virtues from a sample of children.

From a virtue perspective, it is of much greater interest whether there were *some* children who reliably acted honestly and whether there is an identifiable trait of honesty. Hartshorne and May's results do indeed suggest that the honesty of a significant minority of children was not situationally determined. The real question is whether a subset of children could be identified who are consistently honest rather than examining the overall correlations in an aggregate sample.

If the aggregate sample is to be used, it is best to conduct analyses likely to directly test for the presence of an honesty trait. Burton (1963) reanalyzed the original results using factor analysis. He found that situational factors were important but concluded that an underlying trait of honesty was present. In addition, Rushton (1984) pointed to the relatively high correlations (range .50–.60) between the more reliable measures of honesty and teacher ratings of honesty. In another reanalysis, Epstein and O'Brien (1985) aggregated a variety of measures of honesty and produced strong correlations with honest behavior. This aggregation of measures may represent a much better test of the presence of character strengths, because we would look for virtues in a consistent pattern of behavior across a variety of assessments rather than merely in the relationship between any two indicators. These results indicate that the conclusion that character traits did not exist was ill founded.

Baumeister and Exline (1999) suggested that there is no reason that one cannot study virtue concepts using currently available research methods. Indeed, there are many instances of this kind of research, including the study of virtue in general (Cawley, Martin, & Johnson, 2000; Hawkins, Fowers, Carroll, & Yang, in press; Walker & Pitts, 1998), gratitude (Emmons & Crumpler, 2000; McCullough, Emmons, & Tsang, 2002), generosity (Fowers, 2004), what makes a life good (King & Napa, 1998), and practical wisdom (Kramer, 2000; Staudinger, Lopez, & Baltes, 1997; Sternberg, 1985). The recent upsurge of interest in virtue has been accompanied by many studies in this previously neglected area. The promising results of this research are just beginning to emerge, and it is already clear that virtue can be studied empirically. I examine this research in detail in subsequent chapters as I explore each topic.

Does Virtue Require Adopting a Particular Religious or Political Outlook?

Many worry that introducing terms and concepts related to the moral dimension of life, particularly virtue terms, will unavoidably involve the introduction of specific religious or political viewpoints. Although this is certainly a possibility, there is no necessary relationship between religion, politics, and virtue. Conceptually and practically, they are quite distinct. There are virtue frameworks in widely different religious traditions, and there are virtue frameworks that are quite independent of religion. The classical sources of virtue were not religious in conception and predate the modern forms of major Western religions. Similarly, although some prominent conservatives such as Bill Bennett (1993) have espoused virtue concepts, no political position has exclusive ownership of virtue ethics.

Studies of folk understandings of morality have shown that ordinary individuals are able to differentiate relatively clearly between what it is to be a moral person and a religious or spiritual person (Walker & Pitts, 1998), and between moral and religious rules and issues (Nucci & Turiel, 1993). Both of these studies suggested that ordinary individuals see the moral dimension as independent of religious life but that religious life requires moral behavior. These results indicate that ordinary individuals are able to differentiate morality from religion in reliable and meaningful ways, suggesting that psychologists can also make this distinction.

Does a Virtue Approach Lead to a Judgmental Attitude?

It is important to separate the everyday necessity of making judgments and decisions about how to relate to others from being judgmental or condemning. As social beings, humans can and do recognize what is admirable, noble, or fine in ourselves and others and differentiate these qualities from what is deplorable, base, or vulgar. In our private and professional lives we must attend to whether someone is trustworthy or unreliable, compassionate or callous, fair-minded or exploitive. It is impossible to prosper in the social world without making these kinds of judgments about the people with whom we live and work, and we are well aware that others need to assess our reliability, responsiveness, and fairness in a similar fashion. By assessing one another in this way, we want to determine whether individuals are, for example, honest or generous in a characteristic way or only once in a while or just when it suits their immediate purposes, which helps us to decide how to interact with them. Individuals need to know whether and how much to trust each other, whether and how much to rely on one another's loyalty, whether and how much to put their faith in one another's sense of justice. In short, they are interested in ascertaining what sorts of character traits others have.

From a virtue ethics perspective, if one decides that a family member or associate is untrustworthy or cowardly, this indicates that one should not expect this individual to keep a confidence or come to one's defense in a difficult situation. There is no need to condemn or criticize these shortcomings, only to modify one's decisions and actions in accordance with them. To ignore such limitations or to act contrary to one's recognition of them would be foolish.

The purpose of character assessments is not to sit in judgment of others. Rather, it is to decide how best to live and work with them. If I have reason to believe that Person A is characteristically honest, I will tend to believe what A tells me as a matter of course. If I have reason to see Person B as honest intermittently, when it suits B's agenda, then it would be wise for me to be aware of B's agenda so that I can evaluate the truthfulness of B's statements. It is not necessary to vilify or reproach B, only to decide whether and how much to trust this person so that I know how to act toward B to foster the most desirable results. Of course, I will probably be disappointed and angry the first time I feel deceived by B, but recognizing B's limitations is one way to resolve these negative feelings. The old saying "Fool me once, shame on you, fool me twice, shame on me" captures the judicious and responsible assessment I am suggesting.

These assessments of each other serve an orienting rather than judgmental purpose. They are similar to personality and diagnostic assessments that identify less than desirable characteristics without blaming or condemning the individual who demonstrates them. I could, of course, go beyond the essential assessment of B's trustworthiness by seeing this person as despicable and myself as superior, but taking a judgmental and superior stance is neither necessary nor desirable from a virtue perspective. It is so much wasted energy. It seems obvious that the best sort of person would not be interested in seeking the cheap gratification of condemnation or superiority.

SUMMARY

Given the promise of virtue for psychological theory and practice, and the recent attention it has received, a thorough and scholarly treatment of its definition and scope is sorely needed. This book provides a necessary systematic, theoretical framework for virtue in psychology. It brings to light the integrative possibilities of character that are crucial to fully understanding and most beneficially applying the insights of virtue ethics. The virtue framework that I present here offers a far more social and integrative way to understand human affairs than is common in psychology. It transcends the tired dichotomy of self and society and highlights our inherently social nature and the ways that acknowledging the socially embedded character of our lives helps us to see our activities and aims in a much richer light. I show that virtue can be very broadly applied, from understanding optimal human living and how to attain it to clarifying the best professional practices and how to teach them.

This book offers an innovative way to see psychology as a discipline devoted to helping people to flourish as human beings by cultivating their best selves. I present research results, clinical vignettes, and teaching and supervision experiences to illustrate how, individually and collectively, virtues make a very practical contribution to individual physical and psychological health, the quality of personal relationships, social harmony, and social capital, as well as improving the political process. Readers will see, through a variety of examples, how a virtue perspective provides a deeper, richer account of many psychological topics than current theory is able to generate and can thereby enhance psychological theory, research, and practice. The next step in this exploration is to spell out more fully what I mean by virtue, the topic of chapter 2.

2

DEFINING VIRTUE

I say that habit's but long practice, friend,
And this becomes men's nature in the end.
    —Evenus, as quoted by Aristotle in the *Nicomachean Ethics*

What is virtue? Is virtue its own reward? Is it a kind of self-denial, moral superiority, self-righteousness, or self-absorption? Does it underwrite a judgmental attitude, a rule-bound mentality, or a refusal to enjoy life? The short answer to these questions is a simple "no." In a word, a virtue is the form of excellence that allows an individual to pursue worthwhile ends in everyday activities. This chapter presents a systematic discussion of virtue that sets the stage for understanding how character figures in psychology and for seeing how a psychology informed by virtue ethics helps us to better understand and foster the best in our students, our clients, our society, and ourselves.

As more and more psychologists become interested in a virtue perspective in their work, it becomes increasingly important to have a clear and systematic articulation of virtue theory that can guide research and practice. The initial forays into a psychology of virtue have tended to focus on a few, somewhat idiosyncratically chosen traits that are intriguing and have some beneficial outcomes, but these accounts lack a fully articulated coherence or overall unity (e.g., Chang & Sanna, 2003; Doherty, 1995; Keyes & Haidt, 2003; Nicholas, 1994; Seligman & Csikszentmihalyi, 2000). Moreover, authors frequently use the term *virtue* either without explicit definition or with a cursory characterization (Baltes & Staudinger, 2000; McCullough & Snyder, 2000; Sheldon & King, 2001) as though everyone already knows what it means. This will not do, because there are many different ways that we can define and use the term, and there are many misconceptions and prejudices about it. The way we define virtue will go a long way toward clarifying or further mystifying its role in human action. Our ability to theorize, investigate, and practice virtue depends on our ability to define it in a clear, well-grounded way.

This chapter emphasizes the overall coherence and unity of a virtue framework drawing on Aristotle's (trans. 1998) original work in the *Nicomachean Ethics*. (Unless otherwise noted, all citations of Aristotle refer to the 1998 translation of the *Nicomachean Ethics*.) There are many traditions in which we could find definitions of virtue, including warrior societies like the Lakota (Sioux) and Homeric Greeks, Eastern traditions such as the Buddhist and Confucian views, and more recent Christian, Jewish, and Victorian versions. Each of these traditions can provide helpful, albeit differing perspectives on virtue. I am not claiming any special authority or standing for the views I present here beyond the merits of whatever clarity and cogency of exposition I can muster.

If we are to come to grips with virtue, we must start somewhere, and I have chosen to focus on Aristotle for several reasons.[1] The most important is that Aristotle created the most systematic and wide-ranging account of virtue per se. His presentation of virtue and its role in human flourishing is subtle and powerful, and, in my view, unsurpassed. He was the originator of virtue theory in Western civilization, and all subsequent approaches owe a very large debt to his views. His is the most accessible perspective to the majority of psychologists in the West because it has been strongly engaged in our historical cultures. In addition, the Aristotelian tradition has received a great deal of historical and recent scholarly attention, making it a rich and well-articulated source for an examination of virtue and psychology. Although Aristotle's thought was incorporated into the Judeo-Christian tradition, his views predate Christianity and modern Judaism and provide a perspective that does not rely on those religious doctrines. Of course, Aristotle did not have the last word on virtue, and neither will I. One of the very best signs of success for this book will be the emergence of an extended and rich disciplinary discussion of the best way to understand character and how to find its place in psychology.

---

[1] It is important to acknowledge and disavow Aristotle's views on men and women and on slavery. He saw men as morally superior to women by nature and, like virtually all ancients, did not see any difficulty with slavery. From the viewpoint of antiquity there would always be an inequality in male–female friendships, and slaves were part of the natural social order. There is no reason to retain the notion of inequality in the moral worth of the sexes or of the acceptability of enslaving others. These views were so thoroughly ensconced in Aristotle's cultural context that ancient authors seldom questioned them. People today rightly repudiate his views on these inequities, but it is anachronistic to expect him to have done so. His account of the virtues does not require these inequalities. My discussion of the virtues assumes the moral equality of men and women and the unacceptability of slavery and exploitation.

In this chapter, I define virtue in terms of several interwoven themes:

1. Humans act and fashion our lives as a whole through our pursuit of what we see as worthwhile goals (or pursuit of what is good in virtue parlance).
2. This pursuit requires virtues, or well-established personal strengths, that make it possible to seek those goals successfully.
3. Virtues manifest themselves behaviorally in actions.
4. These actions are based on a clear understanding of how best to act.
5. These actions are pursued willingly and spontaneously.
6. Virtues are learned through guidance and feedback.
7. Enacting virtues requires wise choices about how to pursue what is good in specific circumstances.

This definition suggests that virtue is a multifaceted topic that is concerned with many key topics in psychological theory, research, and practice—virtue has goal-directed, dispositional, behavioral, affective, cognitive, developmental, and wisdom-based aspects. I address each theme of virtue in turn in what follows.

VIRTUE AND WHAT IS GOOD

The first and most central thing that we need to understand about virtues is that they are the character strengths that make it possible for human beings to pursue uniquely human aims or goods successfully. I use several terms to refer to what is good. The terms *good* and *goods* refer to relatively abstract accomplishments or states of affairs that are worthwhile. Examples include knowledge, democracy, well-being, flourishing, and mutual understanding. I use terms such as *goals* and *aims* in reference to more concrete accomplishments or states of affairs such as getting a college degree, having cooperative relationships, and traveling safely. In chapter 3, I describe a hierarchy in which shorter-term, concrete goals are components of longer-term, higher-order goals, which are in turn components of our abstract concepts of what is good.

I begin with the pursuit of goodness because a virtue is a valuable characteristic inasmuch as it facilitates the pursuit of worthwhile goals and goods. As discussed in the last chapter, honesty is a scientific virtue because it makes science possible, and we see the expansion of our knowledge as a worthy aim. Honesty is also a key virtue in personal relationships in that it makes trust possible and allows for a deepening and strengthening of the relationship that is not possible in the presence of significant dishonesty. It is the value of the aims (knowledge and friendship) that we pursue that make honesty worth enacting. The same relationship holds between valued ends and virtues in general—virtues are the traits necessary for successfully pursuing what we see as good.

Aristotle began the *Nicomachean Ethics* with the reflection that all human activities have some goal: The end of medicine is health, of shipbuilding a vessel, and of war victory. Individuals and groups engage in some activities for their own sake, such as certain forms of friendship and knowledge seeking. They participate in some activities as stepping-stones on the way to higher-order aims. For example, students study for an exam so that they can pass a course, earn a degree, and pursue a career that will provide fulfillment and the means to live well. Seldom is studying for a test an end in itself, but this effort is part of an integrated plan to reach higher-order goals such as preparation for a career and having the financial wherewithal to support a flourishing life. In the same way, what counts as acting well as a psychologist will depend on how well one fulfills the goals and goods of the profession, and the goodness of the profession is determined by how well it contributes to the goals of the society in which the profession is active (Oakley & Cocking, 2001). Psychology's commitments to human welfare and to understanding human behavior are important goods and help to justify the prestige, financial support, and standing we have in society.

One of the most important features of any contemporary discussion of what is good is the recognition of the diversity of goods, both within mainstream American society and in other cultural groups. This is often referred to as pluralism. It is important to remember that even though individuals have some choice among these plural goals, as human beings, we do not choose our cultural heritage. Individuals are shaped by their participation in a historical culture and adopt culturally based convictions that form the background for their choices. As cultural beings, we select among the culturally available visions of what is good, and we pursue those aims as life projects. For the most part, these are everyday pursuits such as raising children or providing good education. There are also extraordinary endeavors such as stretching the bounds of an art or the promotion of democracy or cultural understanding. There are many goods that are worth seeking, and I address the relations among multiple goods later in this chapter and again in chapters 3 and 4.

Dealing With Value Anxiety

Before proceeding, let me address a question that arises in nearly every discussion of what is good: "Whose goods, values, or morality will predominate?" Another form of this question is "What values are you promoting? What stand are you taking on what is good?" Given prominent concerns about individual autonomy in our culture, these are natural questions, but they are, in some respects, fundamentally misguided. The answer to these questions is that people in reasonably coherent societies are always guided by a more or less shared understanding of what is good. I included the weasel words "reasonably" and "more or less" in the previous sentence because cultural values are multivocal and dynamic, and they tend to resist precise formulation. For example, we in the United States share various versions of the ideals of individual freedom, self-government, self-expression, and so forth. We often disagree about the details and our understandings of these goods have evolved over time, but we are deeply committed to them in the course of our socialization into this historical culture.

Hermeneutic philosophers (Gadamer, 1975; Heidegger, 1962; MacIntyre, 1981; Taylor, 1985, 1989) have illuminated this vital aspect of human existence by pointing out that humans always operate from within a moral tradition because our conception of what is worth pursuing is conditioned by our membership in a given society at a particular time. We cannot stand entirely apart from our heritage. I am no exception to that. For example, I am committed to, even if highly critical of, contemporary individualism, and I think that some form of pluralism is indispensable. In other words, I am a creature of my time and place, and my implicit values are substantially similar to those of many other participants in contemporary American culture. One can, and should, be critical of some facets of our way of life, because cultural values can be misguided, exaggerated, exploitive, or otherwise problematic. Indeed, MacIntyre (1981, 1998) has argued that ongoing debate about the meaning and expression of cultural values is normative in living cultures. Yet one can only question the ideals one finds problematic from the standpoint of other cultural assumptions. For better or worse, there is no possibility of stepping outside the flux of history and culture to obtain a purely objective perspective.

As I discuss virtue, I rely on some version of the same goods and valued aims that are predominant in American culture. Virtue ethics does not propose a specific moral content or some singular idea of the good, a kind of Platonic form that is superordinate to cultures or a replacement for the ordinary aims of individuals (cf. Aristotle, p. 8). The purpose of this book is not to convince readers to adopt new values. Instead, virtue ethics takes cultural values as an initial definition of what is good and attempts to illuminate the character strengths that make it possible to pursue those aims and ideals. Therefore, I want to show how understanding, cultivating, and enacting virtue can help individuals to better pursue the worthwhile aims they already have.

In the process of gaining greater clarity about cultural values and the character strengths necessary to pursue them, critical questions about those values will arise. For example, in the discussion of goods in chapter 4, I raise questions about the exaggeration of a one-sided emphasis on goods that can be possessed by individuals. This critique can help us to reclaim and expand our understanding of goods that can only be held in common with others (e.g., harmony, solidarity). These shared goods are not new, but they are often obscured by the predominant individualism in Western societies.

I cannot overemphasize this point. Our socialization into a society that values individual autonomy above everything else predisposes us to be highly suspicious of any discussion of what is good and right. This socialization leads us to fear that any such discussion is a cover for some moral coercion, to wonder *whose* ideas about what is good and right are being promoted. This book is not about promoting some new set of goods and ideals, it is about how we can better pursue (or reclaim) the ones we already have. This requires us to recognize the morality we *already* embody in our profession and our society, to examine carefully how we promote it, and to remain open to questions about the wisdom of engaging in these endeavors. In other words, I am advocating a greater degree of openness to questioning our ethical commitments as a profession than is typical, rather than imposing a particular set of ideals. (Although it is clear that this openness to reflection and critique of cultural and professional values is itself a value.)

Discussing goods and ideals, even if in a noncoercive manner, runs counter to the discipline's standard arm's-length relationship with human goals as personal or subjective concerns. It is ironic that it is our shared commitment to the good of individual autonomy that gives rise to this powerful inclination to protect individuals from an unwarranted intrusion on their choice and pursuit of ultimate ends. Adherence to this key moral commitment has created one of the most glaring flaws of most psychological discussions of virtue: the nearly complete neglect of the concept of what is good. Questions regarding what is good are generally treated as personal choices outside the purview of the profession. Neglecting questions of what is good is fatal for any discussion of character, however, because virtues are the traits needed to pursue worthwhile aims, and inattention to what is good negates the central purpose of cultivating character.

In this context, it is important to note that Aristotle left the concept of flourishing open-ended, because *no one* can possibly define what is best for all people in a final or conclusive way. Any perspective on what is good for humans is bound to be incomplete and flawed in important ways. I am in full agreement with keeping an open mind about the best way to live. Questions about what is good for humans have been extant from the beginning of the species, and there is no reason to think that humanity has become wise enough to stipulate goodness in a final way. All people can learn from perspectives that differ from their own, and changing circumstances often require new insights to deal with unforeseen constraints in the pursuit of one's aims. Any concept of what is good for humans is debatable and subject to ongoing scrutiny and revision. In fact, one of the key features of the good life is the continuing dialogue about what is best for human beings as individuals and as a species.

This discussion suggests that the full development of the human capacity to reflect on, critique, and dialogue about the moral aims and activities of psychology requires the cultivation of character traits such as modesty and openness. Modesty is entailed in the acceptance of ourselves as culturally embedded participants whose knowledge and experience are unavoidably limited. Acknowledging the diversity of goods requires accepting that we do not have final or certain answers to questions about the good life and that others may have much to teach us. Openness is necessary for dialogue about what is good because real dialogue places our own cherished ideals at risk and requires us to acknowledge that it is possible to learn from others.

Although virtue ethics does not provide a once-and-for-all concept of what is good and of the virtues to pursue that good, it is not entirely relativistic. For example, those who promote racism, genocide, and domination and exploitation of others can and do claim to be virtuous. They also claim to pursue goods that they argue are worthwhile (i.e., racial purity, a utopian vision, or the protection of their way of life). Such claims are as obviously fatuous as the rigged elections that are designed to present the continued rule of tyrants as democratically legitimate. The convoluted arguments put forward to justify such goals provide one indication of how wrong they are. A clearer sign of how wrong such groups are is that the murder, cruelty, exploitation, and dissimulation that serve such goals cannot be construed as expressions of the best in us or of our highest humanity. Even though there is no final word on what humans are at our best, it is clear to all but a deluded few that the murderous racists and tyrants of this world are examples of the worst in us. It is not necessary to have (indeed, I think it is wise to avoid) a final statement of what is good to be able to differentiate between what is better and worse in this way.

Psychology's Exploration of What Is Good

Psychologists have, in fact, been studying the human good actively in a number of ways throughout most of the discipline's history (Austin & Vancouver, 1996). Personality, motivation, and cognitive psychologists have studied goals and goal striving. Other researchers have focused on subjective well-being as the defining feature of what is good for individuals (Ackerman, Zuroff, & Moskowitz, 2000; DeNeve & Cooper, 1998; Diener, 2000; Emmons, 2003). Humanistic psychologists describe and study creativity (Arons & Richards, 2001), self-actualization (Privelte, 2001), self-determination (Maslow, 1971; Ryan & Deci, 2000), and meaning (Kasser & Ryan, 1993; McGregor & Little, 1998; Sheldon & Kasser, 1998). Interest in prosocial behavior has grown from a fringe topic to a major literature in developmental, personality, and social psychology (Eisenberg & Mussen, 1989).

More recently, the positive psychology movement has reinvigorated the discipline's interest in promoting optimal living (Seligman & Csikszentmihaly, 2000). Recent works have focused on human flourishing (Keyes & Haidt, 2003), virtue (McCullough & Snyder, 2000; Peterson & Seligman, 2004; Sandage & Hill, 2001), flow (Csikszentmihaly & Csikszentmihaly, 1994), optimism (Peterson & Chang, 2003; Snyder, 2000), creativity (Cassandro & Simonton, 2003), elevation (Haidt, 2003), and wisdom (Baltes & Staudinger, 2000; Sternberg, 1990, 1998).

Positive personal experiences predominate in this catalogue of research on what is good for humans (with the obvious exception of prosocial behavior). This tendency to make individual experience the center of the good life is an outgrowth of psychology's attempt to remain aloof from questions of what is good by relegating moral questions to the subjective realm. For this reason, it is common to portray the human good in terms of life satisfaction, the presence of pleasant emotions, and the absence of unpleasant emotions (Emmons, 2003; McGregor & Little, 1998; Oishi, Diener, Suh, & Lucas, 1999). Although any account of what is good for humans has to include positive emotional experience, individual affect is only one indicator of a life well lived and cannot be taken as the definitive picture. One obvious reason for the insufficiency is that it is not hard to imagine a happy, satisfied organized crime boss or a thoroughly contented couch potato. Of course, it is good to be satisfied and happy, but mere emotional well-being cannot suffice as the primary indicator of the best that human life has to offer. Surely, the best kind of life has an active dimension through which we pursue various tangible, valuable, and socially relevant ends. Aristotle expressed this by saying that the highest good "does not lie in amusement," noting that "it would, indeed, be strange if the end were amusement, and one were to take trouble and suffer hardship all one's life in order to amuse oneself" (p. 262).

Other authors (Doherty, 1995; Nicholas, 1994) introduce virtues as character traits that promote an interpersonal morality through which one acts benevolently toward others. There is a lot to be said for benevolence and for these authors' pioneering work in demonstrating the relevance of virtue for psychotherapy, but benevolence is not the primary focus of virtue as it is classically conceived. Doing well by others in general is often praiseworthy, but only when the end goal of the benevolence is worthwhile. In other words, actions are only truly beneficial when they lead to genuinely good ends, and therefore the nature of the goals is pivotal for the practice of benevolence. Many attempts at benevolence go awry by misconstruing what is in others' best interest. Moreover, the emphasis on benevolence relies too much on the dichotomization of what is good for the actor and the beneficiary. The emphasis on benevolence is a preoccupation of Christian and Victorian perspectives, whereas a classical virtue framework suggests that both the actor and the social group benefit from excellence in action and that the best goods are held in common rather than individually (e.g., friendship, democracy), a primary topic of chapter 4.

Flourishing

Aristotle uses the term *eudaimonia* to designate the ultimate good for humans. *Eudaimonia* has been translated as happiness, but is better rendered as flourishing, because happiness has primarily emotional connotations for us. *Eudaimonia* is not just a positive feeling or even an overall sense of well-being. Instead, he defined it as an activity to emphasize that the best kind of life consists in habitual excellence in action. In other words, humans flourish by engaging in uniquely human activities in a praiseworthy manner. Living a good life has similar formal properties to being a good musician or a good carpenter. Doing well in music or carpentry means that one is able to *perform* admirably in those pursuits. Therefore, the best place to find the human good is in uniquely human activities that allow the emergence of excellence such as art, athletics, scholarship, citizenship, and so forth (cf. Aristotle, pp. 13–14). It is in these kinds of activities that we have the possibility of fully expressing our humanity because they involve us in exercising our rational capacities in pursuit of our socially relevant ends in a way that can bring out our best selves. From a virtue ethics perspective, humans are goal-seeking, rational, social creatures, and I have much more to say about these characteristics in the next two chapters.

Flourishing consists in cultivating excellence in action, bringing out the best in oneself, and living the best kind of complete life. We seek many goods, from pleasure, honor, and wealth to good relationships, community, and beauty. If the overall aim is to embody the best in one's human nature, then all of the other goals we seek are valuable to the degree to which they contribute to this overall good. Although goods such as honor, pleasure, and virtue are worthwhile, they are subordinate to the aim of living well overall.

This is a highly abstract concept of what is good for humans, but it is not an empty one. I can examine whether I have a good grasp of flourishing by reflecting on whether I am bringing out the very best in myself in the pursuit of the goals I am currently seeking. For example, can I, on reflection, believe that directing my life primarily at the perpetual acquisition of the latest, greatest new gadgets is the best kind of life? Or is a continual pursuit of honors bestowed by others, in competition with my peers, the very best kind of life? There is, of course, nothing wrong with having gadgets or receiving honors. The question is, are gadgets and honors ends in themselves or are they subsidiary to some higher, more comprehensive end? For example, do great scientists work primarily to win the Nobel Prize or to expand our knowledge in important ways? The Nobel Prize is indeed desirable, but most premier scientists see their primary purpose in their contributions to knowledge with or without awards. In contrast to most other ethical theories, virtue ethics emphasizes that the goals I seek reveal a great deal about the kind of person I am. Am I someone whose life is made up primarily of a series of pleasures, honors, and material acquisitions, or does my life consist of a habitual pattern of admirable actions in the service of ends that are worthwhile in themselves (e.g., high-quality friendship, scholarship, citizenship)? Our answers to this kind of question do not just consist of words but emerge in the quality of our everyday activities throughout our whole lives.

Virtue ethics emphasizes the overall integrity of the individual's character and life as a whole. Perhaps the ultimate test of whether the individual is flourishing is to reflect on whether one can look back on one's life with pride and affirm that the aims and activities that characterize it expressed the best in oneself. Before we accept this perspective, we have to reckon with the prime contender in psychology for the ultimate good for humans: pleasure.

Pleasure as the Human Good?

There is a very strong tendency to take pleasure as the highest good in psychological theorizing as well as in some philosophical quarters. There are several advantages of pleasure as a primary good. It is inherently desirable and encompasses a wide range of experiences. Another attraction of pleasure as the central human good is that it is a subjective affair that seems to allow a highly desired theoretical objectivity. If the goal (pleasure) is determined by the individual, then our theory and practice can focus on the relative effectiveness of various means for attaining that goal and ostensibly remain morally neutral about human ends. In addition, pleasure has the appearance of a measurable construct. For these reasons, pleasure seems to provide a good fit to the traditional split between objective science and subjective values.

Given the straightforward character of the hedonistic account in psychology, why would we seek more complex sources of human motivation? Aristotle suggested that the very simplicity of the pleasure account is deceptive by asking "What do you mean by pleasure?" On reflection, it is relatively easy to see that there are many kinds of pleasure and that the tendency in psychology and in some philosophies to lump them all together obscures some essential and enlightening distinctions.

The contexts and sources of pleasure suggest a concept with multiple categories rather than one general experience. Sexual pleasure provides a clear example of this. Having sex with a prostitute differs from sex with a casual lover, and both differ dramatically from making love with a longtime partner. In the case of sex in a long-term relationship, the enjoyment is inextricably embedded in a relationship that has significance beyond that instance of pleasure. Whereas more casual sex is oriented to pleasure as the goal, sexual relations in relationships are an integral part of what makes the relationship good. It simply makes no sense to place the enjoyment of a luscious dessert on the same metric as the pleasure of bestowing an appropriately generous gift on a dear friend. One can also think of compliments offered by a flatterer, a stranger, a friend, and someone one admires but does not know well. The enjoyment of these compliments will again have very different characters depending on their sources, meaning, and context. Ignoring these distinctions for the sake of having a simple hedonic calculus does not represent a workable approach to psychology because it trivializes and obfuscates the very experiences and actions it attempts to explain.

Pleasures also differ in that the character of the enjoyment is related to the kind of person one has become. Being capable of participating in an activity well will tend to increase the pleasure, whether it is eating, sex, friendship, appreciation of art, or leisure pursuits. By becoming a better friend, lover, or connoisseur, one becomes capable of greater pleasure and finer enjoyments in these activities. The appreciation of art is enhanced by knowledge of art and by cultivating a sensibility for various forms of expression. The better a friend one is, the deeper one's friendship can become and the richer one's enjoyment of it will be. It is better to receive a compliment from an honest and respected friend than a stranger not only because one is pleased by the positive feedback but also because it comes from someone one values and the compliment resonates with the quality of shared activities that define the friendship.

As Erich Fromm (1941/1965) pointed out long ago, it is important to keep the proper relationship between pleasure and what is good. If pleasures are seen merely in terms of individual preference, desire becomes the test of value rather than value the test of desire. In other words, is enjoyment the last word in deciding what is worth doing, or should we see some pleasures as worthwhile and others as unworthy? Surely the best kind of life is comprised by desires and pleasures that bring out the best in us. If we see pleasure as nothing more than subjective choice, we are unable to differentiate between better and worse pleasures because the evaluation of the ends is a matter of ungrounded personal preference. By contrast, a virtue ethics perspective on pleasure recognizes that some pleasures are better than others. Aristotle remarked, "It is the mark of virtue both to be pleased and to be pained at the right objects and in the right way" (p. 82).

Virtue ethics sees the objects of pleasure as a manifestation of the nature of an individual's character. One of the clearest ways to recognize a person of character is that he or she will find pleasure in the finest things and the best states of affairs. Pleasures related to noble activities differ significantly from pleasures attendant to unsavory sources. Put another way, some pleasures elevate and others degrade us. For example, the pleasure of a wine for a connoisseur is qualitatively different from the pleasure found by those who drink solely to become inebriated. Some pleasures are objectionable or detrimental, such as gratifications associated with an overweening self-importance, self-absorption, taunting a defeated opponent, or exercising an illegitimate dominance over others. Some find pleasure in cruelty, domination, and exploitation. Having wealth is pleasant, but if one attains it through betrayal, the associated pleasure is different than if it is gained through industry or creativity. In other words, the quality of the pleasure cannot be separated from the nobility or baseness of the activity.

This suggests that pleasure is too varied an experience to serve as a unifying aim for living. In addition, the nature of pleasure seems to be closely related to the kind of person one is, the nature of one's knowledge, tastes, and character being key contributors to the kind and depth of enjoyment that is possible. Finally, some find pleasure in admirable activities and others seek enjoyment in deplorable pursuits. According to virtue ethics, human flourishing cannot be equated with the transitory subjective experience of pleasure, because flourishing has a much broader scope. Flourishing refers to the way an individual's life as a whole is shaping up, which includes experiencing emotional happiness and pleasure, but it cannot be reduced to affective experiences. All of this suggests that the sources and experience of pleasure are dependent on the kind of person one is and on the kind of goods in which one finds enjoyment.

VIRTUE AS AN ACQUIRED DISPOSITION

One of the key aspects of virtue is that it refers to a characteristic excellence, a habit of acting in ways that embody the virtue. That is why many authors see character as an individual's particular configuration of virtues and vices (Drane, 1994; Hursthouse, 1999; McCullough & Snyder, 2000; Meara et al., 1996; Sandage & Hill, 2001; Tjeltveit, 2003). One finds virtue in people who act well characteristically rather than intermittently. For example, one would not consider someone who gives away money or gifts episodically, because of ulterior motive, or under duress to be generous, whereas an individual who gives consistently enacts generosity as a character trait. Although even occasional acts of generosity, loyalty, and fairness are beneficial, one would not consider them evidence of good character unless they are part of a reliable pattern of action, which indicates an acquired disposition to pursue what is good. A person of good character is not easily dissuaded from virtuous actions by difficulties, distractions, or temptations because these actions have become "second nature." The individual is firm in what he or she is doing and stands by it (Broadie, 1991). Encouraging trainees to have this kind of reliable disposition to act well ethically, therapeutically, and scientifically is a central goal of all psychology training programs. Even if we do not generally describe excellence as a psychologist in terms of virtue, we do hope that our graduates will act well characteristically.

Our answers to the question of how human beings should live are not simply expressions of subjective preferences or inherited temperament. Rather, we shape our character through the aims that we believe are truly worth pursuing in our characteristic choices and actions. Agents choose how to act, and the choices we repeatedly make become habits; habits become, in turn, acquired dispositions. Endorsement of many similar choices over time makes each of us one kind of person rather than another. We become brave by acting courageously, generous by giving, brutish by following our lower impulses, and so forth. In other words, we *characterize* ourselves because our habitual acts shape who we are as individuals. As I discuss more fully below, good character is an achievement that individuals cultivate over a long period. Therefore, my use of the term *disposition* does not refer to naturally occurring states, but to cultivated habits.

Acting well consistently in the ordinary activities of life is one of the hallmarks of character, but some critics have questioned the existence of virtues on exactly these grounds. In an articulate recent critique of virtue ethics, Doris (2002) argued that because social psychologists have shown, in many and varied experiments, that human behavior is responsive to situational factors, neither global personality traits nor character traits can be substantial sources of behavior. To cite a few examples, participants are more willing to be helpful after they find a small amount of money in a phone booth, less likely to be helpful if the experimenter tells them that they must hurry, and so forth (Carnevale & Isen, 1986; Darley & Batson, 1973; Isen & Levin, 1972; Latané & Darley, 1970). Doris concluded that this responsiveness to the situation rules out character traits as an independent source of behavior. There is no question that situations influence how individuals act (virtue ethicists also insist on this). Doris questioned whether individuals have identifiable, reliable, and global character traits like honesty or courage. He believed that the evidence he presented contradicted theories proposing character traits.

The argument and evidence Doris presented cannot answer the question about character because those studies did not actually examine the presence or absence of a reliable disposition to act well. These experiments consisted in a single observation of participants' responses to strangers in chance encounters. A single instance of behavior with a stranger does not give us much evidence of the presence or absence of a virtue. Moreover, character strengths are traits that allow the individual to pursue some good. It is highly unlikely that the contrived circumstances of these experiments related to the overall aims that the participants pursue in the ordinary course of their lives. It is entirely unclear how chance encounters with a stranger figure into the important aims of the individual.

If we are serious about exploring whether character strengths actually manifest in behavior, a very different approach to the research is necessary. Investigators have to assess three essential components of a trait or character strength. First, there must be individual differences on the characteristic. Second, evidence for consistency in trait-associated behaviors is needed across situations. Third, there must be consistency in trait-associated behavior over time. In the case of virtues, additional evidence is necessary regarding whether the individual has the proper motivation, affect, and cognitive understanding to consider actions virtuous. The study of virtue is in its infancy, and such demanding studies have not as yet been conducted. Some research on what we might see as protovirtues suggests that admirable behavior appears to emerge in ways that are consistent with a trait perspective. The connections between this research and virtue ethics are very tenuous and suggestive rather than definitive, however.

For example, many researchers have successfully identified what they call *prosocial* behavior using multiple measures and sources of data over significant periods of time (Davis, 1994; Davis & Franzoi, 1991; Eisenberg, Carlo, Murphy, & Van Court, 1995; Eisenberg et al., 2002; Eisenberg et al., 1999; Eisenberg, Miller, Shell, McNalley, & Shea, 1991; Eisenberg & Shell, 1986; Kochanska, Padavich, & Koenig, 1996; Penner & Finkelstein, 1998). These investigators have documented individual differences in helping behavior, moderate consistency across situations, and consistency over a 19-year span, providing evidence for all three of the features necessary for a trait.

The term *prosocial* is a rather vague and colorless way to refer to various kinds of helping behavior. From a virtue perspective, helping behavior is a form of generosity, but these researchers did not approach their study of helping behavior under this rubric. Nevertheless, Eisenberg and her colleagues did identify affective (sympathy and empathy), attitudinal (prosocial values), and cognitive (prosocial and higher-level moral reasoning) concomitants of helping behavior that are strikingly consistent with seeing this helping behavior as evidence of the character strength of generosity. The naturalistic settings, multiple sources of data, and absence of clever experimental manipulations all lend credence to these results and suggest that they tell a more realistic story of character strengths than the more stilted experimental studies cited by Doris.

I am not claiming that research on prosocial behavior demonstrates the existence of generosity, much less virtue in general. Yet these carefully constructed studies indicate that admirable traits can be studied and that greater attention to investigating character strengths is promising. There is mounting evidence that we can identify and measure positive behavioral dispositions. Although the cross-situational and longitudinal stability of these traits varies depending on the methods and sources of measurement, they are consistently found. The best available evidence suggests that a settled disposition to act well is observable and relatively stable in some individuals, contrary to Doris's contention.

ACTION

Action is critical to virtue, because there is no virtue without concrete activity. This is immediately clear if we imagine someone claiming to have courageous thoughts or generous feelings that are not reflected in his or her actions. These thoughts and feelings do not count for much without actions that demonstrate courage or generosity. This emphasis on action distinguishes virtue ethics from much contemporary talk about "values" as an internal, personal possession. In contrast, virtues are always evident in the concrete world of activity.

We can examine the virtue of loyalty to clarify this point. Loyalty includes feelings of attachment and fidelity, recognition of the value of the person or group to whom one is loyal, and remembrance of what one owes to them. None of this counts as loyalty if one fails to stand up for the people to whom one is bound, if one betrays confidences or relationship norms, if one fails to keep one's promises, and so forth. Loyalty is an activity, a way of acting so that one is true to those with whom one has essential ties. This emphasis on overt action is an important affinity between virtue ethics and mainstream psychology's interest in observable behavior.

The activity of loyalty is exemplified in the story of the brilliant philosopher and novelist Dame Iris Murdoch and her husband, John Bayley. They met, fell in love, and lived a long life together. From the mid-1990s, Dame Iris suffered from Alzheimer's disease and her brilliance and exuberance faded tragically and cumulatively. Bayley remained devoted to her throughout the decade until her death in February 1999, caring for her and struggling through the long twilight of her decline. He remained devoted to her throughout this time and wrote two beautifully loving books about her (Bayley, 2000, 2001).

Bayley's loyalty is unquestionably admirable. Most people would hope that they could manage to remain true to their spouses and other loved ones in this way. The question is, can we account for Bayley's devotion with our standard theories of relationships? Where do we find his motivation for such fidelity in social exchange theory, for example? Was it that he expected so little from a relationship (his comparison level)? Was it that he had so few alternative possibilities that staying with a wife with Alzheimer's seemed like his best relationship option (his comparison level for alternatives)? Was it that the relationship with someone with dementia was terribly rewarding or that it entailed no significant costs? Did he believe that her condition could miraculously improve so that they could renew their old relationship? The obvious answers to these questions make it abundantly clear that social exchange theory cannot begin to help us understand this kind of loyalty. Virtue ethics provides a clear and thorough explanation of this devotion that is fortunately not uncommon.

This instance is well-known because Dame Iris was such a brilliant and captivating person, and Bayley is a writer as well. Yet countless spouses and children care for their aging and debilitated loved ones in a very similar way in spite of the costs and the despair attendant on the slow death of dementia. Clearly, Bayley's loyalty was evident in his actions, not just his sentiments or thoughts. If he had written his elegies to her without offering the extended and loving care that he did, we would not consider him loyal as much as opportunistic. Fortunately for Dame Iris and for all of us, he did live his loyalty.

VIRTUE AND REASON

There is an essential cognitive element in virtue because acting well involves acting for the right reasons. In the absence of good reasons for acting as one does, one's actions may be accidentally similar to virtue or whimsical in nature rather than part of a settled disposition. The necessity of a good understanding of virtue highlights the essential role of cognition in character. Knowing what counts as courage or justice is essential to enacting those virtues in a consistent manner.

Generosity offers a classic example of the importance of the right kind of thoughts and intentions in character excellence. When individuals give money, time, or talent, they might have many reasons for doing so, including a genuine wish to share their abundance, a desire to appear generous and receive accolades, a plan to reduce their tax burden, or an intention to make up for past wrongs. Only the first counts as generosity, because the other reasons define the act as public relations, an accounting move, or as penance.

Acting for the right reasons grows out of three sources. First, character includes having an intellectual understanding of the virtue in question, knowing, for example, what generally constitutes generous or just action. Second, one's intellectual grasp of the ends one seeks helps to inform one's actions. Recall that the virtues are character strengths that make it possible for individuals to seek what is good. In the absence of a clear concept of one's aims, one will be more likely to flounder and flail about than to pursue one's valued aims in a focused and deliberate manner. Finally, one's intellectual capacities are engaged in the wisdom to see what is vital in the situations one faces and how one can act to best address what is important rather than what is trivial. I discuss the centrality of this wisdom for the practice of virtue at length in chapter 5.

One of the ways that Aristotle distinguished between natural virtues, those that some people are born with, and fully acquired character strengths is that the latter include an understanding of the virtue. Young children can be very generous, for example, but they do so from impulse, without necessarily understanding why they act in a generous manner or how to modulate their generosity to make it appropriate to the situation (Grusec, 1991). The transformation of the natural capacity for virtue into real character strength requires the cultivation of an intellectual grasp of the virtues and vices to avoid a hit or miss approach to acting well.

Even though a good intellectual grasp of virtue is important, Aristotle made no bones about virtue being an intellectual exercise. He noted that "intellect itself . . . moves nothing" (p. 139). It is one's *desire* to reach worthy aims that moves one to act well, and one's understanding of good action and the ends one seeks helps to focus and direct one's efforts. This means that acting well involves a concordance of emotion and understanding. The person of character acts in a well-informed and well-motivated way, which brings us to the question of how emotions function in virtue.

EMOTION AND VIRTUE

Aristotle saw emotion as a key component of virtue:

> For instance, both fear and confidence and appetite and anger and pity and in general pleasure and pain may be felt both too much and too little, and in both cases not well; but to feel them at the right times, with reference to the right objects, towards the right people, with the right motive, and in the right way, is what is both intermediate and best, and this is characteristic of virtue. (p. 38)

Character shows in how one's emotions are aligned with one's actions, and in this section I explore various ways that one's feelings figure in acting well, beginning with the idea that virtues are enacted gladly rather than reluctantly or grudgingly. The motivation for this wholehearted engagement in virtue grows out of emotional attachment to the goods one pursues. In the next section and in chapter 3, I also describe how generally virtuous individuals, in the unusual cases where they are not able to act well wholeheartedly, can transform their motivation and emotion so that they can gladly do what is best.

Emotional Concordance

According to virtue ethics, one's affective experience grows out of the kind of person one is, and the best kind of character results in acting well wholeheartedly, gladly doing what seems best. This understanding of emotion as an expression of the kind of character one has cultivated stands in contrast with the two dominant contemporary perspectives on emotion. The Romantic philosophical tradition has taught us to see emotions as spontaneous experiences that are beyond our control and that arise naturally out of our inner nature. Humanistic psychotherapy theories, inspired by the Romantic outlook, portray emotional experience as a guidepost to exploring and understanding our deepest selves. According to these approaches, allowing one's emotions to unfold naturally and unedited is crucial to self-understanding, self-expression, self-development, and fulfillment. According to Romantic thought, we promote our well-being best by receiving our affective experience with reverence, and if we are appropriately open to these inner expressions our deepest selves can be read from them.

In contrast, cognitive therapies and cognitive psychology generally, inspired by the Enlightenment tradition that extols rationality over emotionality, see affective life as largely secondary to patterns of thought and behavior. This means that emotions are to be regulated rather than reverentially received and interpreted. One can manage affective experience by eliminating irrational and self-defeating thoughts in the service of increasing contentment and enjoyment over against unhappiness and misery.

A virtue ethical perspective on emotion transcends the dichotomy presented by the humanistic and cognitive schools of thought. In virtue ethics, emotions are indicators of one's nature, but the relevant nature is not a primordial "true nature," as in Romantic thought. Rather, emotional reactions reflect the current state of one's character. If one's feelings are consistent with acting in a praiseworthy manner, they indicate a well-developed character, but if one's emotions run contrary to behaving in a way consistent with what is best, then one will be unable to act well wholeheartedly.

Emotions reveal the kind of person one is in the kinds of things that elicit feelings of delight or pleasure and by the sorts of things that cause pain. To take a simple example, a person can compliment someone's excellent performance gladly or grudgingly. Complimenting them wholeheartedly indicates an emotional concordance with the compliment reflective of a joyful recognition of the other's talent or accomplishment. Giving the compliment grudgingly suggests a smallness of character accompanied by envy or mere conformity with social expectations of praise. This harmony of emotion and action is a necessary component of virtuous activity, because one's motives for action and one's emotional experience of the activity can either resonate with and enhance what one is doing or create disharmony and thereby undermine one's actions. The person of good character acts with a concordance of emotion, thought, and action. There may be times when that concordance is something of an achievement and other times when it comes spontaneously, but this concordance differentiates an excellent character from that of someone who is learning virtue or from the merely self-controlled (continent) individual.

The process of character development, which I describe in more detail later in this chapter, involves schooling one's emotions so that they are consistent with acting well. The schooling of emotions is similar to cognitive therapy approaches in that individuals pursue affective shifts by altering their thoughts and behaviors. Yet this affective training is unlike the management of emotion suggested by cognitive theorists, because it is not pursued for the sake of increasing the ratio of pleasure to displeasure. Rather the point of training oneself to be properly affected is to heighten one's attachment to what is best and to increase the strength of one's attraction to what is good so that one will naturally act virtuously (i.e., seek what is good).

Emotional experience is not just a reflection of one's state of character, however. When properly attuned, emotional reactions can be very informative about the nature of the situations a person faces. The experience of fear, indignation, puzzlement, and joy can help one to see aspects of one's circumstances that may not be otherwise fully apparent (Sherman, 1989). Put another way, the emergence of a particular emotional experience is a necessary indication that one has seen a situation rightly. For example, if a person observes an egregious injustice and does not experience some degree of indignation in response, one might wonder if that individual has a good grasp of justice.

The Love of What Is Good

The primary source of the emotional concordance previously discussed is found in learning to love what is good. Virtue ethics suggests that a proper recognition of what is good naturally inspires a desire to act in the service of that good. Individuals of character are spontaneously drawn to the good, and this concept of moral attraction encourages the best kind of desires and feelings. This enormously appealing idea of wanting to act in the best ways simply because one loves what is best is one of the central concepts of virtue ethics. For example, good scientists act honestly out of love for truth; good therapists persevere with difficult clients because they value human flourishing. Thus, when individuals have cultivated a love for what is good, they do not have to struggle with inner conflicts about acting well. They *want* to do what is best wholeheartedly.

When individuals are involved in pursuing something that they genuinely love, they experience pleasure in its pursuit and in their progress toward their goal. Those who devote themselves to scholarship love to learn and to create knowledge, and they enjoy their scholarly work as a labor of love. Those who love to build take pleasure in their construction work and in the completion of a building or a bridge. Fervent teachers are deeply pleased by sharing their learning and by their students' growing capacities and knowledge. When a good is dear to one, one spontaneously wants to pursue it because one sees it as valuable, enjoys its pursuit, and can act wholeheartedly.

Two recent studies suggest that individuals of character are intrinsically motivated to act in admirable ways. In their study of 23 individuals identified as moral exemplars according to well-articulated parameters, Colby and Damon (1995) concluded that the *"unity of self and moral goals . . . provides the most central key to understanding the unwavering commitment"* these individuals showed to their goals.

> The close relationship of personal and moral goals that we saw in our exemplars means that they do not see their moral choices as an exercise in self-sacrifice. To the contrary, they see their moral goals as a means of attaining their personal ones, and vice versa. This can only be possible when moral goals and personal goals are in synchrony, perhaps even identical. (p. 362, italics in original)

The authors went on to say that this exceptionality is a matter of degree and "is an extreme version of a developmental process that accounts for self formation and growth in every normal individual." Similarly, Hart, Yates, Fegley, and Wilson (1995) reported that a group of inner-city adolescents who volunteered extensively differed from a matched control group in that they saw their moral aims as central to who they were as individuals and they described a much closer relationship between their actual and ideal selves. Both studies indicate that the worthwhile aims that their participants pursued were deeply integrated into their sense of themselves and that they pursued these aims wholeheartedly and gladly.

Of course, no one is perfect, so becoming the kind of person who wants to act in the best way *all* of the time is something of an aspiration in ordinary human life. Within the limitations of human fallibility, however, a preponderance of interest in pursuing what is good is possible and can simplify decision-making and action. There are circumstances that can make it very difficult to see what is best or to act consistently with one's overall aims. In these trying situations, individuals with strong character can transform their emotions to attain an emotional harmony with the best actions.

I explore this transformation of emotion in the next section. It is also significant that no one is born with a spontaneous love of what is good. In fact, learning to recognize and appreciate what is valuable, beautiful, and good is a very important part of socialization. Virtue ethics recognizes the necessity of education to develop human ethical potential, and I turn to the process of character education now.

THE CULTIVATION OF VIRTUE

In his account of the acquisition of virtue, Aristotle did not dichotomize nature and nurture, saying, "The virtues are implanted in us neither by nature nor contrary to nature; we are by nature equipped with the ability to receive them, and habit brings this ability to completion and fulfillment" (p. 33). There are two important points here. First, virtue is a possibility for everyone, but one cannot count on some innate goodness to automatically give rise to excellence. Nor is developing character a matter of struggling *against* a contrary nature. It is a matter of cultivating naturally given capacities. As mentioned earlier, character strengths are those qualities that make it possible to embody one's full humanity. Second, individuals acquire character through practice, through which acting well becomes the natural or habitual response.

Because virtue is a kind of activity, humans learn it by performing virtuous actions. We learn to be brave by acting courageously, to be generous by giving, and so forth. One can acquire the habit of virtue only through practice. Because virtues exist only in action, they must be cultivated through enacting them. But acting as a person of character would act is not the same as acting virtuously. This practice helps one to become comfortable with courage and generosity and to identify emotionally with these actions. One acts in the way that a person of character would act while one is on the way to developing character (Broadie, 1991). The process is analogous to learning a skill in that the initial attempts to do something like woodworking tend to be halting and lead to mixed results. It is only through practice and guidance that one can become adept at making attractive objects with wood. Creating a few pieces of furniture would not qualify one as a furniture maker, only a novice. Similarly, the beginning of practicing courage or generosity would not be considered virtue because these actions have not yet become second nature but are consciously done because they seem good. Someone would be counted as courageous or just or temperate only when courage, justice, or temperance characterizes their actions in a reliable and coherent way. The cultivation of excellence in character is a result of developing habitually virtuous responses to such a degree that it becomes second nature to do them.

Choice and Character

Even though virtue becomes habitual, it is still a matter of choice, not blind habit. Character is a result of choice because making virtue second nature occurs only by repeatedly deciding to act in the desired way over a significant period. One way to describe this is that individuals habituate themselves to acting in a particular manner. Another way to describe it is that when they decide, over and over again, to act in the best way, they are *characterizing* themselves as virtuous persons. That is, they build their characters, for better or worse, through the myriad choices they make in the course of their everyday lives. We might refer to this as "the accretion of character" because each time one acts, one contributes to the formation of one's character, even if only slightly in each instance. From this perspective, one's decisions and actions are not just a series of episodes independent of the rest of one's life and character. They *make up* that life and character.

Habituation is an active, conscious process in which one makes choices explicitly for the purpose of learning to act nobly or basely, developing one's character through these choices and actions. The repeated choice to act well is a result of reason, not due simply to mindless or causally determined habits.

This highlights the fact that every action has a past and a future. The ways I have acted in the past influence what is possible for me now, what I can do easily and what takes effort. The choice I make at this moment helps to ease or impede future decisions and actions through the accretion of character. Each action reinforces or undermines my dispositions to act in particular ways. Each circumstance provides new opportunities to hone and refine one's ability to become wise and to act well or to act foolishly or viciously.

Virtue ethics is concerned with an individual's life as a whole and with how that life comes together through the decisions and actions the person undertakes. The crucial thing is to cultivate one's character by firming up one's disposition to act well across circumstances. In this sense, virtue ethics is *agent-centered*, highlighting the ways in which the individual's character is involved in deliberation and action. An individual's character at any given time is the accumulation of a lifetime of decisions and actions, which lead the person to face the present circumstance with ethical resources that have or have not been developed. The best kind of character positions the individual to pursue an integrated life in pursuit of a coherent set of human goods.

For example, the habitual truthfulness of honest individuals rests on the decision to endorse their honest dispositions in each situation they face. It remains possible for these individuals to act dishonestly, but the long series of choices to be truthful has created a kind of character momentum that makes it easier to be honest as a matter of course (Annas, 1993). The strength of habituation developed through repeated choices to act well is illustrated by a story told by Hursthouse (1999) about a Dutch woman who risked her life by harboring Jews during the Holocaust. When someone commented on the courage that it must have taken to help the Jews, she said, "I don't think it such a courageous thing to do. For certain people it is a self-evident thing to do" (p. 127). This suggests a high degree of habituation that made her actions seem like the only real alternative in spite of the tremendous risks she ran.

Although virtue consists of acting well habitually, virtues are not enacted by rote, without thought. It is not always clear how to act courageously or generously in a particular situation. Moreover, it is not always immediately evident whether one's actions should be characterized more by generosity or justice. In such instances, the individual must deliberate about how best to act given the situation. This process of deliberation and choice is known as practical wisdom (the topic of Part II of this book). Being able to wisely discern and choose a course of action is indispensable to virtue.

Once it is evident that ethics involves character, one cannot reduce it to making correct decisions and acting rightly on isolated occasions that are somehow especially "ethical" in nature. Possessing virtue is deeply relevant to all of one's activities, from the way one spends money, to the kind of jokes one tells, to the things that interest one, and to the things in which one takes pleasure. Individuals reveal, refine, and solidify who they are in all of their activities, not just in a circumscribed domain of "ethical" behaviors. In this way, virtue ethics is far more comprehensive and integrative than other approaches to ethics. Virtue and practical wisdom are relevant in all of one's activities, because all of them together, whether work or leisure, family life or the life of the citizen, contribute to or detract from living as a whole, flourishing human being.

Just as virtue is exercised in all aspects of one's life, so is it taught through engaging in ordinary activities in an excellent manner. Learning virtue in connection with learning all of the other roles and skills necessary for a successful life is nothing other than learning how to engage in those activities well rather than badly (MacIntyre, 1999).

Goodness Requires Training

Individuals can acquire virtue-sensitive emotions through moral education, also known as habituation. Contrary to a central tenet of Romanticism, we require training to learn what is best and how to promote it through our actions. Infants are not born with a natural appreciation for what is good, beautiful, or true. Human beings are born with the *capacity* to grasp what is fine and noble, but without the ability to appreciate specific instances of what is best. These capacities need to be cultivated and refined. For this reason, virtue ethics has much to say about education and parenting. Aristotle is one of those rare philosophers who never forgot that we begin our lives as children and that our experiences as children are crucially related to our moral capacity as adults. He commented that children "ought to have been brought up in a particular way . . . so as both to delight in and to be pained by the things that we ought; this is the right education" (p. 32).

Let me give you an analogy to illustrate this point. Although humans are born with the capacity for language, we are not born with the ability to speak. We learn speech through a long process of shaping vocalizations into meaningful utterances under our caretakers' guidance. As speech becomes available, the possibility to appreciate poetry or beautiful prose emerges. But children also have to learn to recognize and enjoy excellent expressions of language through a long process of education. Similarly, infants and young children naturally respond very positively to music, but the ability to make or even enjoy high-quality music must be taught. There is no guarantee that children will grow to appreciate the finest written or musical art simply because they have an innate capacity to do so, but these capacities are available for cultivation. In the same way, we are not born knowing what it is to be the best kind of person. Humans have to learn what is best and highest in ourselves because it is not given in an obvious and instinctive way. This learning is obviously culturally mediated, and concepts of beauty and nobility vary across historical cultures, hence there are many models of what it is to have good character.

Schooling Emotions

Just as we must learn to appreciate beauty, we also cultivate our emotional responsiveness to goodness and virtue. In our upbringing, we are taught to enjoy some activities over others, to respond positively to particular customs and habits and to experience others aversively. To give a few simple examples, one learns to spontaneously commend or condemn belching during a meal, to trust or fear someone who maintains eye contact, and to feel joy, shame, or indifference to nakedness. It follows that individuals learn to recognize and be attracted by the particular goods that are prized in their historical communities.

In an interesting empirical example of the kind of affective prompting that might encourage emotional development, Haidt (2003) reported that he could differentially elicit happiness and what he termed *elevation* by presenting different video clips. In the elevation condition, participants viewed a 10-minute video about Mother Teresa. This group reported warm, pleasant, "tingling" emotions and a desire to help others, improve themselves, and to affiliate with others. In contrast, video clips meant to evoke happiness resulted in individuals expressing desires to engage in self-interested pursuits. These very brief prompts in an artificial setting are suggestive of how emotional experience can be altered through the presentation of exemplars. Virtue ethics proposes that ongoing exposure to individuals who exemplify the best in human nature can have a pervasive and long-lasting positive effect on ethical behavior. Eisenberg (2002) summarized a great deal of research on children's empathic responses and prosocial behavior in just this way, citing the important influences of parental modeling, encouragement, guidance, and discipline in the cultivation of these protovirtues in children.

Emotional Schooling of Racism and Multiculturalism

We can examine the substantial and consequential examples of racism and multiculturalism as a way to further clarify emotional schooling. Hursthouse (1999) discussed the extent to which racism is the result of training in emotional responses to the rejected race. It expresses itself in highly emotional ways through hatred, contempt, spite, suspicion, and fear. Children do not naturally experience these emotional reactions to people who look and act differently than they do. They have to be taught to see these differences as elicitors of contempt and mistrust, to enjoy the despised others' suffering or oppression, and to resent it when the other does well. Children are taught to see the hated other as dangerous, cunning, and devious, as incapable of appreciating finer things, as unable to feel pain as they do, as lazy, as cheats, and so forth. Training for racism occurs over a long period and is often thoroughly inculcated in its trainees. Those unfortunate enough to receive extensive training in racism may be unable to ever spontaneously and wholeheartedly trust or admire someone from the despised group. Although it is possible to overcome racism, it is unclear whether it can ever be entirely erased.

Training efforts to reduce racism and prejudice are also very much concerned with altering emotional responses. Much of multicultural training takes the form of learning facts and hearing arguments against prejudice. However, these efforts are directed not only at providing information but largely toward retraining one's emotional response to people from other races and backgrounds. Personal transformation from an ethnocentric perspective to an acceptance of and interest in the culturally different is a central aspect of training in multiculturalism (American Psychological Association [APA], 2003b; Fowers & Davidov, 2005; Sue, Arredondo, & McDavis, 1992). This can be seen clearly by considering what the most successful multicultural training would be. Would the most fully multicultural psychologists be the ones who have to overcome an aversion to people who are different from themselves to respond to them with decency and respect, or psychologists whose decency and respect are spontaneous and occur as second nature? Obviously either is better than someone who has not acquired a sensibility for responding respectfully to cultural differences, but equally obviously, it is preferable to be wholeheartedly engaged in cultural sensitivity than to find oneself struggling frequently to attain it. The habituation of a culturally open behavior pattern requires time, effort, guidance, and exemplars. The combination of emotional retraining, knowledge acquisition, and appropriate action suggests that learning to truly value those who are different from oneself is really an acquisition of a virtue, not simply skill or knowledge.

This example also makes it clear that humans can receive emotional schooling toward racism or cultural sensitivity, toward cruelty and domination or mutual respect. Virtue ethics calls our attention to the profound importance of intentionally cultivating the love of what is good in children so that they will be moved to pursue it spontaneously.

PRACTICAL WISDOM

The elaboration of a general virtue framework has great promise for enriching our views of the discipline of psychology and improving clinical and research practices. The perennial difficulty with any general framework, however, is in knowing how to apply it appropriately to the specific circumstances that we encounter. One of the great strengths of virtue ethics is that it devotes considerable attention to elaborating how to enact virtue in the various situations that make up everyday life. The capacity to recognize the essentials of what one encounters and to respond well and fittingly to those circumstances is known as *phronesis*, often translated as practical wisdom, or judgment.

One of the most interesting aspects of virtue ethics is the nearly complete absence of rules for appropriate behavior. There is, of course, a general injunction to act virtuously, but virtue is not a matter of following rules but of cultivating excellence in character, from which fine and noble action will naturally ensue. Because the circumstances one encounters are endlessly variable, no set of rules or guidelines could provide one with enough direction to know how to act in every situation, and individuals have to rely on their ability to choose wisely. In practical situations, the virtues require good judgment to know which traits are appropriate for a given situation and to know how to enact them, given the circumstances. This practical wisdom is so important for virtue that I have devoted chapter 5 to describing it and chapters 6 through 8 to exploring the ways in which practical wisdom is central to acting well as a psychologist.

Practical wisdom is necessary because choosing to act well is sometimes far from simple, even for those who have cultivated an excellent character. Deliberations about how best to act can be broken down into three components for simplicity of presentation even though these components are inseparable in practice. The first component is the ability to see what is important in the particular circumstances one faces, to sort out what is central and what is peripheral so that one can respond to what is essential rather than being distracted by less important concerns. The second is to understand how one can make wise choices about how to pursue one's overall sense of what is good in a particular situation. For example, a parent who is committed to teaching a child self-responsibility will respond to the child's misbehavior in a way designed to increase responsibility rather than simply reacting angrily or punitively. The third component is the ability to choose the appropriate action, given the specific situation and the goals that are relevant to it.

Take a common situation involving generosity as an example. To be generous in a reliable way, a person has to be able to recognize occasions when generosity is an appropriate response, such as a situation in which gift-giving is called for. In choosing a fitting gift, the individual has to have a clear understanding of the nature of the relationship with the recipient as well as an appreciation of the relevant social norms for gifts on such occasions. The presentation of the gift also requires similar capacities for making good judgments to be appropriate. Practical wisdom involves this kind of appreciation of the situation, understanding of relevant customs, and ability to act in a fitting way toward worthwhile goals. One can enact the virtue of generosity only when one is guided by practical wisdom in this way.

Practical wisdom is all the more important in thornier, less well-defined situations. For example, academic departments often have tenured faculty members whose research productivity has dropped off, and who may be relatively inactive out of alienation from or weariness of the concerns of the department. Some administrators and faculty may believe that the professor does not serve the department or the students well. These individuals may seek subtle or not so subtle ways to make it uncomfortable for a senior faculty member to remain and try to enlist others in an effort to oust the professor. Practical wisdom helps one to discern what is most important in such situations and choose a course of action. Although some may recognize only the value of research productivity, it may be important to consider the loyalty this faculty member has earned through long service, or the value of the unique contributions this individual makes to the department. How serious are the allegations of inadequate teaching? How important are the budgetary considerations of replacing this highly paid individual with a junior professor? Is there some way to reinvigorate the professor and find useful contributions he or she could make at this career stage? How should a colleague respond to the pressures exerted on this individual to retire early? Questions like these and the choices they require call on one to distinguish what is central from what is peripheral, to deliberate thoughtfully about what goals one should pursue and how best to accomplish them, and to choose well from the competing alternatives. I elaborate on the critical topic of practical wisdom in chapters 5 through 8 and provide an approach to address such difficult questions.

SUMMARY

Good character is constituted by a characteristic capacity to spontaneously and gladly act well for the right reasons, in the service of a worthwhile goal, and in ways that are appropriate to the situation. Character is an achievement that individuals attain through learning and feedback. As human beings, we are dependent on our caretakers, educators, and heroes to learn all of these elements of virtue. This chapter has illustrated many affinities between psychology and virtue ethics in the scientific and applied areas of psychology, exploring psychological descriptions of goal seeking, romantic relationships, and parenting, and addressing issues raised by racism and multiculturalism. I now turn to a more thorough exploration of the way that virtue provides an organized and integrative framework for understanding individual action, affect, motivation, and cognition.

3

THE CONCEPT OF AN INTEGRATED LIFE

If you want a description of our age, here is one; the civilization of means without ends.

—Richard Livingstone, *On Education*

In chapter 1, I call attention to the pursuit of what is good as the centerpiece of virtue ethics. The focus in this chapter is on understanding how individuals achieve cohesion and overall purpose in their lives by integrating their pursuit of various goods into a meaningful whole. In particular, I distinguish between two general kinds of goods. Finally, the ways in which individuals orient themselves to these goods leads to four different kinds of character.

The first kind of good is known as an *external good*, and it refers to objects or states of affairs that one can possess such as money, prestige, or a job (MacIntyre, 1981; Sherman, 1989). These goods are important to living well. They are known as external because the way that an individual pursues these goods is not intrinsically tied to the good. These goals can be pursued in many ways and individuals tend to choose the least costly way to achieve them.

The second kind of good is referred to as an *internal good* (e.g., friendship, democracy). These goods are known as internal because the means for achieving them are inseparably tied to the good. For example, the only way to have the best kind of friendship is to be a good friend. Similarly, the only way to have a democratic society is to engage in democratic practices including free and fair elections, majority rule, and so forth. Internal goods involve individuals in enacting the goods as much as in achieving them. I have much more to say about the distinction between these kinds of goods in the following section.

Many psychologists have studied goals that fit under the rubric of external goods, and, for reasons I describe below, the discipline has proceeded as though this is the only kind of goal. The focus on external goods is also characteristic of modern Western societies. The tendency to limit our understanding of goods to the external type has been called *instrumentalism* (Richardson et al., 1999; Fowers, 2005), and I describe it more thoroughly in the next section. The recognition of internal goods and the ways in which they contribute to a coherent, meaningful life is a signal contribution of virtue ethics and offers a dramatic way to enhance our discipline.

INSTRUMENTALISM

Instrumentalism, a general conception of the relationship between goals and the ways individuals approach them, has several key features. First, it makes a sharp separation between means and ends in human activity. In this scheme, individuals or groups choose their goals subjectively according to their own lights and values. These aims can arise from impulses, needs, authentic inner promptings, or from advertiser-induced desire. Instrumentalism portrays all human activity in terms of strategies, methods, or techniques that are directed toward reaching a goal. The predominant modern understanding of goal seeking depicts it as a means–ends relationship in which individuals possess or decide on certain ends and then select methods to reach those ends from an array of available strategies.

Second, there is no necessary connection between one's goal and the means that one adopts. Means, including skills and techniques, are viewed as neutral with respect to chosen goals, so that they can be applied dispassionately in the service of any number of aims. This instrumental separation of means and ends gives rise to the common rationalization that the ends justify the means. This construal of behavior often describes such strategies as technical skills that can be acquired through training.

Third, the instrumentalist perspective construes strategies and means as valuable only to the extent that they help one to reach one's ends. Individuals and groups select the means to their ends on the basis of cost-effectiveness, accessibility, or ease, and the actor has little or no attachment to a specific means aside from its effectiveness. If an alternative strategy appears more effective or less costly, it should be adopted.

Fourth, instrumentalism generally portrays individuals' and groups' strategic expertise in reaching their goals as independent of the kinds of persons they are. Strategies, techniques, methods, skill sets, and so on are spoken of as tools that can be acquired by anyone with the resources to do so. In an instrumental framework, communication skills, leadership skills, interviewing skills, diagnostic skills are no different from house-painting skills or driving skills. These technical capabilities are separate from the quality of the person possessing them. In fact, one of the attractive features of an instrumental approach is the possibility of enhancing individuals' lives through training them in skill sets that will help them to attain their goals.

Let me illustrate an instrumental approach to action with the goal of becoming wealthy. This is a subjective choice, because no one is required to be wealthy and many people choose not to pursue wealth avidly. There are many paths to wealth, including hard work, innovation, luck, inheritance, marrying someone wealthy, fraud, theft, exploitation of others, and so forth. Any of these approaches is equally valuable in terms of the sheer possession of wealth, as long as it is successful. Individuals have used all of these strategies. From a purely strategic point of view, theft or exploitation can be at least as effective as hard work or invention. If an individual successfully obtains and retains wealth through immoral means, the wealth itself is no different than wealth attained in any other way. Of course, our conventional moral codes and laws make a relatively clear distinction here between legitimate and illegitimate wealth acquisition, but instrumentalism generally views these moral or legal considerations only as strategic impediments (i.e., theft may be less efficacious because it may lead to legal difficulties and loss of the acquired wealth). Indeed, moral and legal codes are often seen as necessary to curb the "natural" instrumentality of humans in choosing the most efficacious approach to their goals. Within instrumentalism, the reason that theft is not a good strategy is that it is likely to lead to negative consequences, not that it is inherently wrong.

There is no question that much human activity falls within the instrumental realm and picking the best strategy to accomplish a particular goal is often an obviously rational approach. When I plan a route to a destination, means–end reasoning is generally perfectly appropriate. The difficulty is that instrumentalism has become so pervasive in the way people think in the modern West and in psychology that we can scarcely conceive of an alternative. Within the perspective of instrumentalism, external goods are the only type that have any firm reality. Although a good deal of human activity is instrumental in nature, we must recognize that some actions are inherently tied to the goals individuals seek and are therefore valuable in themselves. Such actions are required to pursue internal goods.

Internal Goods

My favorite example of an internal good is friendship. Aristotle (trans. 1999) highlighted the importance of friendship for living well when he said, "No one would choose to live without friends, even if he had all other goods" (p. 214). Many people do think of friendship as an external good that can be obtained through strategies. Dale Carnegie's *How to Win Friends and Influence People* enshrined a strategic approach to friendship, and psychologists often frame friendship as an exchange relationship. Such approaches distort the best kinds of friendships and obscure their central features, however. The way one develops friendships profoundly affects the kinds of friendships one can have. The best kind of friendship is one in which the friends are deeply interested in one another's welfare, act on one another's behalf, share important common interests, are honest and loyal, and so on. Individuals cannot purchase these friendships, hire someone to do the work for them, or achieve such friendships through deception, pretense, or any means other than by mutually acting in one another's best interest over time. The internal relationship between bosom friendship and acting as a friend acts means that this kind of friendship is only possible when the individuals treat each other as bosom friends.

To the extent that you the reader find yourself inclined to reinterpret this example of friendship as an internal good by construing it as an instrumental activity whose *real* (as opposed to illusory) activity consists in the exchange of benefits (e.g., pleasure, security, social support), you may be in the thrall of instrumentalism. If so, you are in very good company, because it is an extremely powerful, pervasive, and hidden bias in Western culture, so much so that it has shaped psychological science and practice without our being aware of it. The danger of instrumentalism is that it can be a self-fulfilling prophecy that leads individuals to devalue activities that are intrinsically worthwhile, but lacking significant external payoffs, and tempts them to treat everything and everyone as means to their desired ends. I see this as a profound impoverishment of our social world. Fortunately, intrinsically valuable activities have not disappeared. They simply operate behind our backs and we generally interpret them instrumentally to reassure ourselves that we are hard-headed realists, rather than fuzzy-headed idealists. Virtue ethics reminds us of the centrality of internally valuable activities in a life well lived and suggests that instrumental actions play a subsidiary, if indispensable, role in such a life.

Psychology and Instrumentalism

Some psychologists prefer an instrumental perspective because it seems to leave the questions of goods and values to the individual and frees researchers and therapists to focus on more value-neutral strategies. Yet instrumentalism is itself an ethical framework because it dictates that choices of values and goals *should* be left to individuals. The injunction to leave goals and values to individuals is at the core of the modern project of increasing individual freedom of action and potential for success. Instrumentalism is a moral position because it defines the nature of individuals' relationship with the world and with each other in means–ends terms, suggesting that strategically pursuing desired objects and experiences is the central business of life. One way to recognize the ethical nature of this stance is to see it as a contrast to Kant's ethics, in which individuals may not ever be treated as a means, only as ends in themselves.

A major consequence of this promotion of individual autonomy and the portrayal of human activity in one-sidedly instrumental terms is that our discipline has become preoccupied with identifying and describing more or less efficient means–ends relations with the choice of ends left to individual preference. In doing so, psychology supports the expansion of our instrumental capacities, but does not contribute much to our ability to deliberate together about the worth of ends (discussed in chap. 5), because they are often portrayed as outside the purview of the discipline.

Most psychological theories, from social exchange theory to cognitive theories, characterize individuals as self-interested actors who seek to maximize their outcomes through instrumental means. To give a few examples, some researchers have proposed that the problem of human aggression is simply a matter of individuals adopting problematic aggressive strategies to reach their personally defined goals. The solution is to replace aggression with "prosocial" strategies that are both more effective and less socially destructive (Eron, 1987; Eron et al., 2002). Similarly, many marital researchers and therapists believe that the way to overcome marital distress is to teach spouses better communication skills so that they can have more satisfying interactions and develop greater intimacy (Baucom, Epstein, & LaTaillade, 2002; Markman, Resnick, Floyd, Stanley, & Clements, 1993; Stanley, Blumberg, & Markman, 1999). Cognitive therapists devote a great deal of attention to replacing problematic cognitive strategies like overgeneralization and catastrophizing with the skill of empirically assessing one's beliefs to increase one's effectiveness in attaining one's ends in the social environment.

It goes without saying that reducing aggression, increasing marital satisfaction and intimacy, and enhancing clients' ability to engage their world realistically are, in many ways, worthy goals. However, the advocates of these approaches virtually never explicitly consider the flaws or shortcomings of this instrumental outlook or inquire as to whether there are other frameworks for understanding human activity. Moreover, as long as our attention is focused solely on methods for reaching individual aims, it is impossible to raise important questions about those ends. Are there times when aggression is appropriate, such as self-defense, police work, or resisting tyranny (Fowers & Richardson, 1993)? Are marital satisfaction and intimacy the best ways to think about marital quality or might the presence of teamwork, shared goals, and character provide a more solid basis for strong marriages (Fowers, 2000; Fowers, Bucker, Calbeck, & Harrigan, 2005)? Is the cautious rationality promoted by cognitive therapy always the best approach to life (Richardson et al., 1999)?

Our cultural emphasis on identifying and using the most efficient means for subjectively or politically defined ends has underwritten an unprecedented instrumental prowess, and there is a good deal to be said for the ability to pursue *some* ends strategically. Nevertheless, a one-sided instrumental view of human action with its attendant moral outlook seems to be deeply self-undermining. Many critics (Bell, 1978; Bellah et al., 1985; Lasch, 1978; Sandel, 1996; Selznick, 1992) have pointed out that the pervasiveness of this instrumental, exchange-oriented way of thinking tends to trivialize cultural meaning, dissolve the capacity to respect and cherish others, and undermine the pursuit of common goals, thereby eroding the very social foundations necessary for effective instrumental action in a complex and interdependent society.

A purely instrumental portrayal of human activity may create a kind of self-fulfilling prophecy of highly effective but exploitive individuals who seek the most efficient means to satisfy their desires regardless of the costs to others. Because instrumentalism portrays the goals in one's life as individually chosen, there is little common ground for seeking any sort of shared good, unless it benefits the individual directly or cooperation appears to be a better strategy for each individual involved. Through an instrumental view, personal, social, and political relationships take on a contractual cast in which humans engage in mutual involvement and attachment solely because the relationship provides benefits to us as individuals. If those benefits fail to compensate for the costs of the relationship or compare unfavorably with other alternatives in the present and foreseeable future, the only rational response is to terminate it.

The predominance of an instrumental portrayal of human action in psychology also seems likely to reduce the likelihood that we will recognize the presence of noninstrumental activity and describe it accurately in our theories. An uncritically accepted instrumentalism is deeply problematic for psychology, because our theories are influential in the world and an unacknowledged instrumentalism can actually undermine worthwhile noninstrumental activity such as parenting and friendship.

From an anthropological perspective, Fiske (1991) concluded his discussion of the relative importance of instrumental motives by saying,

> In most cultures, including Europe before the modern era, people take sociable motives for granted, and it may be something of a peculiarity of our own modern culture that we think it plausible to imagine that rational self-interest might be the ultimate motive underlying even the most compassionate sociable acts. (pp. 203–204)

He cited Udy's (1959) summary of fieldwork in 150 cultures that indicates that social relations are much less frequently organized along the lines of strict economic exchange than along the lines of communal sharing or authority.

Fiske did not argue that individuals are never self-interested or instrumental in their actions. Clearly, a good deal of human activity is instrumental in nature. Buying groceries, maintaining one's living quarters, and performing many work tasks are simply means to the end of having the wherewithal to live comfortably and pursue higher-order goals and goods, but, as I argue in this chapter, many important goods are not attainable through instrumental means. Some goods are internal, or inseparably related to the way the goal is achieved.

THE PSYCHOLOGICAL WHOLENESS OF CHARACTER

In contrast to instrumentalism, virtue ethics claims that the best kind of life is characterized by the overall integrity and harmony of the individual's aims and actions. This harmony is evident in the ways in which such a life is organized around internal goods that one pursues primarily by being the kind of person who embodies those ends. Virtue ethics suggests that external goods are also important, but subsidiary to internal goods. I explore this psychological wholeness in the following section by considering the ways in which an integrated life is crucial to human flourishing.

An Integrated Life

An impressive array of psychologists have devoted their scholarly attention to studying goal seeking (see Austin & Vancouver, 1996; Karoly, 1999 for reviews). These researchers have studied many facets of goal seeking, such as goal content or type, goal hierarchy or structure, goal dimensions, goal importance, goal difficulty and specificity, the temporal range of goals, and goal processes (establishment, planning, striving, monitoring, and affective responses). All of these features of goal seeking have some bearing on virtue ethics, but I focus particularly on goal hierarchy and goal type to show how virtue ethics can contribute to our understanding of goal seeking and psychological wholeness.

Goal Hierarchies

Clearly, individuals have multiple goals and pursuits in their lives, and these aims generally do not have a preordained or automatic organization or harmony. Research suggests that organizing and harmonizing one's aims is an important aspect of goal attainment (Ford, 1992; Powers, 1973). The more discordant or incompatible one's goals are, the more inner conflict and inconsistent or self-defeating behavior one will likely manifest. Karoly (1999) argued that goal harmony is essential to individual well-being and described mental health as "a process of goal-directedness that is flexibly self-regulated, unconflicted, balanced as to content, socially responsible, and consistent with core values" (p. 279).

According to virtue ethics, flourishing is not merely the possession of a bundle or collection of discrete goods or experiences, the amalgamation of which produces a good life. This is obvious when we reflect on the dispersal and fragmentation that result when a life is characterized by disparate, uncoordinated ends (Sherman, 1989). A helter-skelter pursuit of incompatible aims could not possibly qualify as the most desirable kind of life. The best kind of life has to be one in which a significant degree of harmony exists between the many aims and activities that constitute it. Even more, we might expect the best life to involve endeavors that are mutually supporting. This harmony will include the meshing of current goals and activities and the coordination of our aims and efforts over time (Sherman, 1989).

Studies of goal coherence suggest that individuals who are happy with their lives tend to have harmonious goals whereas those who have conflict among their goals experience lower levels of well-being (Emmons & King, 1988; Sheldon & Kasser, 1995). McGregor and Little (1998) found that the meaningfulness of one's life is related to the consistency of life goals and one's identity. Emmons (1986) reported that conflict among goals and ambivalence toward goals are associated with negative affect. Medical students with high motivation for both power and intimacy were more depressed, neurotic, and self-doubting than those with high motivation for intimacy only (Zeldow, Daugherty, & McAdams, 1988). Emmons and King (1988) found that goal conflict and goal ambivalence were associated with negative affect, depression, and anxiety. Conflict among goal strivings was related not only to self-report measures of affect but also to health center visits and the number of illnesses experienced. For this reason, King (1996) argued that an important aspect of self-regulation and adaptation is using processes to reduce conflict among one's goals.

What might this organization of aims look like? Clearly, many goals have merit simply because they help one along to other, more important aims. A student studies for an exam to pass the course, obtain a degree, and finally pursue a chosen career. Our hypothetical student may not see very much inherent value in studying for the exam, but this activity is an essential element in the higher-order aims of gaining knowledge and preparing for a career. Psychologists studying the structure of goals have identified this kind of hierarchical structure with higher-order goals pursued through short- and medium-term subgoals (Austin & Vancouver, 1996; Karoly,

1999). Although there is broad agreement among researchers about the hierarchical structure of goals, there is less consensus on the placement of particular goals in a hierarchy and the relationships between aims that are not directly linked in a particular hierarchical relationship.

Once we look beyond the simple and uncontroversial relation of subgoals and larger goals, what kind of relationships might there be between two higher-order goals such as career success and having a thriving family? There are many ways to work out the relationships among these higher-order ends. For some individuals, their career success is simply a subgoal that supports the family life they wish to have, and conflicts will consistently be resolved in favor of family life. For others, career aspirations have top priority and they fit family life in where possible as a lower priority. For still others, the ongoing harmonization of the two priorities may be more a matter of which arena of activity is most pressing—meeting a crucial deadline may take precedence on one occasion and attending a child's school performance on another.

The key point is that individuals need to work out some relationship among the higher-order goals that guide their lives. Those who do not have such an arrangement are likely to experience frequent, paralyzing conflicts, frustration, and a disorienting tendency to lurch back and forth between them, doing none of them justice. Obviously, no one would see a life characterized by interminable indecision and inner conflict about the relative priorities of various pursuits as the best kind of life.

I am not suggesting that one should aspire to a seamlessly harmonious life in which there are no difficult decisions or dilemmas. The relationships among life goals are undoubtedly fluid in a number of ways. An individual's pursuits have greater and lesser salience at different times. Career concerns may have a higher priority during professional training and prior to marriage, with marital and family plans remaining important, but somewhat dormant. The aims a person has are likely to change over the course of a lifetime, through goal achievement or an evolving sense of what is desirable, possible, or admirable. Aspiring to complete harmony among a static hierarchy of goals is unrealistic, but it does seem both possible and desirable to have a relatively clear sense of what takes priority over what, even if that prioritization may not be fully explicit or final.

Focusing on One's Life as a Whole

Virtue ethics offers an interesting organizing principle for the overall arrangement and harmony of one's ends. It focuses on questions such as "What is my life amounting to as a whole, or what do I hope that it will amount to?" "What holds my discrete activities and short-term goals together?" "What gives them purpose and worth as a whole?" These questions grow out of the central question of virtue ethics: "What kind of person am I?" Having an overall sense of how one's life is shaping up is essential to one's ability to have a cogent answer to these questions.

This focus on the kind of person one is and on the overall picture of one's life is a key aspect of virtue ethics that stands in contrast to instrumentalism, which emphasizes external goods such as possessions, achievements, experiences, and feelings of happiness as the measures of a good life. Of course, these good things are worth having, but possessing them is not enough to constitute a good life. The mere possession of material goods is a dubious indicator of a life well lived, because human beings can acquire possessions and achievements fraudulently or accidentally. Moreover, if these possessions are the mark of a good life, then losing them would obliterate the goodness of our lives. Good experiences and emotions are also worthwhile, but they are evanescent and cannot provide a stable source of worth in our lives. The virtue ethics emphasis on the overall shape of our lives and our characters provides a more substantial and reliable indicator of the quality of our lives. This focus on wholeness also encourages us toward greater integration of our lives and of the important goals that guide us (Annas, 1993), in contrast to the relatively discrete and episodic pursuit of a series of external goods.

What Is Good for Humans?

Virtue ethics approaches the question of defining what is good for us as human beings in terms of considering what it means to be human. Human flourishing consists in living fully and cultivating the best in oneself as a human being. The best life is one in which an individual seeks excellence in ordinary human activities that involve uniquely human capacities. This suggests that we will find what is good neither in an ethereal, otherworldly experience nor in pleasures taken as a reward for and respite from ordinary tasks. Human goods are thoroughly intertwined with our everyday lives, with our work and our leisure, our personal relationships and our public involvements. Character is a matter of *how* we participate in these ordinary human activities and endeavors and how all of them constitute an interrelated whole. Human goods are found in the exercise of our full capacities in meaningful activity toward worthwhile aims and in the pleasure we take in that exercise and its ends.

The virtue ethics framework I am describing suggests that the best kind of life is one in which there is a well-established, even if not fully articulated, goal hierarchy. At the pinnacle of this hierarchy is the development of the individual's full capacities as a human being, and the pursuit of worthwhile aims that give that life shape and direction. I discussed this as flourishing in chapter 2. Individuals have different ideas about the specific aims that they place at the center of their lives, but, within a given cultural group, the place and value of the various aims is recognizable. The subgoals necessary for the accomplishment of one's overall ends will be arranged hierarchically, and some harmony will be established among higher-order goals. This perspective on goal hierarchies makes a key assumption about the content or type of higher-order goals that are most conducive to living well. The next section will describe higher-order goals as *internal*, in contrast to the *external* goals, which are subsidiary goods that are pursued instrumentally.

Internal and External Goods

External goods are the outcomes or products of some activity, but they are separable from the activity (MacIntyre, 1981; Sherman, 1989). The product is external to the activity because there are usually a variety of ways of producing the outcome and its attainment is not necessarily directly linked to which approach one uses. For example, a financier arranges a merger between companies for the sake of the profit it will bring, and a factory worker builds automobiles to earn a wage. The financier could also earn a profit by investing in companies, building or liquidating a factory, and so forth. As far as the profit outcome goes, it does not matter which strategy the financier adopts as long as it brings an acceptable return. Similarly, the factory worker could work in an automobile, steel, or airplane factory as long as the primary outcome of the wage is acceptable. The success of these kinds of activities is solely evident in whether they produce the desired result. If the production of the end fails or miscarries, then the efforts were misspent.

In contrast, one can attain internal goods only by acting in the ways that embody those goods. One pursues internal goods by participating in the activities that constitute those goods. To give a few examples, the only way to be an expert craftsperson is to learn and practice the skills of the trade. The sole pathway to becoming a connoisseur of wine is to devote oneself to learning to appreciate the variations in fragrance, texture, and taste of wine. One can promote democracy only by actively participating in democratic practices (becoming educated, being informed, voting, abiding by election results, and so on).

With external goods, the goal of the action is something that is separate from the activity itself, whereas internal goods are partly found in the worth and enjoyment of the activity itself. The importance of this distinction between internal and external goods cannot be overemphasized. In the instrumental approach to external goods, one searches for means to achieve one's goals. For example, one might run to be healthy or help a friend so that one can get something in return. In contrast, Guignon (1993) explains that internals goods,

> are not just routes to achieving external ends, but instead are experienced as central to *constituting* a particular way of life, a way of life that is good *because* it consists of this and comparable sorts of activities. Action here is undertaken *for the sake of being* such and such: I run as a part of being a healthy person, or I help someone for the sake of being a good friend. (p. 230, italics in the original)

Guignon goes on to point out that, to the extent that one's life is characterized by a long sequence of instrumental pursuits of external ends, that life will have an episodic nature lacking cumulative worth or larger purpose. The activities themselves do not have any meaning and may be onerous chores. I might detest running but suffer through it because it is the most efficient way to stay fit, or I might dislike someone but cultivate his friendship only for what he can do for me. This instrumental view of relationships is very common in psychological theories such as social exchange theory (Fowers, 2000; Huston & Burgess, 1979) and interdependence theory (Rusbult & Van Lange, 1996), and in the literature on social support, which portrays social support primarily as a buffer that protects us from adverse events (Stroebe & Stroebe, 1996).

Psychological research and theory also frequently portray friendship as an instrumental activity. That is, the purpose of friendship is to provide pleasure, benefits, or advantage to the individual. From this point of view, the real motive one has in the relationship is the individual pursuit of rewards or benefits from the friend. If those rewards are not forthcoming, then the individual's efforts in the relationship have been unsuccessful and further investments are ill advised.

In contrast, a richer quality of life can be attained when one's actions are an integral part of being a certain kind of person. If I exercise as part of being a healthy person or do a favor because that is what it means to be a good friend, my actions help to make me that kind of person. My actions and my goals are one and the same, and this gives my activity continuity, wholeness, and cumulativeness that is not possible if I see my actions as mere means to some reward.

If friendship is seen as an internal good, the relationship has a very different character than if it is viewed instrumentally. When friendship is an internal good, friends take an interest in each other, give one another support and encouragement, enjoy one another's company, participate in activities together, and so on because that is what it means to be a friend. Friends do not undertake these activities with a view to receiving benefits or rewards from their friends—mutual participation in the activities themselves is worthwhile. The primary concern is the degree to which they are truly acting as a friend, not whether or not they receive benefits in return. The primacy of the friendship over benefits does not reduce the value of the pleasure, support, or intimacy, however. These rewards of friendship actually resonate more deeply within the shared bonds and loyalty of friendship. Given this contrast, it is not hard to see which kind of friendship most of us would find most valuable.

The same internal relationship is present in the link between acting well and virtue. Virtues are embodied. What counts most in matters of character is *how* one acts, whether one acts as a courageous or just person would in the circumstances. For example, courage is characterized more in the way that someone undertakes a risk than in whether the venture is successful. Of course, a soldier acts courageously for the sake of victory and winning the battle or the war is not a matter of indifference, but the key point is that an act is courageous whether or not victory is forthcoming. Courage is, in this sense, its own end, because what the person of character cares most about is whether he or she is acting nobly. That does not mean that victory is irrelevant to the brave soldier or scientific progress is meaningless to the honest scientist. What it does mean is that military victory or scientific progress is only praiseworthy if gained through courageous or honest actions (Sherman, 1989).

This idea that virtuous action is good for its own sake, or that virtue is its own reward, is perfectly compatible with virtue ethics, but it is important to recognize that that understanding of character is incomplete. It is not the case that virtues are sufficient in themselves. Rather, one must keep firmly in mind that virtues are good in themselves *because* virtues are the mode through which human beings can be our best selves. In other words, acting well is internally related to living the best kind of human life and virtues make that life possible. Virtues do not have independent value in the absence of an overall pursuit of a good life.

External Goods as Goods of Competition

The distinction between internal and external goods illuminates another enlightening aspect of virtue ethics. External goods such as wealth, power, or prestige are limited commodities. These commodities are divided up among individuals in some way and held as possessions. Because their supply is finite and divisible into possessions, they are objects of competition and the more one person has, the less is available for others. Internal goods, on the other hand, are neither finite nor divisible. The internal goods that result from the practice of any true excellence benefit all (MacIntyre, 1981). Practicing generosity is good for both the recipient and the giver, justice benefits everyone, and the goods of friendship are, by their very nature, good for both friends.

Internal goods operate very much like artistic ability. When an artist or a musician produces great art, it enriches all who enjoy the art and can even elevate or expand the practice of the art itself. This is a nonfinite kind of good that all participants share. Of course, the prestige and wealth that can accrue to the artist constitute external ends that might accompany greatness, but it is not primarily for the sake of such external goods that most art is practiced. These external goods are secondary to the goods internal to the art itself for great artists or, for that matter, for Sunday painters. It is the same with virtue. To the extent that virtue results in power or wealth, these external goods are secondary to the practice of excellence because the pursuit of goodness is worthwhile whether or not virtue is rewarded with external goods.

Research on intrinsic and extrinsic goals has illuminated important differences between them that are similar to, if not identical with, the distinction between internal and external goods. Kasser and Ryan (1993, 1996) found that participants' ratings of the importance of extrinsic goals such as financial success, social recognition, and physical attractiveness correlated negatively with several measures of well-being. Moreover, the importance of these extrinsic goals was positively associated with anxiety, depression, narcissism, and symptoms of physical illness. Individuals who espoused intrinsic goals such as personal growth, family security, and community contribution reported greater subjective well-being. Similarly, Emmons (1991) reported that personal strivings for power, which he defined as desires to control, impress, or manipulate others, were positively correlated with negative affect and distress. Two longitudinal studies of goal attainment found that progress toward intrinsic goals was more strongly related to enhanced well-being than progress in attaining extrinsic goals (Ryan et al., 1999; Sheldon & Kasser, 1998).

The distinction between intrinsic and extrinsic goals is not identical with the difference between internal and external goods that I have discussed. Extrinsic goals correspond well to external goods, but the intrinsic goals studied by these researchers involve internal states of individuals as well as "community contribution." In virtue ethics, internal goods are more substantive and are related to ongoing practices and specific communal projects that require personal excellence. In other words, internal goods are inseparably related to activities directed toward goods that transcend the individual (e.g., scholarship, democracy), and intrinsic goals are largely experiences that reside within the individual (e.g., personal growth).

The group of investigators who have studied intrinsic and extrinsic goals reported intriguing results that match the virtue ethics account rather well as far as they go. It is possible that some of the "personal growth" that their participants reported would correspond to character development, but their data do not address this question directly. Additional research investigating more extensive involvement in these kinds of practices and virtues is needed to identify whether internal goods are accompanied by the enjoyment and fulfillment predicted by virtue theory.

The Primacy of Internal Goods

We are now in a position to reckon with the relationship between internal and external goods as a whole. One of the contributions of a virtue ethics framework is the acknowledgment of the presence and importance of internal goods. This contribution is heightened by the recognition that internal goods are of a higher order than external goods. I have implied this already, and it is not hard to recognize this hierarchical relationship between these goal types. In the first instance, virtue ethics takes flourishing to be the highest good and the one for the sake of which individuals seek all other goods in life. Recall that flourishing is activity characterized by excellence. This means that flourishing is the kind of good that can be obtained only through enacting our human capacities in an admirable way. We flourish by being fully human. Flourishing is an internal good because it can be obtained only through the activities that constitute it. There are no methods, techniques, or strategies that produce flourishing; it emerges only through living a full and excellent life.

There are other ways to recognize that internal goods are of a higher order than external goods. There are many people whose work has the character of a calling, in which they feel called to create art, teach, advocate for the downtrodden, and so forth. These individuals are, in general, paid much less than a comparable commitment of time and energy would earn them in other pursuits. They are manifestly unwilling to trade the internal goods they experience in their callings for more money, because their sense of doing inherently worthwhile and necessary work is incomparably richer than external goods such as financial rewards, power, or social prestige. Well-funded researchers face conflicts between the internal good of seeking knowledge for its own sake and temptations to embellish their results or accomplishments in pursuit of additional funding, prestige, awards, and so forth. Clinicians sometimes have to make decisions about making referrals, terminating unproductive but lucrative therapy arrangements, and practicing ethically. In all of these examples, the pursuit of a calling, seeking knowledge for its own sake, and offering appropriate therapeutic services represent internal goods, the pursuit of which is incomparably higher and more admirable than money, awards, or prestige.

When I claim that internal goods have a more central role in a life well lived, I am not suggesting that external goods are unimportant. The possession of some measure of external goods is essential. A moderate level of money and social standing is necessary to support the pursuit of internal goods. No one expects an individual to work without being paid, and some level of social recognition for the value of one's work is also important. The important point is that external goods provide a platform for seeking the internal goods that are integral to flourishing. In the best kind of life, external goods are secondary even though they are necessary as infrastructure to make the pursuit of internal goods possible.

This hierarchical relationship of external goods as infrastructural or subsidiary to internal goods shows up well in the example of a college student. Students complete coursework for the external good of grades, and grades contribute to the external good of a degree, which in turn facilitates obtaining a job, another external good, which provides other external goods such as money and prestige. If that were the end of the story, most people would be very disappointed. It is not the end of the story because all of those external goods serve the internal good of living well. In the best case, they serve the internal good of flourishing, for which a certain amount of money is necessary. Of course, our hypothetical student could enrich his or her life greatly by focusing on internal goods throughout life, such as getting joy from learning irrespective of grades or degrees, developing a capacity for useful contributions to society that transcends a certificate of achievement, finding a calling or vocation rather than simply a job, and pursuing meaningful and valued work rather than simply working for a paycheck. From a virtue ethics perspective, this focus on internal goods does not merely add value to a life, it transforms a life into something incomparably better.

DUTY ETHICS VERSUS VIRTUE ETHICS

Individuals seek internal goods because they are attracted to them as worthwhile ends, and because of this attraction, they enjoy the activity involved in pursuing those goods. In this way, virtue ethics proposes that individuals act in the best ways when they are genuinely drawn to seek what is good. In contrast, there is a strong Enlightenment strand of moral reasoning that views morality as a corrective for self-interested or wayward emotion and impulse. This is exquisitely clear in Kant, who taught that moral behavior requires an act of will in accordance with universally applicable maxims that often run counter to our natural inclinations. These maxims are rules stipulating behavior that a rational person would see as valid for anyone in similar circumstances (e.g., return a wallet to someone who drops it). In a famous passage, Kant claimed that a coldhearted rich man could be a praiseworthy philanthropist through rationally understanding a maxim directing him to benefit others even if he gave grudgingly. Kant (1785/1964, p. 66) claimed that "It is precisely in this that the worth of character begins to show—a moral worth and beyond all comparison the highest—namely that he does good, not from inclination, but from duty." This emphasis on acting rightly by following abstract principles appears prominently in psychology in Kohlberg's theory of moral development (Kohlberg, 1994; Richardson et al., 1999; Sullivan, 1986) and in the Ethics Code of the American Psychological Association (APA, 2002).

The distrust of emotion and impulse is also apparent in utilitarian ethics, in which the right thing to do is determined by calculating what will be most beneficial to the most people. This calculation of benefits is designed to overcome one's natural inclination to an overeager pursuit of short-term pleasure for oneself. Kantians and utilitarians see emotions as either inherently contrary to moral action or simply unreliable and changeable as motives for acting well.

These philosophers assume that this internal conflict is an inescapable feature of human existence. The assumption of unavoidable inner conflict implies a powerful constraint on how coherent and integrated one's life can be. Virtue ethics does not adopt this assumption. Aristotle's discussion of four kinds of character clarifies that the best kind of life is free from pervasive conflict between desire and duty and thereby more fully integrated than the way Kantians and utilitarians conceive of the best kind of life.

Four Kinds of Character

Whereas Kant described the situation in which the moral individual must act against his inclinations as universal, Aristotle saw this struggle between will and desire occurring in only some individuals, but not in those with the best characters. He described four kinds of character: virtuous, continent, incontinent, and vicious. As I describe in the following sections, virtuous and vicious individuals do not struggle with duty and inclination conflicts. The continent and incontinent types do struggle with conflicts between duty and inclination.

The Continent Character

Individuals who match Kant's highest form of morality are those who know how to act well and decide to do so, even though this decision is contrary to their desires. Aristotle considered those who act well in spite of their desires continent individuals. There is obviously a lot to be said for acting well as opposed to following one's less than worthy feelings and acting badly. Continent individuals behave ethically as an act of will because they understand what is right even if they are somewhat reluctant to act for the best.

In a similar vein, Baumeister and Exline (2000) took the position that self-restraint is the "master virtue" (p. 29) and thereby put forward a duty-based view of moral behavior. They saw self-restraint as necessary to curb egoistic desires and impulses in the service of morality. Therefore, they viewed acting morally as an act of will over desire, which positioned them as theorists of moral continence. Peterson and Seligman (2004) also described self-restraint as a virtue. I took a similar position in my earlier writings (Fowers, 2000, 2001), but have since revised my views. Self-restraint is a distinctly Victorian virtue that portrays character in terms of resisting temptation. Research on self-restraint is interesting and provides a valuable picture of continent individuals who face conflicts between duty and inclination, but not of virtuous individuals, who are not conflicted in this way.

An example of continence would be a researcher who carefully follows informed consent procedures but does so reluctantly. The reluctance may grow out of a conviction that the consent procedures may hamper the recruitment of participants, but the continent investigator resists the temptation to cut corners out of a belief that informed consent is an important principle for protecting the rights of research participants.

The Incontinent Character

Individuals who know what they should do but cannot bring themselves to do it are called incontinent persons. The incontinent are less praiseworthy than the continent, because they do not decide to act well even though they understand how to act properly. Incontinent individuals experience significant conflict between desire and duty, but desire wins out over duty. They frequently feel guilt, remorse, and shame about their inability to act in the ways they think are fitting. The incontinent scientist would be unwilling to follow informed consent procedures if they presented substantial difficulties. If, for example, proper consent procedures hampered participant recruitment, the incontinent researcher would cut corners in spite of understanding the ethical importance of consent.

The Vicious Character

Worst of all are vicious individuals, who are so misinformed that they are mistaken about what is good in life and how they should act. In contemporary usage, vicious often refers to malicious or mean behavior, but in virtue parlance, the vicious are greedy, deceitful, exploitive, or self-indulgent in a characteristic way. Individuals with vicious characters seek external goods such as power, social status, pleasure, and wealth exclusively. Moreover, they pursue their goals with every available means, with success as their primary criterion for choosing means. Vicious agents have developed a second nature that leads them to act wholeheartedly in these kinds of ways and to see such actions as the correct and sensible way to act. To follow our example, a vicious investigator would blatantly disregard informed consent requirements out of a belief that they are illegitimate, pointless, or simply inconvenient. This researcher would deceive others about this disregard to avoid consequences and have no real qualms or regrets about acting in this way. The only concern would be to pursue his or her deplorable goals expeditiously and to avoid detection.

The Virtuous Character

The fourth kind of character, the virtuous individual, knows how to act well and does so gladly. A person of good character *wants* to act for the best and generally experiences harmony between desire and duty. The emotional harmony of the virtuous person is clearly preferable to the conflicted emotional state of the continent person when it comes to moral decisions. The emotional concordance found in individuals of character means that there is no need to struggle or agonize between what one wants and what one should do and to succeed in acting well only at the cost of an act of self-control. As Baumeister and Exline (1999, 2000) documented, self-restraint (required by the continent person) is hard work that can exhaust the psychological resources of the individual. From a classical virtue perspective, then, self-restraint is not a virtue at all, because it requires the individual to overcome contrary desires to act well. As Woodruff (2001) put it, "Virtue, after all, is supposed to be the capacity to have the right emotions from the start. If you have emotions that need to be controlled, you are already in trouble" (p. 29).

There is something to admire in the continent achievement of self-control and the overcoming of unsalutary desires and emotions. Yet if one can choose (and one can) between having a division of will and desire and a harmony of will and desire, it seems obvious that one would prefer the ability to act wholeheartedly for the sake of what is worthwhile. This concordance of goal, desire, and action is central to the integrated life that virtue ethics highlights as conducive to human flourishing. Clearly, the scientist with good character would comply with the requirements of informed consent willingly, on the basis of a wholehearted endorsement of the rights and needs of research participants. If acting in this way is inconvenient or difficult, the investigator readily bears the cost because the welfare of the participants is more important than his or her convenience.

Emotional Concordance

One of the chief signs of excellence in character, then, is for one's emotions to be in harmony with the actions that are most fitting in the circumstances. This emotional concordance with moral behavior both simplifies and enriches those actions, because the activity is free from struggle against inclination and the emotions resonate with the action and add affective impetus to it. In the incontinent person, the will to pursue worthwhile aims is too weak and is defeated by the ignoble desires. In the continent person, the rational will controls refractory desires, and in the virtuous person, the rational will and the desires operate in a harmonious partnership. Virtue ethics focuses on one's attraction to what is good as the source of motivation for acting well rather than "the notion that morality is a life harassed and persecuted everywhere by 'imperatives' and disagreeable duties, and that without these you have not got morality" (Bradley, quoted in Annas, 1993, p. 4). The idea that individuals act best when they act willingly because they want to bring some goodness into the world is one of the most attractive aspects of virtue ethics and dramatically illustrates the psychological integration that this perspective offers.

Ryan and Deci (2000) summarized research results suggesting that activities that are intrinsically motivated (when a person has "self-authored or endorsed" motivation, p. 69) lead to enhanced process and outcomes as compared to extrinsically motivated activities. Experimental evidence suggests that intrinsically motivated individuals have greater interest, excitement, confidence, vitality, self-esteem, and general well-being. Although intrinsic motivation is not identical with internal motivation, these findings are consistent with the crucial difference between the virtuous and continent character types, and the outcomes described in the literature on intrinsic motivation are exactly what virtue theory would predict.

How can people be expected to gladly act virtuously when virtue is sometimes difficult for anyone? Consider the soldier who is called on to undertake a mission that will greatly benefit the army and his country but is very likely to result in his death. How can he accept the mission *gladly*? To give a more prosaic example, one not involving life-or-death issues, think of the professor who is called on to nominate a student for an award. She has two students, one of whom is superior to the other in terms of the qualifications for the award, but the professor has a very strong mentoring relationship with the second student, who has also done the professor significant service as a research assistant. How can this professor *gladly* nominate the more qualified but less favored student?

These two examples, particularly the one involving the soldier, put a great deal of pressure on the idea of *gladly* acting virtuously. It is not hard to see how one can learn to give compliments or charitable donations gladly, but it is a little more difficult to see how ordinary human beings can gladly risk their lives. In such cases, the word *gladly* has connotations such as happily or spontaneously that may be somewhat inappropriate. When the situation facing the individual is one that has grave import or requires significant deliberation to arrive at a clear sense of what is best under confusing or difficult circumstances, the attendant emotion will not likely be spontaneous joy in the action. Yet once an individual with good character decides on the best course of action, he or she does pursue it freely, ungrudgingly, and resolutely, and this wholeheartedness is a key to virtue. It is this firmness that attends difficult actions in persons with strong character. The ability to firmly and willingly take a stand grows out of the clarity of purpose derived from pursuing an important good.

The Transformation of Emotion

When acting well is difficult, individuals can bring their emotions into harmony with acting finely through a transformation of those feelings. Because no one is perfectly virtuous and consistent, everyone will, at least occasionally, have emotional responses that may not be entirely harmonious with what they see as good. Individuals may find themselves annoyed or impatient with someone in an ill-fitting way. Or they may be unusually fatigued or strained and have difficulty responding as they characteristically do. If these kinds of feelings are given free reign, the acts that follow will not be virtuous in character. Alternatively, individuals can respond in a way that is contrary to their feelings but consistent with better behavior. Such a response would be self-restrained or continent and is preferable to acting in an undesirable manner, but less praiseworthy than actions undertaken wholeheartedly for a worthy purpose.

When facing refractory emotions, individuals of character bring their feelings into harmony with the requirements of virtue by reminding themselves about the goods they are pursuing and recognizing what is at stake in that situation. The act of recalling what is truly important can transform their emotional reactions to the situation into an experience that is more consistent with wanting to pursue their valued ends.

For example, a father was considering what he wanted to do on a Saturday. His wife suggested that he take their children to see a movie that the children wanted to see. The father did not particularly want to see this movie and his initial reaction was to decline. Then he thought about what it was that he really wanted that day, and it turned out that he had wanted to spend time with his children because he had been very busy and relatively unavailable to them recently. Seeing that this was his aim, he reconsidered the movie as an opportunity for them to spend some enjoyable leisure time together. In view of what he thought was most important for that day, his feelings about the movie were transformed into a desire to go with his children. He did not particularly enjoy the movie, as he had known he would not, but he did enjoy spending the time with his children, especially seeing their delight with the show. His initial emotional reaction was transformed by a consideration of one of his primary aims in life—that of being a loving parent.

Clinicians are frequently faced with this kind of situation. It is not unusual for therapists to feel irritated or bored by a client. Good therapists do not act out such feelings, nor do they simply dismiss the feeling and pretend that they are interested in and comfortable with what the client is saying. Rather, a beneficial therapeutic response requires a transformation of the experience into one that pursues therapeutic goals. Therapists do this by noticing the irritation and considering what it means that they are irritated. If it turns out that the client is doing something that elicits irritation, then they examine what the client is doing and why he or she might be acting in that way. In this way, the therapist transforms the irritation into curiosity, which leads to exploring the actions of the client that elicit irritation. The intent of this exploration is to understand the reasons for those actions and to see if they are related to the concerns for which the client is seeking assistance. Therapists do all of this in the service of the therapeutic goals that both the therapist and client are pursuing. With practice, this kind of self-reflection and exploration becomes second nature, and therapists' emotional reactions become reliably responsive to their therapeutic aims.

Our emotions require schooling and transformation at times. Fortunately, our emotional reactions are responsive to rational reflection on our valued aims. It is this transformation that allows therapists to help difficult clients, researchers to revise their cherished theories in light of contrary evidence, and parents to discipline and guide recalcitrant children in a loving way.

Recent evidence suggests that the transformation of emotion may be very important in relationship maintenance. Finkel, Rusbult, Kumashiro, and Hannon (2002) described the process of transforming initial behavioral impulses that may be detrimental to relationships into a more constructive response. They termed this *transformation of motivation* (Rusbult & Van Lange, 1996). The transformation involves altering narrowly self-interested motives and inclinations to be more consistent with longer-term, broader goals that are beneficial to one's partner or friend, and relationship enhancing. In good close relationships, this transformation is characteristic and relatively quick (Agnew, Van Lange, Rusbult, & Langston, 1998; Aron, Aron, Tudor, & Nelson, 1991). In contrast, transformation of motivation requires more deliberation than self-interest with strangers in experimental settings (Dehue, McClintock, & Liebrand, 1993). Finkel et al. noted that at times this process is automatic and habit-driven, whereas at other times it requires active deliberation and effort.

As evidence for the transformation of motivation, Rusbult, Davis, Finkel, Hannon, and Olsen (2001; as cited by Finkel et al., 2002) reported that participants given more time to formulate reactions to hypothetical betrayal incidents tended to behave more constructively than individuals with less time to provide their reactions. In a study of actual betrayal incidents, Finkel et al. (2002) also reported that forgiveness occurs over time, suggesting that some time is necessary to transform motivations. In one of their studies, they also performed an experimental manipulation that increased the participants' commitment level, which was, in turn, related to more constructive responses to hypothetical betrayals. They also reported two studies on real betrayal incidents and found that the more committed relationship partners were, the more positive their immediate and delayed responses were to the betrayal, and delayed reactions were more positive than immediate responses. Thus, individuals who valued their relationships more tended to be more forgiving. The participants' reinterpretations of the betrayal mediated the relationship between commitment and forgiveness of betrayal. This process of reinterpreting the betrayal in more benign terms helped partners to alter their feelings and forgive their partners. These authors did not study whether forgiveness was earned or well justified, but it is clear that a reinterpretation of the betrayal incidents is a key part of forgiveness and this reinterpretation grows out of the value that the relationship has to the forgiver. To the degree that one can assume that forgiveness was appropriate, this process is consistent with the transformation of emotion described by the virtue ethics account of pursuing important aims in the face of problematic circumstances and emotions.

In a similar manner, McCullough, Worthington, and Rachal (1997) defined forgiveness as a set of motivational changes that *decrease one's interest* in retaliation and estrangement, and *increase one's interest* in conciliation and goodwill. McCullough et al. (1998) studied the motivational shifts that lead to forgiveness in some detail and found that forgiveness was most likely when partners experienced empathy for the offender and did not avoid him or her. Empathy was predicted by prior relationship closeness and the degree of apology from the offending partner. This series of studies is consistent with Finkel et al. (2002) in suggesting that a positive reinterpretation of the offense and a transformation of emotion are important aspects of forgiveness. McCullough et al. (1998) also studied offender apology and found that it was an important contributor to empathy for and forgiveness of the offender.

The growing literature on forgiveness indicates the centrality of transforming the initial negative emotional reaction to an offense into a more relationship-enhancing interpretation. Forgiveness is very strongly related to relationship commitment (Finkel et al., 2002; McCullough et al., 1998).

The centrality of commitment indicates that individuals engage in this difficult transformation for the sake of relationship preservation and enhancement, both important life goals.

SUMMARY

Virtue ethics highlights the idea that the best kind of life is one in which there is a significant degree of harmony and synergy among the various aims and activities that make up that life. In this chapter, I have discussed four aspects of this psychological integration in particular. The first is a harmoniously integrated life, which is an achievement, particularly in the hurly-burly of the contemporary world. The primary source of integration in life is a reasonably well-organized set of goals and goal-related activities. Goal hierarchies are important in the research literature on goals, and harmony among goals is an important predictor of individual well-being.

Virtue ethics highlights a second area important in the literature on both goals and motivation. This perspective emphasizes a distinction between means–end instrumental activity and an internal relationship between goods and actions and portrays instrumental activity as subsidiary to internal goods as an important part of the best kinds of goal hierarchies. Pursuing internal goods such as friendship, scholarship, and democracy represents higher-order activity because these ends are valuable in themselves and not simply for the sake of something else. The overall goal, according to virtue ethics, is flourishing, defined as the full development of oneself as a human being, clearly the highest aspiration possible, but a goal that remains open-ended and subject to ongoing inquiry and debate.

Third, an integrated life is best pursued through cultivating virtue, partly because virtuous activity involves a harmony among an individual's thoughts, emotions, actions, and goals. The four character types illustrate this with individuals of character being capable of acting wholeheartedly in seeking internally valuable aims, whereas continent and incontinent individuals are torn between desire and duty, and vicious individuals can only act instrumentally in pursuit of the goods of competition.

Fourth, emotional concordance is an essential element of good character, and the nature of one's spontaneous response to circumstances provides a measure of character strength. One can achieve this emotional integration through learning to love what is good. On some occasions, even the noblest of individuals will not have the best immediate affective response, and some transformation of emotion will be important to allow them to act wholeheartedly. In this situation, recollecting what they believe to be good and worth pursuing can help them to act well even in difficult or conflicted circumstances.

In this chapter, I have focused primarily on the psychological integration that virtue ethics highlights and promotes. There is a corresponding social integration of individuals in virtue ethics that emphasizes the ways in which individuals are embedded in communities, are deeply dependent on one another, pursue shared goals, and experience some goods only in concert with others. In the next chapter, I turn to this social dimension of character.

4

THE COMMUNAL NATURE
OF CHARACTER

True love in this differs from gold and clay
That to divide is not to take away.
—Percy Bysshe Shelley, *Epipsychidion*

In the previous chapter, I explored the important distinction between internal and external goods as a way to expand our understanding of what is good. In this chapter, I focus on a second distinction between individual and shared goods to further augment our conception of what is good. In brief, individual goods are those that an individual can possess, such as money, talent, or pleasure, whereas shared goods are those that can only be possessed together with others, including democracy, solidarity, or teamwork. There is a strong tendency in American society and in psychology to focus exclusively on individual goods, which places deep limitations on our cultural self-understanding and on our theory, research, and practice. This tendency is fueled by individualism.

INDIVIDUALISM

Alexis de Tocqueville (1830/1969), that most observant of visitors to the United States, sounded a prescient warning in the 1830s about a growing trend toward individualism in America. He feared that the emphasis on individual freedom and fulfillment in the young republic might undermine the traditions and practices that create substantial connections between individuals and the kinds of civic bonds that nurture a free and democratic society. Since that time, many have concluded that de Tocqueville's anxiety was well founded, as individualism has become more and more pronounced in our way of life. Observers of American society continue to voice concerns that American individualism may have grown to cancerous proportions, unraveling the social fabric necessary for the institutions and practices that support self-government (Bellah et al., 1985; Lasch, 1978; Rieff, 1966; Sandel, 1996; Wolfe, 2001).

There are several key features of individualism (Bellah et al., 1985; Cushman, 1990, 1995; Fowers, 1998, 2000; Richardson et al., 1999; Sandel, 1996; Wolfe, 2001). First, the individual is taken as the primary social reality, with relationships among individuals having a secondary status. Second, the individual's autonomy is central in that individual choice in lifestyle is paramount. Third, values, preferences, and meaning are seen as matters of individual taste and judgment. From this perspective, individuals evaluate their choices and activities according to their preferences and perceptions regarding the benefits that they provide. Finally, individualism portrays the principal human motivations as egoistic, with individuals pursuing their self-interest primarily and social interest secondarily. This viewpoint also suggests that self-interest and social interest are likely to be in frequent conflict and that this conflict is most likely to be resolved in favor of individual interest. Self-interest can be long-term as well as short-term, and it can lead to benefits to others on the way to benefiting oneself. Individualism simply emphasizes that self-interest is the primary motivation and the most rational source of behavior.

The emphasis on individual autonomy is a bedrock premise in contemporary American society, and the ethical importance of this individual autonomy seems indispensable. The primacy of the individual is so widespread that there scarcely seems to be an alternative.

Individualism's Self-Undermining Tendency

As admirable as the individualistic vision of self-direction and personal fulfillment is, "American cultural traditions . . . leave the individual suspended in glorious, but terrifying isolation" (Bellah et al., 1985, p. 6). Such freedom may make it difficult to engage in meaningful attachments because those relationships entail obligations that constrain one's autonomy. The avoidance of constraint and obligation not only undermines the stability of personal relationships but also limits the ability of the citizen to engage in the hard work, self-sacrifice, and commitment necessary to participate in and support democratic practices (Beiner, 1992; Sullivan, 1986; Taylor, 1985).

A thoroughgoing individualism is self-undermining because the excessive reliance on individual resources for the definition of a worthwhile life leads to a sense of arbitrariness and anxiety about the meaning and value of one's pursuits (Cushman, 1990, 1995; Rieff, 1966). This anxiety can be resolved through a kind of egoistic solipsism: "My decisions are best because I say that they are and no one has the right to question them." Alternatively, and more commonly, doubts and uncertainties about the life choices one makes are resolved through seeking external validation or guidance from fads, advertisers, celebrities, cults, and experts—the very "interference" from which individualism seeks to protect individuals. As a last resort, individuals can escape from this burden of autonomy by seeking perpetual distraction (Cushman, 1990).

The more we as Americans separate our identities and aims from others, the thinner these self-defining features become, the more arbitrary they appear, and the more difficult it is for us to sustain these pursuits. There is intriguing evidence that the occurrence and severity of depression and anxiety have increased in the United States in the latter half of the 20th century as individualism has become more pronounced (Klerman & Weissman, 1989; Lewinsohn, Rohde, Seeley, & Fischer, 1993; Twenge, 2000). Increases in depression and anxiety were related strongly to birth year and had moderate to strong effect sizes for age cohort. In Twenge's analysis of the increases in anxiety among children and young adults, she found that indicators of overall threat (crime, social change) and decreases in social connectedness (percentage of people living alone, trust in others) substantially predicted later levels of anxiety. (Threat and social connectedness were too strongly correlated to be analyzed separately.) Although it seems obvious that decreased social connectedness and increased levels of threat would correlate with increased anxiety, the powerful cohort effects and population level analyses Twenge presented are quite compelling and take us well beyond the psychology of individuals. Combined with other indicators of increasing social fragmentation (Bronfenbrenner, McClelland, Wethington, Moen, & Ceci, 1996; Fukuyama, 1999; Putnam, 2000), the emphasis on individual separateness and autonomy in American culture seems to be associated with significant psychological distress. The net outcome of excessive individualism may be isolation as much as freedom, meaninglessness as much as self-definition, anxiety as much as self-direction, emptiness as much as possibility.

Individualism and Psychology

One of the key features of most psychological theorizing, research, and practice is an insistence on individual choice of goals and desires (to the extent that agency is granted) that mirrors contemporary individualism (Richardson et al., 1999). It is up to each individual not only to decide what the best kind of life is but also to select the criteria for that choice independently. Contemporary individualism dictates that all of this should occur with little or no interference from family members, communities, or therapists. Indeed, the autonomy to make these self-defining choices is central to what we in contemporary America take to be the good life. These essential decisions emanate from within the individual, whether that is a matter of simply registering what is pleasant or unpleasant or of ongoing attention to the promptings of a deep inner nature seeking to express itself spontaneously and creatively.

Standard experimental methods in psychology fit hand in glove with the assumption that individuals exist prior to social relations because the individual is the natural unit of analysis in this approach. Moreover, when investigators are interested in social interactions, they most frequently conduct experiments with participants "interacting" with invisible, nonexistent others who are actually represented by preestablished research protocols, with a confederate who manipulates the participant in some way, or, at the pinnacle of social representation, with one-time encounters among strangers. It is difficult to imagine an investigatory approach that would make it more difficult to appreciate fully the depth of the social nature of human beings. Of course, these procedures have been adopted as a means to control variation so that investigators can rule out alternative explanations of the findings. Although this approach has its merits, the relative priority of experimental control over fidelity to anything resembling actual human social intercourse is striking. By so commonly foregrounding the individual in our theories, methods, and practices, we psychologists have tended to neglect or at least dramatically understate the essential social context that makes individuality possible.

To the extent that the cultural morality of individualism suffuses our professional activities, as many authors have painstakingly documented that it does (Bellah et al., 1985; Bruner, 1990; Cushman, 1990, 1995; Danziger, 1990; Fowers, 2000; Richardson et al., 1999; Sampson, 1977, 1985; Sarason, 1981; Spence, 1985), our discipline is as much an expression of a particular historical culture as it is the pursuit of universally applicable knowledge. (I rely on these authors' evidence and my own argument in chaps. 1 and 2 rather than repeat them there.) Because psychology has adopted individualism as its bottom-line account of human nature, we have blinded ourselves to the depth of our social embeddedness and dependency on others. Moreover, the scientific imprimatur that we have placed on individualism reduces our ability as professionals to support the necessary social bonds that make robust individual choice and identity possible. Although individualism has been roundly criticized and has virtually no empirical grounding as the fundamental basis of human behavior, it has stubbornly retained its centrality in psychological theory and practice.

I have discussed the fallacy of value neutrality throughout the book, and I believe that the intertwining of cultural values and social science is inevitable. Therefore, I am not suggesting that we should or even can sanitize our professional activities of ethical commitments, but that we should acknowledge that we do have some stance on how best to live and present these views for critical scrutiny and debate. The intermingling of cultural values and psychology is most problematic when it is denied, because that renders the underlying moral projects of the discipline beyond criticism. This gives individualism the status of an unacknowledged dogma.

The primary focus of this chapter is an exploration of the rich social world that individualism obscures and neglects. In keeping with the theme of expanding our understanding of what is good, I begin by defining and arguing for the class of shared goods, which have no place in individualism. A recognition of shared goods takes us beyond the limitations of individualism by illuminating the deeply social nature of human living and the ways in which this social world enriches and enables the choices individuals make about their lives. Following this discussion, I clarify that the virtues are not just individual characteristics but also social at the core. A discussion of the centrality of the virtue of friendship in living well rounds out this exploration of the communal nature of virtue. Virtue ethics puts us back in touch with modes of living well as human beings through a sense of belonging and wholehearted participation in shared endeavors, and with the ways that genuine involvement with others contributes to rather than detracts from our identities and capacities, gives shape to our choices, and provides an essential arena for our deepest fulfillments.

SHARED GOODS

The standard contrast in psychology between the widely accepted motive of self-interest on the one hand and the dubiously considered motive of altruism on the other obscures the possibility that certain goods, perhaps the most precious goods, can only be held in common (MacIntyre, 1999). In other words, the argument is usually about whether I pursue what is good for *me* or for *you*, but what is good for *us* is seldom considered. These shared goods constitute a crucial component of a flourishing life that has been largely neglected in psychology even by many developmental and social psychologists studying prosocial behavior. There are many shared goods, and their obviousness renders them easy to take for granted. It is manifestly true, however, that many human endeavors come to fruition only through shared goals, mutual effort, ongoing relationships, and abiding social practices. Consider a few examples such as democracy, friendship, solidarity, and justice. No one can possess democracy or experience solidarity on their own. These are shared achievements that individuals can pursue only through sustained participation in communal undertakings.

Active Participation and Shared Goods

Participation in genuinely shared goods grows out of our social nature, which predisposes us to long-term affiliations in families, friendship networks, professional or avocational groups, communities, and tribal or national groups. Shared goods do not ensue from simple membership in any of these groups. Rather, these goods are consequent to mutual participation in ongoing practices that constitute the group in a particular way and make it possible to experience shared outcomes. For example, genuinely democratic government is possible only when there are practices such as regularly occurring elections, accessibility to elective office, voting, secret ballots, trustworthy vote-counting procedures, a willingness to abide by the majority decision, respect for the law, and a loyal opposition. The good of democratic self-rule is dependent on the degree to which citizens engage in these kinds of practices. Ongoing participation in them requires the belief that the practices are efficacious and a shared belief in the value of democracy. These jointly held beliefs and practices are *constitutive* of the democracy. That is, they make self-government what it is, and without them there is no real democracy.

One of the essential aspects of shared goods is that all of the participants possess them multilaterally. For this reason, there is no competition for shared goods and no one can possess more of them than anyone else. It is meaningless to say that I have more democracy, solidarity, or friendship than others who are involved in the relevant group of individuals. These goods exist only when one holds them in common with others and they are indivisible.

The idea of shared goods makes it clear that in some crucial respects what is good for me is inseparable from what is good for others. There is no neat dividing line between individuals when it comes to living within a well-functioning community. Most citizens have to participate with good-will in the community most of the time for it to thrive, and the flourishing of each individual citizen is to some degree dependent on the order, safety, attractiveness, and cooperativeness of the community at large.

Because human beings cannot provide the context for our own well-being entirely by ourselves, each of us is dependent on other people for this ordered community. For that reason, we owe a debt of gratitude to participating others for their role in supporting the environment that is so essential to our well-being. We repay that debt through our own willing participation in the practices that uphold the community and through recognizing others' efforts. This dependency relationship cannot be characterized in simple exchange terms because, much of the time, those who contribute most to our individual development and to the maintenance of the social context in which we thrive are different from the set of individuals whom we are called on to assist (MacIntyre, 1999). Humans cannot reciprocate the gifts that our forebears gave to us in the creation of our society and the sacrifices they made that enabled our freedom and prosperity. Similarly, children cannot give their parents anything like what their parents provide for them. This developmental assistance is inherently asymmetrical. The kindness people receive when their cars break down or when they need directions or need to use someone's telephone often can be repaid only to others who need their help but have given them none.

The concern for and action on behalf of future generations has been studied under the rubric of generativity, which highlights the frequent temporal asymmetry of generosity. This literature documents the tendency to take care of those who need one's help and to contribute to the common good or overall welfare of a community. It is also interesting that the degree to which individuals report generative concern and behavior has been positively associated with indicators of their own subjective well-being in several studies (Ackerman et al., 2000; Keyes & Ryff, 1998; McAdams, de St. Aubin, & Logan, 1993). Ackerman et al. suggested that generativity contributes to individual well-being by promoting actions that foster beneficial interpersonal relationships.

Ordinary compliance with familial, legal, and organizational authorities provides an excellent example of another mode of action that upholds communities. Obedience to authority is widespread in groups and is seldom based solely on the threat of punishment or prospect of reward (Tyler, 1997). Instead, individuals voluntarily behave in accordance with rules because they see the rules as legitimate. Tyler presented evidence from five studies of the relational basis for according legitimacy to a variety of authorities. He reported results suggesting that the way individuals are treated by an authority (with recognition of their status in the group, neutrality, and benevolence) is more strongly related to granting that authority legitimacy than is the favorability of the outcome received from the authority. In addition, the more an individual identifies with the group and with the authority, the stronger this relationship between relational treatment and legitimacy is. These results suggest obedience to authority is primarily a matter of identifying with the group and feeling that one has a recognized place in it. In other words, individuals follow the rules as part of what it means to belong to a group more than for the external rewards they hope to attain or punishments they wish to avoid.

Milgram (Milgram, Sabini, & Silver, 1992) famously demonstrated the dark side of the tendency to grant legitimacy to authority. He showed the dangers of blind obedience, but blind resistance to authority is no better. Appropriate adherence to social norms, rules, and authority is necessary for a well-ordered community. Decisions about how and when to comply with norms and authority are a matter of practical wisdom, which I discuss in Part II of the book.

Of course, I can enjoy the benefits of a well-functioning community without participating in its maintenance. Such a stance might be seen as advantageous from an instrumental perspective because, if I am in the right kind of community, I could reap substantial benefits with little or no effort. As long as there are relatively few members of the community who take this stance, I seem to have it made. If too many people follow my lead, the level of participation in community maintenance will fall below what is necessary for its optimal functioning, but as long as others carry the load, I can come out way ahead by receiving benefits without contributing my efforts.

Although this free ride appears to be a marvelous bargain from an instrumental perspective, it has a much less salutary face in virtue terms. For someone concerned with virtue, the primary question is not what can I get out of this situation, but what kind of person am I? If I am asking for a free ride, I would be compelled to say that I am a freeloader—not much of a citizen at all—if being a citizen means being an active contributor to the life of my community. I am a resident and a beneficiary of the community, but my approach to this commonwealth is one of unilateral benefit seeking rather than full participation. If I could bring myself to evaluate my involvement, I would see that I fall far short of what is admirable in citizenship. Moreover, the benefits I reap from freeloading are limited to external goods. As a freeloader, I place myself outside the richest aspects of communal life, and I cannot experience the solidarity, belonging, or sense of shared purpose (i.e., internal goods) that come only with active communal involvement.

Knowledge as a Shared Good

It is ironic that shared goods should receive so little attention in a discipline such as psychology, because one of its most central and defining activities aims precisely at a shared good: knowledge. The scholarship that is aimed at expanding our understanding of human behavior is deeply communal. Academic scholarship is always conducted within a community, even when those activities are pursued by individual and, to some degree, isolated investigators. Scientific psychology is a community rather than a mere social or professional group because it has shared goals (knowledge production, improvement of human welfare), shared practices (research methods, peer review), and standards (criteria for truth claims, ethical guidelines).

The process of publication, with all of its flaws and errors, embodies the communal nature of scholarship. The point of gathering data, making arguments, and creating theories is to publish one's results and to influence the direction of professional thought and activity by creating knowledge. The process of certifying claims as legitimate knowledge is highly social in that it involves peer review and interchanges between authors, editors, and reviewers. In addition, public discussion and debate about results is a vital aspect of scholarship. Finally, the knowledge itself is a shared good, because privately held information and theories are of little value.

Training psychologists to participate in the production of knowledge is also a shared project in that it involves teachers and students in a personal and ongoing relationship that employs standard practices, exemplars, and shared paradigms to teach students how to engage in scholarly activities that will be recognized as such by their peers. Of course, individual prestige and fame figure into these communal practices, but this personal prominence is primarily attainable through contributions that the profession as a whole or as a significant subgroup deems valuable. The journal articles, books, and other presentations of knowledge that hold prominent places in our discipline do so through being held in common in our discourse, our training, and our research and applied practices.

This is not to say that all scholarly activities are by nature virtuous, or that all knowledge claims, or even those accepted by the profession, are genuine contributions to the common good. The process of academic inquiry can be misguided, distorted, corrupted, or fraudulently pursued. For this reason, we must continually renew our commitment to ongoing collegial scrutiny and questioning, combined with the search for replication, deeper understanding, verification through application, and so forth. The best way to maintain this commitment is to remain cognizant that the internal good of knowledge is immeasurably more valuable than money or fame.

The community of scholars can only correct mistakes and malfeasance through communal action and a shared commitment to mutual scrutiny and ongoing dialogue (Meara & Day, 2003). We uphold the scholarly community by participating in the key practices of knowledge seeking that constitute it. These practices include presenting our results honestly and courageously, engaging in dialogue respectfully, giving opportunity for others' voices to be heard justly, making claims temperately by allowing for the possibility of refutation. We can also perpetuate our scholarly enterprise through good training, by cultivating a love of truth in ourselves and our students, and teaching students to practice knowledge seeking in a characteristically honest, courageous, just, and temperate manner. Clearly, these remedies and preventive efforts can only be pursued collectively and will succeed only to the extent that we pursue them in concert. There is no appeal outside of this community that can provide guarantees of validity or veracity. We do all of this out of our shared devotion to truth, and our individual claims to knowledge and critical questioning of others' claims borrow their authority from that common pursuit rather than from any abstract logic, well-honed method, or personal preference. From a virtue ethics perspective, our commitment to such shared aims and to the virtues required for their pursuit are not external constraints on our scholarly practice, such as we might find in laws or abstract duties. Rather, these moral commitments form the very conditions under which genuine scholarship can unfold (MacIntyre, 1999). In other words, our commitments to truth and scholarly dialogue are constitutive of the communal pursuit of knowledge (Taylor, 1989).

The Relationship Between Individual and Shared Goods

In attempting to make room for shared goods, I am not suggesting that the goods that individuals can hold independently are unimportant. Goods that individuals can possess in differing amounts such as wealth, fame, and achievements or a capacity to appreciate art are also worthwhile elements in a life well lived. In the previous chapter, I described a type of external good that can be individually possessed and of which there is a limited supply, making them goods of competition. It is clear that all human beings seek some goods of competition at the same time that we participate in communal enterprises. From a virtue ethics perspective, it is clear that we need at least a moderate degree of physical and financial resources to be able to live well. When one has the misfortune to be preoccupied with worries about having physical security, food to eat, or a place to live, it is very difficult to attend to cultivating excellence. At the same time, a high level of wealth and prosperity is not necessary for living well. Surveys of subjective well-being commonly demonstrate the limits of wealth as a source of flourishing, because there are very weak correlations between financial prosperity and self-reports of living a meaningful or satisfactory life (Diener, Sandvik, Seidlitz, & Diener, 1993; King & Napa, 1998). In fact, some research suggests that valuing material prosperity over goals such as personal growth or community contribution is associated with lower levels of subjective well-being (Kasser & Ryan, 1993, 1996). These studies indicate that beyond a moderate level of financial resources, material goods do not contribute substantially to the good life. This suggests that the means for providing basic comfort and security are merely the infrastructure of a good life, not its guiding purpose.

This view of what is good in life does not subordinate individual aims to the good of the community, nor are shared goods merely a summation of individual goods (MacIntyre, 1999). These individual goods have an independent value that is not encompassed by what is held in common.

Moreover, individuals are members of multiple groups with a variety of shared goods, and what is best for one's family may or may not be related to what is best for one's community, religious group, or nation. Individuals rightly pursue what is good for themselves as individuals even as they participate in the community maintaining practices that facilitate the good of their groups.

Of course, some individuals aggressively seek to obtain very high degrees of material prosperity, prestige, and notoriety. Some pursue these ends illegally, but many do so within the institutions and practices that form the infrastructure of our democracy, economy, and justice system. As previously noted, research indicates that such avid pursuit of material goods is not conducive to individual well-being. The single-minded pursuit of the goods of competition is also highly problematic for the general welfare when individuals place their possession of these goods above the shared goods that make this pursuit possible. This occurs when political and legal practices are perverted, sidetracked, or abused for the benefit of some people at the expense of others. Financial fraud, political influence peddling, and suborning justice are examples of how individuals seek their personal benefit in ways that actually undermine the very system that makes it possible to pursue the goods of competition they value so much. The process of undermining social institutions in this way was demonstrated dramatically in the steep stock market decline in 2002 that followed the revelation of a series of fiduciary misdeeds by major corporate figures at Enron, Adelphia, WorldCom, and other companies. To the degree that such egoistic activities become commonplace, they can destroy the institutions and practices of democratic societies and free markets, as de Tocqueville (1830/1969) warned us.

The key point is that shared goods form a higher order of ends that provides the context for one's strivings for individual goods. Moreover, the cultivation of a democratic society with free markets and a functioning justice system can be one of the major purposes for obtaining the goods of competition. Attaining a certain level of prosperity is necessary for citizenship and for participation in public life. Although some public figures use their position for personal gain, many statesmen and stateswomen have put their material possessions in the service of society through political activity, charitable giving, and other forms of public service. The institutions and practices of democracy and justice require care and respect to foster personal freedom and the ability to prosper as individuals. When human beings pursue these shared goods, we do so in concert with others, and our success in attaining them benefits all who participate, which takes us beyond the egoistic–altruistic dichotomy (MacIntyre, 1999).

Unfortunately, shared goods are virtually invisible in contemporary psychology, which is almost wholly oriented to portraying individuals in an unencumbered, self-interested manner and focusing its attention on identifying strategies that make it possible for them to succeed in their pursuit of individually chosen and possessed goods. This narrow disciplinary focus may inadvertently undermine the communal pursuits and ends that are indispensable for human flourishing. Therefore, it is vital for us to expand our disciplinary vision to include shared goods and their cooperative pursuit so that we do not promote an excessive form of self-interested individualism.

THE SOCIAL CORE OF THE VIRTUES

As this discussion of shared goods indicates, virtue ethics is a deeply social perspective that acknowledges the importance of individual identity and choice but insists that individuals' memberships in ongoing historical communities shape and give meaning to their identities and choices. Aristotle (trans. 1996) is famous for saying that "man is a political animal" (p. 13), and the virtue ethics tradition that he began is deeply social in ways that challenge the individualistic tenor of psychology and contemporary American society. Virtue ethics is communal in nature because it begins with the premise that humans are by nature social beings, and the social affiliations we have are essential to our capacity to flourish as humans. Although virtues are individual character strengths, individuals learn about excellence and about what is good socially and pursue many of the best activities in life primarily in concert with others. Moreover, there is a class of goods that we can only hold in common with others, and these goods are essential to flourishing and would be inaccessible to us if we were entirely independent individuals.

When humans are born, we enter a fully formed social arena in which long-established projects and practices are already under way (MacIntyre, 1981; Taylor, 1985). As we mature, we play a steadily expanding role in these ongoing endeavors long before we recognize that we do so or that we have any choices about the nature of our participation. This enculturation or socialization is automatic and generally implicit. Our participation in the ongoing stories of our families, communities, societies, and species is an essential aspect of our humanity. In other words, we are already committed to a form of life and a perspective on how to live it appropriately long before it is possible for us to reflect on whether and how we want to continue our involvement.

Geertz (1973) pointed to this social dependency in his famous statement that humans are incomplete animals who must learn how to be human through culture. Cultural psychologists have studied many ways in which cultural perspectives shape individual psychology. One of the most prominent and interesting of these topics is the influence of the cultural value of individualism. Researchers have demonstrated that the primacy of the individual is a cultural inclination rather than a universal feature of humans (Fukuyama, 1999; Kitayama, Markus, & Kurokawa, 2000; Triandis, 1995) and that many cultural perspectives are far more communally oriented.

Psychologically speaking, Baumeister and Leary (1995) presented an impressive and diverse compilation of evidence for what they termed a *need to belong*. They argued that the need to belong is as basic to human nature as any other need because it affects behavior, emotion, and cognition in a wide variety of circumstances, elicits goal-directed activity, has ill effects when not satisfied, and is universal in humans. As a species, we form relationships early and relatively easily, not only on the basis of shared pleasure but also under adverse circumstances. The termination of long-term relationships is accompanied by significant distress. Human cognition has strong relational features, with in-group biases, enhanced memory for details, and frequent attributions related to one's relational status (doing something because one is a spouse or a parent). Social isolation is a primary source of distress, giving rise to anxiety, depression, and stress, undermining immunocompetence, and increasing the likelihood of suicide and other forms of mortality.

All of these scholars suggest, in different ways, that human flourishing is deeply dependent on social relatedness and the individual's participation in culture. One would expect, therefore, that the virtues needed for flourishing as social animals would have a deeply social dimension as well.

The Virtue of Social Animals

It is a common misconception to see virtues in terms of individual attributes that may or may not have a social component. At its extreme, this perception invites the criticism that the virtue perspective leads to a self-preoccupation that undermines one's ability to be fully socially engaged. This is a fundamental misunderstanding of virtue, because individual character and all of the specific virtues are profoundly social in their origin, enactment, and ends.

The dominant individualism in psychology shows up even among psychologists who have taken an interest in virtue. For example, Baumeister and Exline (2000) described virtue as a sacrifice of individual interests for the sake of group harmony and benefit. This is a consequential misunderstanding of virtue based on the assumption that individuals are autonomous beings who are naturally and fundamentally egocentric in the pursuit of their own desires, which places them in ongoing conflict with their social environments. According to these authors, individuals foster social harmony through the self-control of their asocial, egocentric impulses. Each of these premises contradicts the virtue ethics outlook for two key reasons. First and foremost, the need for self-control is a failure of character, because virtue involves wanting to act for what is good. As I outlined in chapter 3, when we choose to act well in spite of our desire to do otherwise, we are acting *continently* rather than virtuously. Second, the individual's good, as I am arguing in this chapter, is deeply intertwined with what is good for the group.

Character strengths do not arise from instinctual or accidental sources. Humans are not naturally virtuous, but we do have the capacity for virtue, and every normally endowed individual who receives the appropriate guidance and encouragement can develop admirable characteristics. Children have to learn what their caretakers and surrounding community consider worthwhile and which character traits make it possible to seek those goods. Children learn about character from their caretakers, teachers, peers, and heroes. This learning is intensely social because one needs models to emulate, teachers to impart a way to understand virtue, and caring others to provide guidance and feedback about one's efforts. It takes practice to learn to love what is good and to develop the habit of acting for the sake of that good automatically, and sustained practice requires encouragement and example from others. Like language, virtue cannot be learned in isolation.

The enactment of virtue is also essentially social. Although the disposition to act well resides in the individual, virtue exists only in action and those actions have an ineliminable interpersonal dimension. As Aristotle noted, "the just man needs people towards whom and with whom he shall act justly, and the temperate man, the brave man, and each of the others is in the same case" (trans. 1998, p. 264). Consider honesty, for example. The primary meaning of honesty is to tell the truth to others, whether that truth-telling deals with the everyday facts of one's life or with one's scholarly pursuits. Honesty shows up primarily in the *interchange* of truth between people. Of course, it is common to speak of being honest with oneself, but self-honesty would count for little if it were coupled with deceiving those who have some claim on the truth from one. Generosity and justice are also social at the core in that they necessarily involve being generous or just with others. Being generous with oneself and doing oneself justice are secondary applications of these virtues and admirable only when they are coupled with their social instantiations.

Nussbaum (1986) described the social dimension of character strengths that are less obviously interpersonal. She suggested that even virtues that are sometimes called "self-regarding" such as courage or temperance transcend the individual in an essential way. Consider the prototypical courage of risking one's life in battle. This kind of courage requires a genuine concern for the well-being of one's country and fellow citizens. Similarly, real moderation (temperance) is based on a clear appreciation of the social norms for the proper degree of eating, drinking, sexual activity, emotional expression, and so forth. Individuals cannot fully express these character strengths without knowledge of and sensitivity to the norms, well-being, and goods prevalent in their social environment.

Woodruff (2001) also emphasized the social dimension of courage by pointing out that soldiers can't be courageous individually. If a single soldier attempts to win a battle by individual action without the support of others in the unit, that soldier is likely to be killed, which amounts to foolishly throwing one's life away, not courage. Similarly, the virtues of loyalty and generosity cannot be unilaterally practiced in families or communities that are fully bent on extracting the most individual benefit possible from others without regard to the cost to those others. In such a circumstance, attempts at loyalty or generosity will amount to inviting exploitation and disrespect, not demonstrating virtue. The ability to recognize when and in what ways to practice these virtues is very much a matter of accurately perceiving the character of one's social circumstances so that one can make wise decisions about what is appropriate in the concrete situation. I have much more to say about the practical wisdom required to decide how to act well in the next chapter, but I want to note that acting virtuously is always a matter of perceptively grasping how one can act well in view of one's situation with others.

Are There Self-Regarding Virtues?

Some proponents of virtue divide the virtues into "self-regarding" qualities such as temperance and integrity and "other-regarding" character strengths such as generosity and loyalty (Frankena, 1973; Meara & Day, 2003; Pojman, 1990). These authors have identified self-regarding virtues as those that benefit the individual and other-regarding virtues as those that are primarily beneficial to others. In the previous section I argued that virtues often considered self-regarding have an inherent social dimension. MacIntyre (1999) gave a more compelling reason to reject this distinction. He argued that the division of virtues into self-regarding and other-regarding categories maintains a split between the individual and the social that is misplaced in virtue ethics. This division is based on the notion that human beings have divided inclinations and passions, some of which are self-regarding and some of which are other-regarding. This often leads to the position that egoists are entirely self-regarding and altruists are often other-regarding and self-neglecting. MacIntyre points out that the task of character education is to transform and integrate those inclinations such that we see and love the *common* good and recognize how our individual welfare is deeply tied to others' well-being. When we understand this deep and inescapable connection, "we become neither self-rather-than-other-regarding nor other-rather-than-self-regarding, neither egoists nor altruists, but those whose passions and inclinations are directed to what is both our good and the good of others" (p. 160). Another way to put this is to see that most of our motives and actions cannot be neatly divided between the categories of self- and other-benefit. In the next section, I discuss how friendship illustrates that many of our actions are embedded in emergent social relationships in which shared goods often transcend the separate interests of the individuals. In the previous section I discussed how the vital concept of shared goods illuminates a primary aim of human action. MacIntyre's reasoning makes it clear that virtue is not a matter of self-sacrifice so much as a way of acting that aims at achieving shared goods, or, at the very least, harmonizing individual and group interests. The virtue of friendship can help us to see this overlap of interests in a concrete and enlightening way.

FRIENDSHIP

The importance of the virtue of friendship provides one of the clearest demonstrations of the centrality of the social in virtue ethics. Aristotle's *Nicomachean Ethics* contains 10 books, and 2 of them are devoted to friendship. This ancient commitment to friendship provides a remarkable contrast to most modern ethical theories, which attempt to define ethics in terms of *impersonal* duties and obligations. Aristotle believed that human flourishing is centrally concerned with ongoing ties of affection and involvement in mutually valued endeavors. His summary comment on friendship is that "Surely it is strange, too, to make the supremely happy man a solitary; for no one would choose the whole world on condition of being alone, since man is a political creature and one whose nature is to live with others" (p. 238).

It is important to recognize that Aristotle's concept of friendship is not limited to voluntary associations among peers but is very broad, including marriage, family relationships, and relations among fellow citizens. There are four ways to see that this broad concept of friendship is at the core of a well-lived human life. First, friendship provides us with companionship and enjoyment. As Baumeister and Leary (1995) have documented, humans have a deep need to belong, and we do not flourish without substantial social involvement. Second, the best kinds of friends are those who bring out the finest in us and encourage us to be our best selves. As I discuss in the following section, friends can help us to cultivate and practice virtue. Third, friends can increase the likelihood that we will be successful in pursuing our aims, because sharing our endeavors with others enriches and strengthens our efforts. We are most able to engage in sustained excellent activity when we participate in those pursuits with well-disposed others.

Finally, friendship is also vital because, as discussed earlier in this chapter, some goods can be experienced only if we hold them in common with others. In all of these ways, friendship is central to the overall project of flourishing as a person.

Instrumental Friendships

In discussing friendship, it is important to differentiate among different types of relationships, as some will be more conducive to some goods and others will foster other goods. As I pointed out in the last chapter, psychology has generally focused its attention on instrumentally based friendships that confer benefits. In general, instrumental friends mutually understand this give and take and do not seek to manipulate or just "use" one another. These friendships often involve genuine positive feelings for one another, which are perpetuated by exchanging benefits and enjoyment. Aristotle distinguished two forms of instrumental friendships. He called the first advantage friendship because it is based on the tangible benefits that the friends exchange. He called the second type of instrumental relationship pleasure friendship because this friendship grows out of and continues on the basis of providing enjoyment for each other.

Many ordinary friendships take the forms of advantage or pleasure friendships. In fact, it is important to have advantage friendships, because people need help from others to get along in life, even if the friendship does not attain any greater depth than the simple exchange of assistance. It is also valuable to have friends whom one simply enjoys, whether or not one's bonds with them have depth and purpose beyond simple companionship or pleasure.

If, however, friendships were truly limited to exchanges of advantage and pleasure, as some prominent psychological theories suggest that they are, humans would be plagued by a deep sense of impermanence and our relational life would become episodic and lacking in coherence. This is because advantage and pleasure relationships have serious inherent limitations. One important drawback is that advantage and pleasure friendships tend to be primarily self-serving in their emphasis on receiving enjoyment or benefits. In other words, it is the enjoyment or benefits that draw me to the relationship rather than the character of the person who is my friend or the inherent value of the joint activities in which we engage. For this reason, these two types of friendship last only so long as the mutual advantage or pleasure endures. For example, if a business associate ceases to be useful and the friendship hasn't taken on a significant alternative basis such as coming to enjoy one another's company, it is very likely that the friendship will fade. The focus on the exchange of external goods like advantage or pleasure leads to impermanence because the friendship is subject to the vagaries of what is pleasant or advantageous, which is likely to change over time.

Advantage and pleasure friendships also have an episodic character because exchanges of these external goods typically happen in discrete situations or contexts. When individuals take stock of such friendships, they will be inclined to examine whether the exchange has been equitable to them, and they will tally the episodes of benefits and compare them to the incidents that were disadvantageous or unpleasant. In this calculus, the more recent past will generally outweigh the more distant past. In other words, they will be inclined to wonder what their friend has done for them lately.

The episodic character of an instrumental approach is particularly problematic in marital relationships, a key form of adult friendship from a virtue ethics perspective. As I have argued elsewhere, a focus on pleasure and satisfaction in marriage is one of the key contributors to the high rate of divorce (Fowers, 2000), for if one's feelings of satisfaction are the primary reason for remaining married and that experience diminishes for whatever reason, it is entirely rational to end the marriage. As long as people lack a coherent and attractive alternative for maintaining such important relationships, there will continue to be a very high divorce rate.

Social exchange theory, for example, has been extremely influential in marital research and therapy. Exchange theorists suggest that relationships are, essentially, a series of exchanges between individuals. Spouses give their time and energy to one another in various ways and, in return, they expect to gain benefits from doing so. Exchange theorists claim that spouses decide whether their marriage is satisfying by weighing the overall balance of costs and benefits in the relationship. Spouses then compare that balance to alternatives to the relationship (being in another relationship, or being single). If their marriages stack up well against the alternatives, they are likely to maintain them. If a relationship is less attractive than the alternatives, social exchange theorists believe that spouses then consider the barriers to ending their marriages. Barriers include such things as laws that make divorce difficult or costly, social disapproval of divorce, the loss of property, and so forth. If a relationship is less attractive than the alternatives and the barriers to splitting up are weak, couples are more likely to split up.

This theory suggests that spouses are logical, hard-nosed relationship comparison shoppers, who restlessly evaluate whether they are getting the best relationship "deal" that the market can offer. According to social exchange theory, spouses have a curious neutrality about whether to leave their relationships. This perspective suggests that they will let the cost-benefit ratio of their marriages tell them whether to stay or leave. Commitment or loyalty would actually be foolhardy or illusory from this point of view, because commitment forecloses the possibility of cutting a better deal in the relationship market (unless the relationship is vastly better than any conceivable alternative).

Social exchange theory provides a reasonably good model for relatively short-term, instrumental friendships, but not longer-term relationships. Social exchange theory emphasizes the kind of reasoning that is more consistent with an individual who is continually evaluating the wisdom of continuing a relationship rather than one who perceives the relationship as a long-term commitment. Experimental evidence suggests that participants do see short-term involvements in exchange terms but that a longer time frame encourages a more communal approach (Clark, Mills, & Powell, 1986; Williamson & Clark, 1992; Williamson, Clark, Pegalis, & Behan, 1996). A longer-term orientation has been shown to be a key feature of successful marriages (Rusbult & Van Lange, 1996; Stanley, Lobitz, & Dickson, 1999; Waite & Gallagher, 2000) and an essential component in partners' willingness to sacrifice for the relationship (Van Lange et al., 1997), accommodate the partner (Rusbult et al., 1991), and forgive relationship transgressions (Finkel et al., 2002). Thus, it appears that an instrumental perspective can capture the tenor of short-term, low-commitment relationships but is inadequate for understanding longer-term, committed relationships.

Research on the concept of sociosexuality provides another window into the limitations of a one-sided instrumentalism in romantic relationships. Sociosexuality is the degree to which individuals are interested in sexual involvement with someone else in the absence of emotional bonding or commitment. Those who are higher in sociosexuality tend to choose partners primarily on the basis of their physical and sexual attractiveness (Simpson & Gangestad, 1992) and frequently seek sexual involvement with multiple partners (Seal, Agostinelli, & Hannett, 1994). Therefore, greater sociosexuality represents the instrumental pursuit of sexual pleasure and beauty over depth or longevity of relationships. Consequently, individuals high in this trait report less investment, love, and commitment to their romantic relationships than those with lower sociosexuality (Simpson & Gangestad, 1991, 1992). In other words, because individuals high in sociosexuality see relationships as a means to the end of pleasure, their relationships are likely to be shorter and have an episodic rather than cumulative character, just as virtue ethics suggests.

Character Friendship

A relational life limited to instrumental forms of affiliation would be missing the kind of friendship that Aristotle saw as most central to living well. He called this *character friendship,* and this kind of relationship has three qualities that distinguish it from pleasure and advantage friendships.

First, character friends share an understanding of what is good or worthy and a mutual commitment to seeking it. This means that character friendships are likely to have greater longevity because the kinds of goals that are central to one's understanding of a good life are likely to be much more stable than what is pleasurable or advantageous at a given time. Friendships based on seeking such worthwhile aims are likely to be long-lasting. Second, character friends come together because they recognize each other's good qualities, the character strengths that each of them possesses that make it possible for them to seek what is good together. The stability of character over time also contributes to the relative permanence of this kind of friendship. Third, character friends work together to achieve their shared goals. This kind of joint cooperation and teamwork adds another dimension of richness and support for continuity in a relationship.

Character friendship is also pleasurable and beneficial, but it transcends these considerations. In other words, the nature of the friendship goes beyond the individual interests or enjoyment of the friends and aims at larger goals. In character friendships, mutual happiness is a by-product of shared commitment and teamwork rather than the primary goal.

Aristotle spent so much time discussing friendship because it is essential to the life of virtue. Character friendship provides more than pleasurable association; it constitutes the best arena in which the individual can actualize virtue and pursue what is good. As Sherman (1989, p. 127) put it,

> To have intimate friends and good children is to have interwoven in one's life, in a ubiquitous way, persons towards whom and with whom one can most fully and continuously express one's goodness. The friendships are not external conditions of those activities, like money or power. Rather, they are the form virtuous activity takes when it is especially fine and praiseworthy.

Sherman highlighted the way in which the most important aspects of character friendships are *internal* to the relationship in that they are not separable from it (e.g., solidarity, shared goods), in contrast to *external* benefits (e.g., pleasure, material assistance) that might result from the relationship but can be sought in other venues. This distinction is another example of the internal and external goods I described in the last chapter. That is, individuals can only obtain the good that comes of character friendship in the process of pursuing shared goals through teamwork and valuing the goodness in one another. The only way to have this kind of friendship is to *be* this kind of friend.

Aristotle called a character friend "another self" because character friendship is based on friends sharing the pursuit of the same good and cooperating in that pursuit. Friends also share similarities and can learn from each other and support each other in pursuing their jointly held aims.

Friends with good character also help one another to improve because they want the best for each other and are committed to one another's flourishing. Beyond that, however, friends "take the mold of characteristics they approve" from each other (p. 247). Friends learn from each other, because having a friend is something like having a character mirror. Individuals can see aspects of themselves in their friends and study them with more detachment than they might have in self-reflection.

It takes time to become character friends, not only because it takes time to get to know each other and to appreciate the good in each other but also because friends must learn to coordinate their activities over time to achieve their ends. This mutual coordination is essential for living well because sharing activities with a friend increases one's joy in them. Moreover, when a friend relies on us to do our part and acts in conjunction with us, it makes it easier for us to act well and to maintain our efforts against obstacles and fatigue.

It is extremely arduous to sustain the pursuit of even worthwhile goals as an entirely individual affair. Solitary endeavors are prone to a creeping sense of arbitrariness, pointlessness, and discouragement. An excessive reliance on one's individual resources gives rise to a pervasive sense of anxiety about the meaning and value of one's pursuits, which simply cannot be justified and supported entirely from within. This self-doubt is all too easy to come by, particularly in a world that is so full of uncertainty and change. The insufficiency of the individual's internal resources is a serious problem for an individualistic psychology, but one that is simply taken as a basic element of humankind's social nature from a virtue ethics perspective.

Persistence in one's pursuit of identified goods is partly dependent on the recognition of those goods by others and on their appreciation or admiration of one's efforts in bringing those goods about. Friendship is a primary avenue for human beings to confirm in each other the value of our pursuits, to coordinate our efforts to succeed in those activities, and to cultivate the best in ourselves and our friends to make that success possible. Indeed, our self-respect and self-esteem depend in no small part on confidence in the value of our activities, and this confidence is extraordinarily difficult to maintain entirely independently. Confirmation from respected others contributes greatly to our belief in the value of our endeavors (Flanagan, 1991; Rawls, 1971).

Our individual good is thoroughly dependent on others in very tangible ways as well. Whether we consider physical health and security, education, appreciation of beauty, or the search for truth, our efforts are supported by and coordinated with myriad others, both those we know and those whose actions benefit us without our knowledge. Others' individual activity as well as social practices and ongoing institutions are indispensable to exercising one's talents and to overall flourishing. For example, seeking excellence as a composer or musician requires a reliance on participating with others in the present and partaking of the musical tradition and practices of earlier generations (Flanagan, 1991). From a virtue ethics perspective, this dependence on others is not a regrettable weakness in our species. It is a significant source of joy, continuity, self-transcendence, and self-extension, all of which opens our lives in important ways that would not be available to us if we were truly self-sufficient. For all of the reasons I have enumerated in this section, a life without character friendship would fall crucially short of flourishing as a human being.

There is some research suggesting that there are two forms of friendships roughly paralleling instrumental and character friendships. Clark and her colleagues have studied two distinct relational frameworks that inform interactions among stranger dyads (Clark et al., 1986; Mills & Clark, 2001; Williamson & Clark, 1989; Williamson et al., 1996). She has called them exchange and communal orientations. In the exchange orientation, individuals focus primarily on the instrumental aspects of the interaction, particularly on the balance of give and take in the relationship, with no special attention to what the other person might need from them. In communal relationships, which are more likely in friendships, romantic relationships, and family relationships, individuals pay more attention to what their friend needs and give benefits or assistance according to the friend's needs rather than on the basis of strict reciprocity. The relationship and the friend are valued and cared for more than are the outcomes that one receives. Other researchers found that an emphasis on the unity between spouses ("weness") in marriage helped to predict marital stability over a five-year period (Buehlman, Gottman, & Katz, 1992; Carrere, Buehlman, Gottman, Coan, & Ruckstuhl, 2000).

The concept of character friendship also suggests that friends would actively support one another's pursuits and well-being. A number of studies using a variety of methods have found that when individuals perceive support for their goals from friends, family, or spouses, they show more persistence and effort, feel greater efficacy in reaching those goals, and are more likely to achieve their goals (Kaplan & Maddux, 2002; Shah, 2003a, 2003b; Zaleski, 1988).

Another line of research has explored a related tendency for individuals to merge their self–other boundaries in close relationships (Aron, Aron, & Smollan, 1992; Aron, Aron, Tudor, & Nelson, 1991; Cialdini, Brown, Lewis, Luce, & Neuberg, 1997). This merger of the self–other boundary involves integrating a partner's "resources, perspectives, and characteristics into the self" (Aron, Paris, & Aron, 1995, p. 1103). This merger means that the allocation of resources to one's partner and offering help to the partner are not clearly separated from the individual's self-interest (Aron et al., 1991; Cialdini et al., 1997). Indeed, as Cialdini et al. pointed out, "When the distinction between self and other is undermined, the traditional dichotomy between selfishness and selflessness loses its meaning" (pp. 490–491). I would add that the more friends pursue shared goals and cultivate character friendship, the more likely it is that what is good for one of them is also good for their friend and their relationship. These studies were not designed specifically to assess the character friendship concept, but they are quite consistent with it and suggest that further research on this concept is promising.

SUMMARY

This chapter has been devoted to two themes. First, I have argued that psychological theorists, researchers, and practitioners have rather unreflectively adopted a predominant individualism that obscures and distorts essential aspects of the shared life central to our humanity. Our discipline must be expanded to more adequately address the essential social nature of what is good for humans. Virtue ethics highlights the ways in which the social world helps to constitute the individual and provides an ongoing and essential context for the possibility of individual pursuits and flourishing.

Empirical sources on subjective well-being, romantic relationships, communal relationships, generativity, and the legitimacy of authority provide multiple indications that virtue ethics provides a useful perspective on the social nature of humans. The virtue framework brings these diverse literatures together in an interesting and novel way that is suggestive of substantial heuristic utility.

Second, virtue is irreducibly and necessarily social. Although character strengths are found in individuals, they are taught socially and expressed in ways that are deeply dependent on social mores and arrangements. Friendship is a central virtue that is essentially social and irreplaceable in a complete life. I have argued that the instrumental portrayal of friendship is an extremely truncated view of this kind of relationship that limits friendships to exchanges of external goods and neglects the communal stance individuals seem to take with friends (as opposed to the instrumental stance commonly adopted with strangers), and the possibility of friendship as a shared pursuit of jointly valued goods.

Virtue ethics suggests that we must enlarge our discipline to encompass a more complete understanding of the kinds of goods that are held in common with others. The multilateral and indivisible nature of these goods tends to render them invisible to us, and to obscure the extensive activity that is involved in maintaining shared goods such as self-government, social solidarity, and family cohesion. A consciousness of these goods makes it plain to us that there is no neat dividing line between what is good for me and what is good for others, and that all of us depend on and owe a debt to others who contribute to our shared good. We can possess many of our highest goods only when we share them in this way.

All of this makes it clear that virtue is inextricably communal. Humans gain an appreciation of character from others, learn the virtues from others, engage in virtuous activity with others, pursue goods we can only hold in common with others, and practice many primary virtues (e.g., friendship, generosity, justice) only with others. Each individual must decide whether or not to engage in admirable activities, but the context, meaning, import, and recognition of fine actions is profoundly social.

The ultimate success of such shared efforts depends on one's ability to recognize what is important and to make wise choices. In the next four chapters I explore practical wisdom as an account of how to choose well.

II

PRACTICAL WISDOM
IN PSYCHOLOGY

5

PRACTICAL WISDOM: THE HEART OF VIRTUE AND PSYCHOLOGY

Those who consider wisdom to be the most valuable of all possessions, are to be regarded as the wealthiest; and that wisdom, seeing that there is nothing which can be balanced against it, confers upon those who value it highly, and upon them alone, a wealth which is the greatest and most secure.

—Solon, quoted in *The Library of History* by Diodous Siculus

So far, my exploration of virtue has focused on the character strengths that make it possible for human beings to flourish and on the goods involved in flourishing. As shown in the preceding chapters, flourishing is a complex topic, involving many different character strengths, the coherence of one's overall life goals and ideals, and engagement with others in activities aiming toward shared goods. The perennial difficulty with any general framework, virtue ethics included, is in knowing how to apply it appropriately to the specific circumstances that one encounters—the devil being in the proverbial details. One of the great strengths of virtue ethics is that Aristotle and his commentators have described an approach to enacting virtue in everyday life through a capacity he called *phronesis*, which is usually translated as practical wisdom or judgment. It is also translated as prudence, but I do not use this term because of its current connotations of caution, calculation, and frugality. In contrast, practical wisdom involves being able to respond well and fittingly to one's circumstances as one seeks what is good. This chapter focuses on the concept of practical wisdom in some detail, and the other chapters in Part II outline the significant role practical wisdom plays in teaching, research, and clinical practices.

In a nutshell, practical wisdom is the ability to make wise decisions about how to act in a specific situation to pursue what is good. It is important to keep goodness, as the centerpiece of virtue ethics, fully in mind as we explore practical wisdom. Human activities aim at specific goods such as knowledge, good relationships, good government, and so forth. Wisdom and goodness mutually entail one another. Making wise choices has everything to do with being able to seek what is good, and one acts wisely only when in pursuit of worthy ends.

In our pursuit of what is good, we as human beings always have to decide whether our actions, in a given situation, should be guided primarily by courage or modesty, generosity or justice, or by some other virtue. In addition, we have to decide what would count as a courageous or generous action in each instance. We choose wisely by separating the important aspects of our situation from the trivial and responding primarily to what is significant. In this way, it is clear that practical wisdom guides the enactment of the virtues. Aristotle famously described virtue as the mean between excess and deficiency. For example, courage is the mean between rashness and cowardice. Practical wisdom helps us to recognize where that mean is for each concrete situation. This is why Aristotle said that "with the presence of the one quality, practical wisdom, will be given all the virtues" (p. 158).

Practical wisdom is more than one virtue among many, as some authors have suggested (Kitchener, 2000; Meara et al., 1996; Peterson & Seligman, 2004) because practical wisdom plays a more general and pervasive role in pursuing what is good than any particular virtue does. Virtue ethicists fully acknowledge the complexity of living well, and practical wisdom is the capacity to mold the multifarious elements of one's day-to-day life into a coherent and vibrant whole. This requires the ability to recognize what is worthwhile and the wisdom to coordinate one's efforts in specific situations to successfully pursue valued aims in a way that conduces to living well overall. The capacity to make good decisions or exercise good judgment in the everyday world is essential for both ordinary living and for professional activity.

It is difficult to overstate how crucial practical wisdom is to professional practice. The psychotherapist must be able to recognize and respond to what is most important in a client's presentation and avoid being distracted by what is trivial. Psychotherapists also have to choose how to intervene in each situation and to adapt those interventions to fit that particular person and occasion. Judgment is also vital for researchers, because choosing the most important questions for study is a crucial aspect of research, as is the perspicacity necessary to match investigative methods to the research question. Investigators must be judicious and focused on what is central as we interpret our results and discuss their implications and applications. Next, I examine the small, but growing psychological literature on wisdom to begin exploration of this topic.

WISDOM IN PSYCHOLOGY

Most psychologists will find the term *practical wisdom* foreign and perhaps somewhat woolly-headed. Psychologists often prefer to trim such high-flying concepts to the more familiar cloth of technical expertise, intelligence, or personality. As Holliday and Chandler (1986) put it when wisdom first became a serious topic in psychology, "wisdom . . . is not a topic openly discussed in the polite society of contemporary social science inquiry" because it "does not fit comfortably into the procrustean bed of contemporary cognitive-developmental theory" (pp. viii, 1) or, I would add, any standard psychological theory. Following decades of studied neglect, wisdom returned to the discipline in the effort of developmental psychologists to understand better the cognitive strengths of the elderly (Holliday & Chandler, 1986) and has received increasing attention recently.

Wisdom Research

Much of the psychological literature on wisdom adopts a generic, undifferentiated concept of wisdom that conflates theoretical and practical wisdom. For the account I develop, it is important to differentiate these two forms of wisdom because they have different contents and uses. *Theoretical wisdom* (called *transcendent wisdom* by Wink & Helson, 1997) is more abstract and emphasizes a well-formulated cosmic perspective that transcends narrow self-concern and contains philosophical or spiritual insights. *Practical wisdom*, in contrast, is more concrete and deals primarily with the capacity to make good judgments in everyday living about how to conduct oneself appropriately. My focus is on such everyday practical wisdom.

Because the concept of wisdom had been so thoroughly eschewed in psychology, wisdom research initially took the form of surveys intended to identify folk concepts of wisdom. For example, Holliday and Chandler (1986) conducted a series of studies to identify the prototypical elements in folk conceptions of wisdom. They asked a set of participants to identify characteristics of wise individuals, then asked a second set of participants to assign prototypicality ratings to these characteristics, followed by a third study in which the researchers used a recognition memory paradigm to assess whether participants recognized the previously identified wisdom characteristics as falling in a single category. Their research was largely consistent with their expectations and suggested that wisdom is an identifiable, interpretable, and robust construct. They identified highly prototypical folk constituents of wisdom, including having learned from experience, seeing things in a larger context, maturity, being a good source of advice, considering all options before deciding, being reflective, seeing the essence of situations, being perceptive, weighing the consequences of actions, and so forth. Other investigators have developed similar lists of wisdom constituents through multidimensional scaling (Clayton & Birren, 1980; Sternberg, 1990) and categorization theory approaches (Baltes & Smith, 1990). All of these researchers have also attempted to organize the concept of wisdom into a limited set of dimensions. Clayton and Birren (1980) identified reflective and affective dimensions. Holliday and Chandler (1986) described five factors, including understanding, judgment, general competence, interpersonal skills, and social unobtrusiveness. Sternberg (1985) derived components such as reasoning ability, sagacity, learning from ideas and environment, judgment, expeditious use of information, and perspicacity.

Given the differences in methods and samples, it is not surprising that these researchers identified different factorial structures or clusterings of wisdom descriptors. So far, no researcher has made a concerted attempt to harmonize these findings, but the similarity in the first-order descriptor lists across studies and the coherence of the descriptors within investigations suggest that there is an identifiable folk conception of wisdom.

The Max Planck group (Baltes & Staudinger, 2000) has developed the most sustained research effort on wisdom in psychology. They use a paradigm in which they ask research participants to comment on life problems or life review vignettes. Trained raters code the participants' responses according to five criteria to assess the wisdom of the responses. These criteria are rich factual knowledge, rich procedural knowledge, life span contextualism, relativism, and uncertainty. In a series of studies, these researchers have found that they can reliably identify wisdom using these methods and that the wisdom ratings appear to have good construct validity (Staudinger, Lopez, & Baltes, 1997; Staudinger, Maciel, Smith, & Baltes, 1998; Staudinger, Smith, & Baltes, 1992). For example, individuals who were independently nominated as wise persons had higher wisdom scores than a comparison group (Baltes, Staudinger, Maercker, & Smith, 1995).

Although individuals who are considered wise will be exceptional (Baltes & Smith, 1990; Kramer, 2000), some degree of wisdom is accessible to any normal individual. In their research on how people make wise decisions about life problems, the Max Planck group found that the highest ratings for wisdom in their studies occur rarely but that wisdom ratings do fall on a continuum. Wisdom is a kind of individual difference variable rather than an all or nothing capacity. Kitchener and her colleagues (Kitchener, 1986; Kitchener & King, 1990; Kitchener, King, Wood, & Davidson, 1989) have shown that reflective judgment, which can be seen as a component of wisdom, varies across individuals and that individual improvements in judgment occur sequentially over time.

Wisdom as Intelligence or Personality

One important aspect of wisdom research has been the exploration of whether wisdom is empirically distinct from intelligence and personality. The Max Planck group has found that their construct of wisdom is related to, but empirically distinct from, various measures of intelligence and personality (Staudinger et al., 1992, 1997, 1998). The modest positive correlations that Staudinger et al. (1997) found between wisdom and personality measures such as openness to experience, psychological mindedness, judiciousness, and a negative association with conservatism follow their theoretical predictions closely and discourage us from seeing wisdom as a derivative of standard personality traits. Other researchers have found that their constructs of wisdom and reflective judgment are empirically distinct from intelligence (Kitchener, 1986; Kitchener & King, 1990; Sternberg, 1985) and a variety of personality measures (Wink & Helson, 1997). Therefore, wisdom does not seem to be reducible to previously identified concepts of intelligence or personality.

The Trouble With Wisdom as Technical Expertise

Wisdom, in everyday and professional activities, is often portrayed as a technical matter. In particular, many psychologists are inclined to see good professional practice as a kind of technical expertise that results from the effective application of well-defined and empirically supported techniques to carefully delimited problems. Good therapeutic and scientific practices, from this point of view, are the dispassionate application of knowledge and skills rather than a matter of wisdom. There are many situations and difficulties that are best addressed in this instrumental fashion, but to see all of human life as manageable by technical means is distorting and limiting, as we saw in chapter 3.

Aristotle saw technical know-how as a form of knowledge and an ability that is appropriate in certain domains. He called this kind of know-how *techne* and designated as its domain those activities that involve concrete action designed to produce a specific outcome or product. Generally, these products can be unambiguously specified in advance by the maker, and the objects have distinct uses that are independent of the activity of creating them (Dunne, 1993). The quality of the product is separable from the quality of the maker, because its quality is dependent only on the skillful use of technique. In contrast, *phronesis*, or judgment, applies in both clear and ambiguous situations, is crucial to one's pursuit of the highest goods, and is central to character, all of which I discuss below. Examples of *techne* include the realm of crafts such as building or making pottery, the production of which serves other human ends (providing living space, storing commodities) with which carpenters and potters do not concern themselves. The only question for the practitioner of *techne* is whether the techniques are applied well or poorly to produce the predetermined product. In other words, technical expertise determines the quality of the product but has nothing to say about the use of the product or its place in the user's life. Many professionals prefer to see the application of their skills in just this way, as technical expertise that serves the objective pursuit of unbiased knowledge, the politically defined goals of society, or the more subjectively defined goals of clients in psychotherapy.

Models of Wisdom Based on Techne

The tendency in psychology to assimilate concepts such as practical wisdom, wisdom, and practical intelligence to technical or procedural expertise is very strong. For example, in their ongoing program of research on wisdom, the Max Planck group has defined wisdom as *"expert knowledge involving good judgment and advice in the domain, fundamental pragmatics of life"* (Baltes & Smith, 1990, p. 95, italics in original). They rely on models of expertise as a basis for their theory and research, and their theory of wisdom is strongly and explicitly related to technical expertise.

Chandler and Holliday (1990) worried that the emphasis on expert knowledge and pragmatics in the Max Planck model of wisdom may represent a contemporary tendency to equate wisdom with technical expertise, amounting to a conceptual impersonation of wisdom by instrumental reason. This concern has some traction because the Max Planck model emphasizes factual knowledge and managing uncertainty, and its core conceptual model of expert systems derives from highly systematized knowledge domains such as chess or physics. Moreover, Chandler and Holliday pointed out that the model excludes ethical terms dealing with character, what is good, and what is moral. Such ethical terms appear with great frequency in studies of folk concepts of wisdom (Clayton & Birren, 1980; Holliday & Chandler, 1986). So the Max Planck group appears to prefer an ethically neutral view of wisdom that portrays good judgment as "sound, effective, practical, and action-guiding" (Dixon & Baltes, 1986, p. 225) and unrelated to goodness beyond the desires and plans of individuals.

The Max Planck group's five constituents of wisdom do have a strongly instrumental cast. Factual knowledge provides "general knowledge about the human condition" (Staudinger et al., 1992, p. 272). Procedural knowledge provides the "strategies and heuristics concerning the management and interpretation of life matters." Contextual understanding allows the actor to recognize "that persons or events are not considered in isolation, but are viewed in their multiple life-span contexts." Value relativism "acknowledges that individuals and societies may differ in their priorities. Persons high on this criterion are able to differentiate and distance themselves with respect to values without, however, losing sight of a small set of universal values [undefined by the authors]." The management of uncertainty encompasses "management strategies and heuristics dealing with life's uncertainties." According to this portrayal, wisdom involves a kind of detachment from firm value commitments with a strong emphasis on pragmatics, strategies, and heuristics designed to help the individual manage contexts, uncertainties, and "life matters." This detached, managerial posture is the very picture of instrumentalism, particularly in the absence of any explicit consideration of the character of the wise person or of the overall good that wisdom is to serve. Therefore, a shrewd, exploitive person would fit this definition as well as an individual with good character because, for these authors, wisdom is detached from any conceptions of character or goodness. This separation of technical prowess and ethical considerations is a hallmark of contemporary instrumentalism.

A further indication of the strength of the instrumental impulse in psychological theorizing emerges in Sternberg and associates' (2000) concept of practical intelligence, a concept related to wisdom. These authors defined practical intelligence as the ability to "find a more optimal fit between the individual and the demands of the environment" (p. 34). Individuals pursue this fit by "maximizing practical outcomes . . . most typically of oneself [because] one's ultimate goal often is to maximize one's self-interest" (Sternberg, 1998, pp. 353–354). Sternberg differentiated practical intelligence from wisdom by defining practical intelligence as the ability to solve practical problems in which one's own interests are primary whereas he saw wisdom as the capacity to balance multiple interests and seek the common good. Sternberg and his colleagues portrayed practical intelligence as a kind of cleverness, shrewdness, or effectiveness in problem solving that is quite detached from the moral dimension of life. Practical intelligence is about problem solving, not about pursuing worthwhile aims or expressing good character.

Interestingly, Sternberg (1998) saw wisdom as a special case of practical intelligence, which inverts the classical view that cleverness is subordinate to wisdom. In a classical vision, wisdom is the superior attainment, and the practical intelligence he described is a deficient form of practical reasoning, one that neglects questions of character and the centrality of what is good. Practical intelligence may be very useful, but it can serve any end, egocentric or cooperative, beneficial or destructive.

Sternberg seemed to be interested in setting apart wisdom as an ethical form of practical reasoning in which one seeks a balance of interests and the common good. He noted that "despots are frequently practically intelligent, managing to control an entire country largely for their own benefit . . .

[whereas] in wisdom, one seeks a common good" (p. 355). He acknowledged the ethical core of wisdom by writing that "it is impossible to speak of wisdom outside the context of a set of values" but he demurred from defining those values, the common good, or the nature of "interests," claiming it was not

> the mission of psychology, as a discipline, to specify what the common good is or what values should be brought to bear. . . . Such specifications are perhaps the job of religion or moral philosophy. I, at least, would be skeptical of any psychologist who claims to specify what people should think. (p. 356)

This series of statements illustrates a central confusion in psychology into which Sternberg fell. The value of scientific objectivity operates as a kind of moral gag order. For instance, I wonder why he would not have been equally suspicious of a philosopher or theologian who wants to tell people what they should value and what goods they should seek. Why should these professionals be freer to speak on what is important in life? Did he believe that they have some authority or arcane knowledge that psychologists do not have? I also find it ironic that he debarred psychologists from discussing values on the basis of his evident commitment to the values of individual autonomy and scientific neutrality. Significantly, because wisdom can only be discussed in terms of values and, according to Sternberg, psychologists should not discuss values, he seemed to suggest that it is impossible for psychologists to theorize about and investigate wisdom, an extremely odd assertion in a theoretical article about wisdom!

Sternberg offhandedly suggested Kohlberg's theory of moral development as a way out of this dilemma. Kohlberg surely cannot help here, because his theory embodies powerful value biases and is completely barren as a resource for understanding values or the good because the stage theory focuses on the *form* of participants' moral reasoning not the *content* (Gilligan, 1982; Richardson et al., 1999; Sullivan, 1986). Like many psychologists, Sternberg faltered on the question of values and goods because he feared that an explicit discussion of values and goods would invariably lead to coercion. There is no reason to believe that individual autonomy must or even can be so complete as to rule out any discussion of what is worthwhile in psychology. Nor is it necessary to see individual freedom as so fragile that any joint deliberation about what is good will necessarily undermine that autonomy. Paradoxically, it is the depth of our *communal* commitment to individual autonomy as contemporary Americans that renders our defense of it so automatic and absolute.

I think it is important to credit Sternberg with taking a courageous step in defining the important psychological concept of wisdom in ethical terms, a step beyond instrumentalism that relatively few are willing to take explicitly. He was squarely in the mainstream in his attempt to avoid matters of values, however. The necessity of redefining psychology in ethical terms is an important subtext of this book. As I have made plain, I do not believe that we can leave questions of the good entirely to philosophers and theologians even as we recognize their specialized knowledge in these domains. Paradoxically, the fear of value imposition has led psychology to submerge its values under a cloak of objectivity, which has made it all the easier to covertly promote the instrumental individualism so prevalent in our theories, research, and practice (Richardson et al., 1999).

The Insufficiency of Techne

Psychological theory, research, and practice do not lend themselves to a neat separation of facts and values or means and ends. The attempt to draw such lines results in the kind of confusion Sternberg demonstrated. We cannot adopt a purely technical approach to our work partly because we cannot specify the precise outcomes in advance, as *techne* requires. In clinical and research practices, psychologists frequently deliberate about the nature and quality of desired outcomes, not just about the means used to bring about those products. We are always, implicitly or explicitly, seeking to promote some human good in our research, social policy, and clinical endeavors. We frequently and rightly find ourselves in extended debates about the nature of the goods we are promoting. The history of psychology has been replete with ongoing discussion about the ends of the discipline, from the early debates about whether psychology should be solely a science or include a practice dimension, to the humanistic challenge to the behavioral hegemony of the 1950s and 1960s, to feminist and multicultural challenges, to the current positive psychology movement (Leahey, 2000). Feminists and multiculturalists have famously challenged psychology to work toward greater respect and justice for women and minorities and questioned the legitimacy of a discipline that is blind to those ends. The advocates of positive psychology suggest that the traditional focus of psychology on the remediation of pathology is incomplete and needs to be supplemented with a clearer understanding of the good of human flourishing (Seligman & Csikszentmihalyi, 2000). Whether or not psychologists participate in such movements is largely a matter of whether they accept the goals of the movement or retain a preference for the traditional aims of psychology. Either way, the choice is one of goals, not means. A psychology that was truly constrained to fit within a narrow technical framework would be incapable of deliberating about its goals, due to its single-minded focus on the means of reaching goals that are defined in advance subjectively or politically.

Psychological practices cannot be reduced to *techne* because we must concern ourselves with the quality of the goods and goals we seek. The traditional aims of psychology involve goods that are worthwhile in themselves (knowledge, human welfare), not just objectives that are means to other ends. Moreover, these goods are not simple products like crockery that may or may not be useful in a good life. Rather, knowledge and well-being are indispensable constituents of a good life. For all its value, technical expertise cannot inform our understanding of what is worthwhile. In fact, we can use *techne* well only when we are clear about what is most important and about what we want our professional and personal lives to amount to. As shown in the following section, *phronesis* is the form of rationality through which one deliberates about the quality of both the methods and the goals that one pursues. *Phronesis* facilitates the clarity about one's goals that is necessary to apply *techne* well and to know when a technical approach is appropriate.

Contrary to contemporary psychological theory about wisdom, wisdom is centrally and indispensably ethical. Wisdom is inherently ethical because wise decisions and well-considered actions are those that help individuals to pursue their valued aims in the best kind of way, not merely as a matter of the pragmatic management of situations. The separation of the capacity to manage knowledge, context, and uncertainty from the quality of the goals this management facilitates is indefensible. Consider an individual who exhibits the very best management of knowledge, context, and uncertainty, but does so in pursuit of a foolish goal (to be a first-class buffoon) or a reprehensible one (racially motivated murder). Such an individual could not possibly be considered wise even if one did acknowledge some cleverness or shrewdness in the pursuit of such deplorable aims. Only a very strong ideological bias toward instrumentalism could have induced otherwise intelligent theorists to try to convince us that the worth of the ends could be disregarded and that wisdom could be located *entirely* in the choice of means. According to such a view, superficiality and rascality count as wisdom as long as the individual is clever in using information and managing situations.

Although their research is impressive and enlightening in many respects, the technical approach to wisdom in the Max Planck and Sternberg groups is yet another example of the widespread instrumental bias in modern psychology. If we remain trapped within an exclusively instrumental perspective, our understanding of human living will be unnecessarily constrained and distorted. In stark contrast, Aristotle repeatedly insisted that "it is not possible to be good in the strict sense without practical wisdom, or practically wise without moral virtue" (p. 158). Given that wisdom cannot be reduced to intelligence or personality and that the technical approach to wisdom has proven inadequate, it seems worthwhile to explore Aristotle's ethical model of wisdom.

PRACTICAL WISDOM

Aristotle defined practical wisdom as *orthos logos* or right reason in moral matters (broadly defined in terms of seeking what is good, not restricted to right–wrong distinctions). There are many ways to unpack this idea of right reason. For example, Aristotle said that virtue is acting according to the mean between excess and deficiency. Unfortunately, it is often difficult to know what the mean is. For example, what is appropriately courageous on one occasion might be rash on another and cowardly on a third. Thus, the doctrine of the mean is a helpful general notion, but it does not give us much concrete guidance, for we need to know what makes an action the mean in a particular situation. For that, we need a more detailed understanding of practical wisdom.

MacIntyre (1999) offered a helpful perspective by defining practical wisdom as follows:

> A chain of reasoning whose first premises concern the human good, whose intermediate steps specify what the virtues require, if the human good is to be achieved, and whose conclusion is the action that is good and best for us to perform here and now. (p. 159)

Following MacIntyre, I discuss practical wisdom as choosing and acting well in the pursuit of what is good in our daily activities. I focus on three complementary components of wisdom: the moral perception of what is at stake, deliberation about what is possible and what actions are called for, and the reasoned choice of the best course of action. Although I present these components separately for clarity, they are inseparable in practice.

Moral Perception

As MacIntyre (1999) suggested, practical wisdom helps individuals to decide how best to act to pursue the goods they seek in a given situation. This kind of deliberation is part of the warp and woof of everyday life. In their ordinary activities, individuals make most of their choices rather automatically unless they face some unusual or difficult circumstance. In other words, practical wisdom is not an exotic or unusual kind of rationality, but one that is central to the successful pursuit of everyday concerns and activities. A simple example of practical wisdom is choosing an appropriate gift for someone, which is based on how one sees the recipient, the nature of the relationship, the occasion, and how one wants to present oneself. A poorly chosen gift misfires because of a misperception regarding the recipient, the relationship, the occasion, or the intentions of the giver. Other common examples of practical wisdom in everyday life include tact in conversation, decisions about which of one's many goals to pursue at a given point in time, and planning the sequence and coherence of a class lecture. Individuals make decisions about such matters in terms of what is appropriate or fitting for the circumstances and for the goals they are pursuing. Kitchener (1999) and Rest (1994) have called this the "ordinary moral sense."

Sherman (1989) pointed out that prior to deciding *how* to act, an individual must recognize the need for action, and this can occur only through a clear-sighted reading of the circumstances:

> Accordingly, much of the work of virtue will rest in knowing how to construe the case, how to describe and classify what is before one . . . in so far as circumstances do not come pre-labeled as this sort of occasion or that, they must be classified by us. (pp. 29, 40)

In other words, one has to recognize that a particular occasion offers an opportunity to be of use to a friend, to be generous to someone less fortunate, to use a particular therapeutic intervention, or to test a specific theoretical premise. This recognition is what I mean by moral perception. It is *moral* perception because the focus is on differentiating what is valuable, significant, or important from what is valueless, insignificant, or unimportant in the circumstances.

Discerning the Essential

Virtuous action begins in the capacity to discern the features of a situation that are most important. An individual's capacity to act appropriately is dependent on this ability to comprehend the essential features of the situation. Moral perception is not limited to seeing what is right or wrong. It cuts deeper in that it illuminates what is most important and valuable. From this point of view, considerations of significance and worth are the basis for decisions about what is appropriate and right to do.

Moral perception is an ethical sensibility that highlights what is at stake in a given situation for the goods that one seeks. Significance always emerges in relation to one's aims, and therefore clarity about what is good and noble is the source of moral vision. If one's understanding of the human good is confused or vague, the ability to see what is most important will be clouded. Indeed, one's reading of a circumstance is largely constituted by one's intentions, for the actual pursuit of an end is only possible when a situation is construed as an occasion to act for the sake of that aim (Sherman, 1989). The philosopher Martin Heidegger (1962) described this phenomenologically in that the life projects that individuals pursue help to create a clearing in which a situation shows up in a particular way. Against the backdrop of one's goals, one sees the details of one's situation with greater clarity and insight, being able to recognize better the salience of both particular features as well as the overall import of the present state of affairs.

In this way, intentionality shapes perceptions of one's circumstances and clarifies how best to respond to them.

One of the most frequently recurring features of the *Nicomachean Ethics* is Aristotle's insistence on the appreciation of the particular case as essential in ethical matters. General concerns about virtue, law, and custom are important, but they hold true only roughly and in general. Moreover, ethical precepts only really come to light in view of the specific features of the situation before one, and these details will serve to qualify the results of any abstract reasoning on ethics. He stated that "matters concerned with conduct and questions of what is good for us have no fixity . . . the agents themselves must in each case consider what is appropriate to the occasion" (Aristotle, p. 30) and "such things depend on particular facts, and the decision rests with perception" (p. 47). The importance of the particular cannot be overstated, because, from a virtue ethics perspective, it is not possible to act ethically solely on the basis of universal principles. What it means to act well is always conditioned by the specific circumstances and how the pursuit of worthy aims can be adapted to the situation. This is the reason for the startling absence of moral rules in the *Nicomachean Ethics* (MacIntyre, 1981).

Moral perception is essential for productive therapeutic work. The psychotherapist must be able to recognize and respond to what is central in clients' lives and avoid being distracted by what is peripheral. One of the most striking things about the therapeutic situation is the overwhelming amount of verbal and nonverbal information that is present at any given moment. Making sense of this information is very difficult because our clients are confused and bewildered, and they usually describe their situation to us in a jumble. Moreover, one of the primary reasons many people need therapists is that they have learned to cope by avoiding, obfuscating, or complicating the central issues in their lives. In the face of these complications, therapists must sift through and organize the information we receive, as well as decide what else we need to know to be helpful. Thus, the crux of therapy is deciding how to construe the "blooming, buzzing confusion" of the therapeutic encounter with our clients so that we can focus on the most important things with a given client at a particular time. This kind of perception cannot be formalized or routinized, although psychotherapy theories and the collective psychotherapy wisdom do offer some general suggestions. Rather, therapists have to cultivate the ability to recognize what is at stake for their clients and to respond in ways that help clients to reach their goals in the situations they encounter. In chapter 6, I give an extended description of how practical wisdom guides good therapeutic practice.

Another way to see the importance of attending to the specifics of a situation is to recognize that it is one thing to know that a good therapist is empathic and an entirely different matter to know what empathy consists of with a particular client at a given moment. Abstract, third-person knowledge about empathy is useless without the ability to act appropriately empathic in the concrete situation. Similarly, it is one thing to know that a good scientist takes action to reduce alternative explanations of the results of research, but an entirely different thing to know what those alternative explanations are for a given study and to know how to design the study to rule them out. Without the concrete perception and contact with the particulars, general knowledge about empathy or alternative explanations hangs inertly in the air. No amount of abstract reasoning can lead to the practical knowledge necessary for wise choices. Practical wisdom always emerges through the direct contact that the agent has with the concrete particulars.

Character and Wisdom

The ability to recognize clearly what is important in a situation is linked to character. For example, if someone fails to notice clear indicators that a situation is one that usually calls for courage he or she would apparently lack that virtue. A generous person is more likely to recognize when and how to give appropriately than a miser or a profligate. Thus, character is revealed as much in what an agent perceives as in what is done. This is not to say that all situations are unequivocally clear even within a given community's standards, but acting well requires agents to be able to discern the importance of courageous action, although the specific ways that courage may come into play might require further deliberation. This connection between character and wisdom is recognized in folk conceptions of wisdom, which frequently contain character terms such as gentle, empathetic, peaceful (Clayton & Birren, 1980), concerned for others, fair, offering solutions on the side of right and truth (Sternberg, 1985), tolerant, mature, moral, modest, and kind (Holliday & Chandler, 1986). I have much more to say about the connection between practical wisdom and character in chapter 9.

Affect and Wisdom

Aristotle also took pains to show that our emotional responses are central to virtue and this is nowhere clearer than in the moral sensibilities required to see one's circumstances rightly. Given the complexities and ambiguities of the human world, we must interpret our situations to determine how to approach them. These interpretations are shaped by our aims and by the contours of our character. Both our aims and our character help to constitute our emotions. Therefore, experiencing the feelings that are appropriate to the salient aspects of what we face is one of the clearest marks of character. For this reason Aristotle comments that emotions

may be felt both too much and too little, and in both cases not well;
but to feel them at the right times, with reference to the right objects,
toward the right people, with the right motive, and in the right way,
is what is both intermediate and best, and this is characteristic of virtue.
(p. 38)

The affective aspects are not mere concomitants of our moral perceptions, however, because right readings of situations are often possible only
when we have certain feelings, whether those emotions are compassion,
anger, love, or revulsion. The affective response of the person of character
is largely a recognition that a situation is of one kind rather than another.
Emotional reactions highlight the ethically salient features of a situation.
For example, indignation in the presence of egregious injustice is a hallmark
of recognizing that injustice. Similarly, fear is directly tied to situations
that pose a danger to us or to something we value, and which may
require courage.

Courage is not the absence of fear, because someone who responds
fearlessly and blithely to a threatening situation is more likely to be acting
rashly than courageously. For example, the vast majority of novice therapists
I have supervised are fearful about meeting clients and engaging them
therapeutically. In my view, these individuals understand that there is a lot
at stake in these encounters and that they are uncertain about their ability
to rise to the occasion in spite of their extensive training. It is fitting to
feel fear in this circumstance, and this fear will help them to be appropriately
circumspect in their initial dealings with clients and in seeking supervisory
guidance. There are a small number of trainees who begin their practicum
work with full confidence in their ability to provide therapeutic service,
and these individuals have always been deeply worrisome to me. Their
confidence is misplaced and indicates an inability to recognize the complexity and moment of therapeutic work. I have seen their lack of appropriate
fear lead to many rash interventions and result in unwarranted risk taking
with issues that are of great importance to their clients. For these trainees,
my primary goal is to teach them a proper respect for their limitations in
view of what is at stake for their clients and the power their clients give
them in therapy. That is, they must develop a more acute moral perception
of the therapeutic situation.

This example illustrates that one might miss some of what is truly
relevant if one sees dispassionately, without engaging one's emotions (Sherman, 1989). When individuals perceive a situation rightly, they experience
delight in what is good and noble and revulsion toward what is base.
These feelings of delight or revulsion are inseparable from the capacity to
differentiate the noble from the base—the absence of such feelings indicates
the inability to appreciate the moral significance of the situation. Sherman
(1989) underlined the importance of proper emotional engagement by saying

that "without emotions, we do not fully register the facts or record them with the sort of resonance and importance that only emotional involvement can sustain" (p. 47).

There has been growing attention to "moral emotions" in psychology (Eisenberg, 2000), but this has largely been restricted to guilt, shame, and empathy. Guilt and shame arise in response to the transgression of a moral standard, with guilt generally seen as leading to reparative behavior and shame to counterproductive self-consciousness and self-criticism (Ferguson & Stegge, 1998; Niedenthal, Tangney, & Gavansky, 1994; Tangney, 1998). According to Eisenberg, situational "guilt involves feelings of tension, remorse, and regret" and "the primary concern is with a particular behavior" (p. 668). In contrast, shame is seen as a sense that "the entire self feels exposed, inferior, and degraded" (p. 667). Consequently, shame is associated with neuroticism, anger, and anxiety, whereas situational guilt is not (Einstein & Lanning, 1998; Tangney, Miller, Flicker, & Barlow, 1996; Tangney, Wagner, & Gramzow, 1992). Situational guilt seems to play a positive role in relationships, leading to apology and reparative behavior following a transgression because the individual responds to the important particulars of the situation. Empathy is an emotional response to another's distress that often leads to helping behavior or acts of restitution if the individual also feels responsible for the distress (Tangney, 1991).

There is a well-documented relationship between empathy and helping behavior (see Batson, 1998 and Eisenberg, 2000 for reviews). The link between empathy and helping behavior can be short-circuited if the individual becomes too distressed and seeks to avoid the other person's suffering. Both guilt and empathy, as well as the positive behaviors that follow from these emotions, are dependent on accurately recognizing that one has transgressed or that someone else is in distress. The experience of the moral emotions that have been studied so far is consistent with the concept of practical wisdom: Positive behaviors occur only when the individual is able to perceive the moral dimension of the situation (one's transgression or another's distress), experience some degree of responsibility for alleviating the situation, and remain focused on the difficulty at hand rather than becoming caught up in self-distress that leads to shame or an avoidant reaction.

Investigations of moral emotions are at a rudimentary stage. Researchers have not yet investigated such complex affects as the emotional attraction to what is good that is central to virtue ethics or more specific connections such as that between injustice and indignation. Affect is central to character because it is one's delight in nobility that moves one to act well. Investigative attention to the affect associated with character could significantly deepen our understanding of the moral emotions.

Deliberation

Moral perception will often result in a clear and immediate response and the appropriate course of action will be immediately apparent. For example, one might be facing a situation similar to circumstances that one has encountered frequently or the import of the occasion might be sufficiently clear that there is no need for further deliberation. In some circumstances, however, the most fitting response is not so obvious and requires deliberation. In such cases, one pauses to reflect and to ascertain how best to realize one's aims, given the circumstances. Many authors interested in developing a psychological account of wisdom focus on the ability to respond well in situations of uncertainty (Baltes & Smith, 1990; Clayton & Birren, 1980; Holliday & Chandler, 1986; Kitchener & King, 1990; Sternberg et al., 2000).

Each situation has a multitude of features, and human beings come to them with many interests and considerations. The complexity of our circumstances means that there may not be a single, obviously correct response to them. It is easy to see why we often err in our judgments about how to act because there is seldom a one-to-one correspondence between our aims and the features of a particular occasion. In complex situations, it is important to identify which goals are relevant and to focus on how we can pursue them in the circumstances. Deliberating well depends on a practiced acuity in focusing on the most relevant of the multiple elements of a situation in such a way that the appropriate concerns about the best kind of life are activated (Wiggins, 1980). Qualitatively different mind-sets for deliberation about goals and implementation of goals were identified by Gollwitzer and colleagues (Gollwitzer, Heckhausen, & Steller, 1990; Gollwitzer & Kinney, 1989; Taylor & Gollwitzer, 1995).

Once we see the possibility of pursuing one or more aims, we have to consider how best to seek them in the particular circumstances we face. What is practically best will inevitably differ from one state of affairs to another, which means that what is best is always constrained by the specifics of the situation. To complicate matters further, there are no set rules or definite procedures for arriving at this judgment, and we must rely on our sense of what is proper or fitting to choose the best course of action. People rightly subscribe to certain general rules such as "do not hurt others unnecessarily" or to general principles of justice, but these considerations are never sufficient to provide detailed guidance in a specific situation. We must relate such precepts to the particulars in a way that is fitting. Any attempt to specify rules for how we are to apply the general principles given the nearly infinite array of considerations and qualifications inherent in living would quickly degenerate into an infinite regress of caveats, considerations, exceptions, modifications, and so on. Living well is not a matter of learning and following a rule book, because, after all, there is no algorithm for life. Instead, we must make the best choices we can given what is possible and what is worthwhile.

Many commentators have interpreted Aristotle as limiting deliberation to simple means–end reasoning. After all, he famously proclaimed in Book III of the *Nicomachean Ethics* that "We deliberate not about ends, but about what is toward ends" (p. 56), and this is often taken to mean that he endorsed the kind of means–end instrumentality so common today. This is an anachronistic interpretation, for the ancient Greeks did not make the kinds of crisp distinctions between means and ends that characterize our modern instrumentalist orientation. Moreover, Aristotle disconfirmed this interpretation in Book VI. His separation of deliberation from ends in the text previously cited is better understood as an affirmation that human beings seek the highest good, *eudaimonia* or human flourishing, naturally and need not deliberate about the value of *that* end.

One of the ways to recognize the necessity of deliberating about goals is to recognize that our aims often have rather vague descriptions and we must deliberate to arrive at a suitable specification of an end (Wiggins, 1980). Deliberation sometimes involves a search for the best specification of my aim in view of what is practicable. Thus, deliberating about how best to seek a particular aim may involve deciding what counts as my end. For example, it is not necessarily obvious what counts as a worthwhile profession for someone deciding on a life's work, a good marriage for a particular couple, or a good community in a given historical society, and extended deliberation may be necessary to clarify these ends. Clarifying the goals of psychotherapy with a client and the aims of a research program are similarly complex and often involve lengthy consideration of what is both worthwhile and possible.

The function of coordinating one's overall ends is another important aspect of deliberation. In many situations, there are multiple considerations and pursuing one aim may undermine or compromise one's efforts to attain other goals. An individual's concerns generally do not allow for a single, unambiguous goal, but rather one frequently confronts a plurality of ends, which sometimes make competing and inconsistent claims on one (Nussbaum, 1986; Wiggins, 1980). Therefore, one of the tasks of deliberation is to evaluate one's planned course of action in terms of overall aims and attempt to harmonize these various ends. In such cases, one has to assess the relative importance of one's ends and to choose that course of action that best serves the most important ends or that best incorporates the largest share of one's aims. These choices cannot be dictated in advance, but must be the outcome of careful deliberation and decision making.

In general, the question is, How can I pursue this goal in this situation in such a way that my actions are acceptable in terms of all else that matters?

The ultimate test of deliberation is whether the decision process brings the most pertinent considerations to bear in such a way that the most relevant concerns carry the most weight (Wiggins, 1980). As Broadie (1991) aptly put it,

> Practical wisdom is not the ability to select effective means to a goal which is rightly seen to be good no matter what. It is the ability to pursue a goal initially worth pursuing in such a way that it continues to *be* worth pursuing. (p. 240, italics in original)

The more successful we, as human beings, are in fashioning our lives into a pattern of coherent, mutually supportive endeavors, the less frequently we will have to choose between them in this way. Some conflict and tension are inevitable, however, unless we sacrifice large portions of our personal, work, or social lives for the sake of simplicity and freedom from such tensions. Our choice of the best course of action requires us to select actions that best address our most important concerns and best harmonize our multiple aims.

I have been describing practical wisdom as an individual attribute thus far, but it is important to highlight several social aspects of wisdom as well. First, wisdom, like character strength, is learned primarily through instruction, modeling, practice, feedback, and interaction with others. Second, when a situation is difficult and calls for deliberation, individuals are very likely to seek others' input and advice before making a decision. Staudinger and Baltes (1996) conducted an intriguing study in which they found that consulting with a valued friend or family member enhanced the wisdom of their participants' responses to a set of life problem scenarios. Moreover, dialogue with someone whose opinion the participants valued increased performance both when it was conducted explicitly with that person and when the participant simply imagined the conversation. Third, many deliberative occasions involve more than one person and require some degree of joint consideration, decision making, and coordination of effort. Finally, as Staudinger and Baltes pointed out, "there are no absolute criteria that define wisdom. Rather, wisdom is recognized and attributed to [individuals] by consensus among a number of people" (p. 748).

Reasoned Choice

Deliberations are oriented toward making choices about the appropriate actions in a given situation. These choices are not merely a matter of plunking for one of the available alternatives, but reasoned in a particular way. Aristotle highlighted this with the term *prohairesis*, which translates literally as "choosing over" or "choosing before." His point was that one deliberates about what is better and worse, for choosing the best course means selecting the best of the available alternatives (Sherman, 1989).

Aristotle further emphasized the combined roles of reason and desire by defining choice as "desiderative reason or ratiocenative desire" (p. 139). These locutions point out that reasoned choice unites desire for what is good with the agent's thoughts to produce the concrete form in which individuals can best achieve their aims at present. The reasoned choice of practical wisdom always aims toward an action that is fitting to the occasion. *Prohairetic* choice involves an effort to harmonize one's several ends with what is currently possible. The conjoint assessment of what is desirable and what is feasible indicates what is meant by the terms *practical* and *wisdom*.

The Max Planck group has highlighted the importance of cognitive flexibility in wisdom (Baltes & Smith, 1990; Kramer, 2000). This flexibility shows up in the ability to consider various perspectives on a given situation and to entertain multiple courses of action before choosing one. When situation perceptions and response alternatives are significantly constrained or rigid, an individual is more likely to respond in an automatic way than to fashion a response that will fruitfully address the specifics of widely varying situations in the service of a combination of life goals.

For example, making reasoned choices is crucial in research endeavors. For seasoned researchers, decisions about which questions to pursue appear to be relatively straightforward, but they are actually the result of a long process of coming to understand an area of study, recognizing what is at stake theoretically and practically, and recognizing what is possible. One of the most challenging aspects of training students to be productive scholars is to help them to recognize which questions are worth asking. Although abstract theory provides a general heuristic for research, it does not, by itself, clarify which of the myriad possible research questions investigators should ask. Some of these questions are crucially important to the theory and its subject matter and some are peripheral. As a discipline, we have focused tremendous energy on developing statistical, measurement, and experimental design technologies that have improved the mechanics of research. These techniques do not, by themselves, guarantee high-quality science, however. The most sophisticated methods cannot compensate for triviality or lack of focus in the purposes of a study, a research program, or a literature. In chapter 7, I make a case for the centrality of practical wisdom in research by showing that the core of good research is the ability to choose high-quality questions and that doing so requires the wisdom to recognize which questions are most worthy of study.

The ability to choose the best available course of action presupposes the capacity to recognize what the options are. Practical wisdom develops in part through the accrual of experience through which one can learn many different ways of responding to one's circumstances. Some of this learning will be highly domain specific, such as knowledge about various methods of recruiting study participants or selecting applicants who are appropriate for a particular training program. Yet the ability to perceive what is at stake in a given situation and to recognize what is and is not possible also transcends the specifics of any domain of action. This is to say that practical wisdom is trait-like, and one aspect of the trait is being able to see alternative courses of action.

A reflective capacity plays a very important role in reasoned choice. Before selecting among the response options, a wise individual will consider the way that the most promising alternatives are likely to play out. This involves a cognitive rehearsal of the various actions and their probable results. The ability to predict, with some accuracy, how well one can carry out a plan and how the actions will be perceived by others is also involved. It is important for individuals to be able to reflect on their own motives and aims as well, because one sometimes chooses a course of action for the wrong reasons (e.g., out of unreflective anger, despair, or social conformity). Critical self-reflection on one's motives can help one to make wiser choices.

Being able to reflect on the results of one's choices is helpful in accruing the kind of experience necessary for increasing one's ability to make the best choices. Although stereotypical notions of age suggest that the elderly will be wiser than younger individuals, there is little support for the automatic development of wisdom with age (Staudinger & Baltes, 1996; Staudinger et al., 1992). Wisdom requires more than the mere accretion of experience. Individuals have to be able to examine and evaluate their actions and experiences to see what they did well, what they did poorly, and what they can learn from the episode.

Critical self-awareness is also important because individuals learn virtue and wisdom through practice. Repeated trials are only beneficial if one has a reasonably clear sense of the criterion and the ability to assess one's success in approximating it. It is only through recognizing mistakes and correcting errors that individuals can learn from them and improve their performance. Aristotle likened learning virtue to learning a craft or a musical instrument. Without guidance and correction, practice may only increase bad habits. No amount of sitting at a piano without guidance and correction will allow one to become a virtuoso. Those who aspire to virtue hold virtuous models as their guide—initially their teachers and later their friends and their heroes.

Reasoned choice also has a social component. Individuals often consider alternatives for action, ponder their motives, and reflect on how a situation played out in discussions with others. It is interesting that one of Aristotle's arguments for the importance of friendship is that friends help people to see themselves more clearly because a friend is "another self." This other self shares one's view of the good and can help one to recognize errors in seeking it. Moreover, one can learn from a friend's approach to living as if one were watching oneself from an external vantage point. Friends are particularly valuable in their ability to foster this kind of self-reflection.

SUMMARY

Practical wisdom is, contrary to current psychological theory, intrinsically tied to an apprehension of what is good. Actions can be considered wise only if they are appropriately directed toward praiseworthy ends. Wise individuals are able to perceive what is most important in a situation with respect to what is good. They recognize what is at stake, what is central and what is peripheral, and they focus on the most important aspects of the situation. They are also able to bring many considerations to bear on their understanding of a set of circumstances, including the way in which acting in favor of one important goal might affect other goals. The affective resonances of the situation at hand also influence how wise individuals choose. Wisdom involves reflecting on which actions will work best to achieve one's ends in view of the relevant considerations. Wise individuals often seek input from others and regularly reflect on their choices and actions as a way to improve their perception, deliberation, and choice making.

It seems uncontroversial that one must deliberate about how best to act in one's personal and professional lives. Naturally, individuals want to deliberate well, and I believe that Aristotle offered us a vivid and compelling account of how to do so in terms of practical wisdom. He reminded us that excellence in deliberation requires excellence in character, for thinking through what one ought to do involves a proper appreciation of the goods one is seeking, acuity in moral perception, and the ability to put reasoned choices into action. These qualities characterize the virtuous person. That is why I believe that we must incorporate practical wisdom and virtue into the curricula that we use to train helping professionals and students of human nature. In the next three chapters, I explore the ways that this portrayal of practical wisdom can help to illuminate important aspects of psychotherapy, research, and professional ethics.

6

CHOOSING WELL IN CLINICAL PRACTICE

We can be knowledgeable with other men's knowledge but we cannot be wise with other men's wisdom.

— Montaigne, *Essays*

I have supervised dozens of novice therapists over the years, which helps me to retain a clear sense of just how difficult therapeutic work is to learn and practice. In my first decade as a supervisor, I frequently found myself with my head in my hands after supervision sessions wondering just what it was that I had been trying to teach my supervisee during the last hour. It was not that I was confused about what I was saying; nor was I doubtful about the value of what I was teaching. I was perplexed because I could not conceptualize what I was teaching neatly into the standard categories of theoretical perspective or specific techniques. At times, I found myself wishing for a simpler world in which a single theory would fully capture therapeutic work and provide clear guidance in each situation. I would fantasize that if I could only adopt a single, comprehensive approach and become sufficiently grounded in it, I would not find myself feeling so perplexed. Of course, this was nothing more than wishful thinking, because there is no such comprehensive and unequivocal guidance available.

As I let go of this omniscience fantasy and reflected on what it was that I was trying to teach, it gradually became clear to me that it was practical wisdom. In the ordinary human world, individuals must frequently act without certain and transparent knowledge and rely on their judgment of what is important and best in the situations they face. As students begin

129

their practical training, most of them have a lot of difficulty differentiating what is central and what is peripheral in their clients' presentations. Students are often so busy practicing the listening skills they have learned, using the required assessment protocol, thinking about the client diagnostically, attempting to apply some theory to the individual, and pondering which techniques might be helpful that their attention is dispersed and they frequently feel overwhelmed. When one combines the complexity of the tasks therapists face with the typical confusion and emotional disarray that clients present, it is small wonder that novice (and sometimes experienced) therapists struggle to find a focus for their efforts.

It is interesting to reflect that success in any one of the tasks that require the attention of the therapist, whether that is the use of listening skills, diagnosis, or theoretical conceptualization, requires the ability to separate the important from the trivial and to apply a generalized knowledge set to a specific individual. Except in unusual circumstances, much of this is automatic for the experienced practitioner, but the perplexity of the novice highlights what an achievement the smooth activities of the expert are. For example, something as apparently simple as reflecting feelings requires us to decide which feelings to reflect, whether to respond in a way that heightens the affect or emphasizes the content of the material, whether to frame the reflection as an exploration or as a normalization of the affect in the circumstance, and so forth. No matter how well a therapist understands the concept of reflecting feelings, this skill depends entirely on whether the therapist can pick the most central affects to reflect and understands the relationships between the feelings and the client's difficulties and context accurately. The more complex therapeutic tasks such as conceptualizing the problem, diagnosing, and treatment planning require the ability to attend primarily to what is central to an even greater extent.

If psychotherapy clients presented us with clearly defined problems that fit neatly into an ordered matrix of difficulties, one that lent itself to a straightforward algorithm of solution generation, our job as therapists would not be so difficult. For some, this algorithmic psychotechnical vision is a dream to pursue avidly through dedicated and painstaking research. For others, it is a nightmare vision of a dehumanizing categorization, labeling, and technicalization of our lives. For me, it is just a fantasy—a good fantasy if one is inclined to highly rational, technical solutions to problems and a bad fantasy if one leans toward a more humanistic view. In either case, it is a fantasy, because human beings stubbornly refuse to be easily categorized and processed, and professional practices recalcitrantly remain complex, uncertain, unstable, and riddled with matters of value. Where can we find guidance for deciding what is most significant in what clients present, for deciding how to understand their difficulties, for recognizing what form to give our interventions? Let's begin with the obvious sources taught in psychology programs: psychotherapy research and psychotherapy theory.

PSYCHOTHERAPY RESEARCH AS DEFINITIVE GUIDE?

Some stakeholders in psychotherapy see the best of all possible worlds in the development of an algorithmic approach that would delineate highly specific, manualized treatments for well-defined client difficulties. Such a system would include a comprehensive and unambiguous classification of client problems that therapists could match with specific treatments designed for those particular problems. Researchers would empirically test the treatments for efficacy and effectiveness and provide manuals to standardize their application and to maximize therapeutic benefit. Psychotherapy trainers would provide training in these manualized procedures.

This approach clearly emphasizes *techne* over *phronesis*. In fact, the aim of those who wish to standardize psychotherapy is to replace, as far as possible, the therapist's judgment with pre-determined intervention packages for specific client problems. To be successful, the *techne* approach must begin with a set of well-defined, clearly diagnosable problems and devise a set of corresponding methods that are specified as treatments for each problem. This *techne*-inspired model has encountered what appear to be intractable difficulties with every aspect of its program, raising serious questions about the possibility of an algorithmic psychotherapy. In the next few pages, I present some representative viewpoints on the challenges facing the standardizers, but I cannot provide anything like a comprehensive overview of this enormous critical literature. I rely primarily on psychotherapy research insiders to tell us how far the standardization project has progressed and to indicate its likely future. I rely on proponents of psychotherapy research rather than external critics, partly out of respect for their intellectual integrity and partly to avoid presenting a polemical argument.

Guidance From the DSM?

The standardization project faces serious complications in the first step of reliably specifying the difficulties that clients bring to psychologists. The taxonomic approach of the *Diagnostic and Statistical Manual of Mental Disorders* (4th ed., text revision; *DSM–IV–TR*; American Psychiatric Association, 2000) was designed specifically to allow client difficulties to be classified in this way. Although researchers typically identify a narrow diagnostic range for inclusion in their clinical trials, few clinicians have that luxury. In their extensive review of research on which therapies work for which patients, Roth and Fonagy (1996) cautioned psychologists that "diagnostic labels have a tendency to create an illusion of homogeneity which fails to mirror the complexity of clinical work. Any particular diagnosis may have a wide variety of clinical implications" (p. 28). They went on to point out that

> comorbidity of Axis I and Axis II disorders is extensive. . . . This fact makes the relationship between diagnosis and treatment more complex than might be indicated by research . . . and certainly makes it unlikely that data from trials can be transferred directly into the clinical context.

This situation is even more critical because "patients with comorbid conditions . . . are also likely to constitute the majority of patients receiving long-term therapy or multiple episodes of short-term therapy" (p. 31). This conclusion has been endorsed by others as well (Clark, Watson, & Reynolds, 1995; Malik & Beutler, 2002). Studies assessing psychotherapy outcome with the comorbidity of depression and personality disorders suggest that clients with comorbid personality disorder have poorer outcomes than those who do not. In anxiety disorders, various personality disorders moderate the effects of treatment in complex ways (see Clarken & Levy, 2004, for a review). The specifics of the various moderator effects are not particularly important here. What is important is that the presence of these moderator effects means that standardizers do not need to specify treatments for a simple list of 11 major personality disorders and 22 major mood and anxiety disorders (an additive total of 33). Rather they need specific treatments for each combination of 11 times 22 disorders (a multiplicative total of 442 plus the 33 simple disorders, for a total of 475), because different combinations have different treatment outcomes.

There is also a dramatic contrast between the apparently neat symptom lists of *DSM–IV–TR* and the relatively ill-defined, nebulous, and confusing picture that practitioners frequently face in their encounters with their clients. Defining the boundaries of what will and will not be addressed in the therapy is a key feature of problem framing, but these decisions are not a matter of scientifically established facts as much as delimitations provided by our therapy theories, our personal predilections, and our pragmatic sense of what psychotherapy can and cannot accomplish. Unfortunately, there is very little agreement about these matters among psychologists, with some defining problems as faulty cognitions, others as attachment difficulties, others as defense mechanisms and internal conflicts, and so forth.

In this process of "problem setting," we "*name* the things to which we will attend and *frame* the context in which we will attend to them" (Schoen, 1983, p. 40). Naming and framing are information management activities that help to constitute the problem by giving it definition. These activities are not neutral in that our choices—about what to include and exclude in our formulation of the problem, whether we see it as an individual disorder or a family dysfunction, whether we view it as a biological or psychological difficulty—make a great deal of difference, and these decisions can be traced to important value and political commitments (Cushman, 1995; Prilleltensky, 1997; Richardson et al., 1999; Woolfolk, 1998). Therefore, it is often difficult to distinguish the degree to which expert knowledge captures the essential features of a situation or tailors its construal of the situation to fit the professional's knowledge, technology, and cultural values. Consequently, the necessary objectivity of diagnostic standardization is questionable.

Naming and framing are creative activities that define the problem as much as any set of symptoms or ostensibly objective facts. In fact, the purpose of *DSM–IV–TR* is precisely to assist clinicians with this naming, and its entire classification system is a massive project in framing difficulties in living in terms of a medical model of pathology and treatment. One way to see the bias of this framing according to a medical model is to attend to the large number of factors important to therapy outcome that are absent from *DSM–IV–TR*. Clarken and Levy (2004) presented a great deal of evidence that client diagnosis is a gross oversimplification of

> many client characteristics that must be considered in planning a treatment intervention [e.g., demographics, psychological mindedness, defensiveness]. . . . If one abandons the simplistic notion that assessment of client diagnosis alone provides a clear road to treatment, one is faced with an overwhelming number of client variables to consider. (p. 214)

They underscored the complexity of this situation by noting that the number and combination of factors makes it "impossible to adequately research all these variables" (p. 214).

If *DSM–IV–TR* were successful in the ways that its proponents wish it to be, it could provide just the naming and framing necessary to guide an algorithmic practice. It does not function this way because there is simply too much dual diagnosis, diagnostic overlap, and diagnostic disagreement, and too many important client factors that have no place in the manual but are essential ingredients in therapy intervention and outcomes.

Guidance From Therapy Efficacy Research?

What about the guidance that treatment efficacy research can provide to therapists? In their discussion of the clinical value of psychotherapy outcome research, Roth and Fonagy (1996) noted the disparity between the goals of research (controlled experimental trials designed to isolate general causal relationships among variables) and clinical practice (improvement in specified aspects of an individual client's life). This means that "by design, research trials underestimate the impact of factors often seen in clinical practice" (p. 52). In the "bible" of psychotherapy research, *Bergin and Garfield's Handbook of Psychotherapy and Behavior Change*, Lambert, Bergin, and Garfield (2004) added that the "comfort" that practitioners and the public may feel about the application of empirically supported treatments is somewhat illusory, because "the fact is that the success of treatment appears to be largely dependent on the client and the therapist, not on the use of 'proven' empirically based treatments" (p. 9). By this, they meant that there is typically more variance associated with client and therapist variables than with differences in treatment approaches.

We saw how the wide variation in clients compromises attempts to standardize therapeutic methods in the previous section. The project of standardization also falters because of the substantial variability among crucial characteristics of therapists, including warmth, adjustment, skill, interest in helping clients, and ability to form high-quality therapist–client relationships. Investigations of the relationship between therapist qualities and client outcomes suggest that variability among therapists is a substantial factor in outcome (Blatt, Sanislow, Zuroff, & Pilkonis, 1996; Crits-Cristoph & Mintz, 1991; Luborsky, McClellan, Woody, O'Brien, & Auerbach, 1985; Orlinsky & Howard, 1980). In most of these studies, there was an explicit attempt to limit therapist variability through training in specific therapeutic approaches as a way to standardize interventions. The fact that therapist differences persist and have an impact—in spite of arduous attempts to homogenize their work—clearly shows the limitations of the standardization effort. As Strupp and Anderson (1997) argued, it is not simply that therapist variability is an independent source of influence on outcome. Rather, therapist personality influences the extent of adherence to therapy manuals and how effectively the techniques are "delivered." According to Lambert and Ogles (2004), "researchers, influenced by mechanistic models [and, I would add, instrumental rationality in general], have placed their bets more on technical factors as the powerful ones in therapeutic change . . . while therapist variability has been ignored to a surprising degree" (p. 168).

A number of authors have attempted to deal with the widely noted gap between research and practice by outlining an evidence-based practice model. Roth and Fonagy (1996) presented a representative model that involves feedback loops between researchers, clinicians, and quality assurance bodies. They suggested that therapy research be used to develop treatment guidelines that would "state that a person with a particular diagnosis should receive a particular therapy" (p. 50). These authors immediately clarified that such guidelines would have "exceptions to the rule" requiring flexibility. Indeed, they said, "the challenge of protocol-driven practice is to ensure that clinicians combine clinical expertise and sensitivity together with their knowledge of the research base, recognizing the value and limitation of each resource" (p. 51).

In their model, the clinician's case formulation is "the critical step" because it offers a "coherent model for the patient's problems," setting the stage for decisions about "the most appropriate mode of treatment" (Roth & Fonagy, 1996, p. 51). Similarly, the Division 12 (Society of Clinical Psychology) Task Force (1995) emphasized that the list of empirically supported treatments they identified "[did] not substitute for educators' and practitioners' own decisions about what [was] the most appropriate treatment for a given client" (p. 5). This entirely reasonable position places the decision about which treatment to offer squarely with the clinician and acknowledges quite clearly that the practitioner's judgment as to the nature of the client's situation is the only way such decisions can be made. I agree with these authors that therapists should make these decisions on the basis of their knowledge of relevant research. However, the value of this research for a specific individual is just as much a matter of judgment as the nature of the client's difficulties is. According to some of the leading lights of psychotherapy research, science cannot provide detailed guidance for many of the concrete situations that therapists face (e.g., Strupp & Anderson, 1997). There is useful information in the results of this research, but the practitioner's judgment is the arbiter of its value in specific cases. If psychotherapy research can make only general suggestions whose ultimate value is a matter of therapist judgment, the attempt to make psychotherapy a form of *techne* has not succeeded, and this endeavor has actually highlighted the centrality of *phronesis*. If psychotherapy research cannot provide the detailed guidance clinicians need, then we may want to look to psychotherapy theories to fill this gap.

PSYCHOTHERAPY THEORY AS DEFINITIVE GUIDE?

One way to see psychotherapy theories is as repositories of wisdom given to us by some of the greatest lights of therapy. There is undoubtedly a great deal of excellent guidance in the corpus of psychotherapy theories. Concepts available in the literature are often quite helpful in making sense of what clients do or say and suggesting how one might address constellations of client actions in a productive manner.

One immediately confronts an embarrassment of riches in this literature because of its sheer size and breadth, however. How is one to choose from the vast number of concepts and the wide array of theories available? Although there are only a dozen or so major individual psychotherapy theories, there are, by some counts, over 400 types of therapy (Karasu, 1992; Kazdin, 1986). The proliferation of therapy theories and the receding possibility of a consensus view on the best approach to helping clients make it clear that unequivocal theoretical guidance is only theoretically available. As Prochaska and Norcross (2002) put it, "A healthy diversity has deteriorated into an unhealthy chaos. Students, practitioners, and patients are confronted with confusion, fragmentation, and discontent. With so many therapy systems claiming success, which theories should be studied, taught, or bought?" (p. 1).

One of the results of this theoretical Babel is that practicing therapists often adopt some form of eclecticism or personalized approach to therapy. Surveys suggest that one half to two thirds of practitioners use more than one theoretical perspective regularly in their work (Jensen, Bergin, & Greaves, 1990; Norcross, Karg, & Prochaska, 1997). Eclecticism is, by its nature, a matter of individual choice of concept and technique, and as Lambert et al. (2004) pointed out, "there is little likelihood that two eclectic therapists would use the same techniques with the same client" (p. 6). At its worst, an eclectic approach is just a potpourri of loosely related concepts and techniques that are selectively applied by the therapist as the situation seems to call for them. At its best, the more fashionably labeled "integrative" approach involves a more coherent and systematic amalgamation of thera- peutic concepts and techniques. Although the latter has a more respectable sound to it, therapists with both well-integrated and more loosely eclectic approaches face ongoing and sometimes difficult choices about which con- cepts and techniques to apply in the great variety of situations they face.

The more loosely organized the therapist's approach is, the more flexibility he or she will have. This flexibility comes at the price of greater indeterminacy in how best to understand and intervene with a particular client. For the fully eclectic therapist, each decision is relatively independent of previous decisions and requires some kind of matching between what is occurring in the session and a relevant concept and intervention method. By definition, eclectic therapists do not have theoretical guidance other than their own judgment to indicate which precepts or techniques to adopt at a given point in time. These therapists must rely entirely on their wits and their sense of a match between what they see before them and one or more ways to understand their clients. The ability to grasp adequately what is important in a given interaction with a client and to interpret it in a helpful manner is precisely what I am referring to as practical wisdom. There are eclectic therapists who are able to flexibly identify and respond to what is central to their clients in highly effective ways. These therapists rely on their natural or acquired practical wisdom and are excellent examples of this ability. To the degree that eclectic therapists lack practical wisdom, their treatment decisions will be arbitrary, hit or miss affairs, however.

Therapists at the more integrative end of personalized approaches have incorporated aspects of various therapy theories in a more systematic way. At the extreme, such personalized approaches might be very similar to formal therapy theories and have many of the advantages of these theories.

At this extreme, an integrative approach might simply graft a single concept from one perspective onto another theory. The chief advantage from the point of view of this chapter is that such integration provides some guidance about which concepts or techniques are likely to be useful in particular situations and how the concepts relate to each other. Some therapists choose a single theoretical perspective and become thoroughly immersed in it so that they are at home with its concepts and methods. Many therapists adopt this single-theory approach and devote themselves to mastering it.

The question is, even when one has a very systematic viewpoint, how much guidance can a general theoretical perspective provide for the decision-making demands of ongoing interaction with particular clients? Even in this relatively simplified and clarified world, the therapist has to work with highly general theoretical propositions that must be applied to a specific client. In each instance, the therapist must decide *which* of the theoretical concepts and interventions are appropriate for this particular client at this specific point in time. Once a therapist has identified a relevant portion of the theory, its application still requires a decision about *how* to apply a given concept or technique to a particular client's situation, for each interpretation of a defense, challenge to a cognitive distortion, or reflection of a feeling must be attuned to *this* particular client at *this* time and in *this* circumstance. The universe of clinical situations, constellations of client difficulties, temperaments, contexts, and therapist strengths and weaknesses has nearly infinite variety. No theoretical structure or system of rules can specify what to do in every instance.

Theories can give us general guidance, but they cannot do our thinking for us when the rubber meets the road in session with clients. General theoretical precepts remain general until they are interpreted for a specific circumstance (Woolfolk, 1998). The interpretation and the interpreter are just as important as the theory when it comes to providing good therapy. Casebooks can be helpful because they show how theoretical concepts and techniques can be applied to specific situations. Similarly, supervision and case consultation tend to be case centered and oriented to helping therapists to know how to apply general concepts to specific cases. Casebooks, supervision, and consultation cannot cover all of the variations in client difficulties, the constellations of vulnerabilities and strengths different clients have, or the unforeseeable vicissitudes of the therapeutic process with different clients. The best these resources can do is to provide *illustrations* of how therapists *can* apply theories and techniques in a particular situation. Mastering the ability to apply theory is a matter of cultivating good clinical judgment.

Psychotherapy combines complexity, uncertainty, and moment, and abstract theories cannot adequately guide psychotherapists unless we supplement them with our ability to apply them wisely. Practical wisdom is the capacity to recognize what is important in a situation, deliberate about how best to understand this significance, and choose a course of action that allows one to pursue therapeutic goals with clarity and purpose. Psychotherapy theories and research can undoubtedly contribute to this decision making, but they cannot replace *phronesis* because clinicians must use their judgment to select among and apply these resources according to the requirements of the situation. I have briefly outlined a few of the reasons that neither research nor theory can provide a standardized approach to psychotherapy practice. Because of their great variety and intrinsic pursuit of what is good, social practices like psychotherapy resist definitive abstract formulation in theory and precise specification of procedure. Clinical judgment cannot be exactly specified and any description will be true only roughly and in outline. As I show in the following section, this judgment or wisdom develops largely through a series of vicarious and personal experiences of perception, deliberation, and decision making accompanied by instruction, guidance, and feedback.

PRACTICAL WISDOM IN PSYCHOTHERAPY

The three major elements of practical wisdom I described in chapter 5, moral perception, deliberation, and reasoned choice, can help us to understand and practice good decision making for the complexity and uncertainty that psychotherapists face. Keep in mind that these elements of practical wisdom are interwoven and operate simultaneously even though I am presenting them as somewhat discrete.

Moral Perception in Psychotherapy

The essence of moral perception is the ability to separate what is central from what is peripheral and to recognize what is at stake in a given situation. This ability makes it possible to recognize what the focus of therapy should be both in the therapeutic moment with clients and over the course of the therapy. Stephen Covey's aphorism about living a focused and coherent life is also apt for the psychotherapist's daily work: "The main thing is to keep the main thing the main thing" (Covey, Merrill, & Merrill, 1996, p. 75). Although it sounds straightforward, it is anything but simple. The ability to recognize and remain focused on the things that count most is one of the most essential characteristics of effective therapists.

The key to maintaining this focus is for therapists to keep the goods their clients are seeking (greater vitality, better relationships, more self-confidence, etc.) firmly in mind. Recall from chapter 5 that practical wisdom is centrally concerned with pursuing what is good and includes the ability to recognize how to do so in particular situations.

A Beleaguered Mother

Let me illustrate the ability to see what is most important with an impressive example from Charles Fishman, a well-known family therapist. He was conducting live supervision with a student who was working with a stepfamily composed of a mother, her 9-year-old daughter and 7-year-old son, and her husband.[1] The session was very chaotic, and the therapist was attending to the wife's criticisms of her husband's unwillingness to help her and his defensive responses. During this discussion, her son was moving around the therapy room playing roughly with the toys available in the room, which frequently distracted the mother and the therapist. Her daughter sat clutching her stomach, moaning, and rocking back and forth until the mother began to attend to her as well. All of this activity was a nearly perfect microcosm of the family's interactions, as the parents were generally at odds with each other, the son was frequently difficult to structure and discipline, and the daughter made frequent visits to the school nurse with stomach pain, which required her mother to leave work to take her home.

The poor student therapist was completely overwhelmed by all of this and unable to gain any traction with this family. After phoning in a few times to offer direction to the student without much success, Fishman entered the session. He saw what was most important in this interaction very clearly and effected a profound transformation with two interventions. First, he introduced himself and commented that as he was watching the family behind the mirror, he was struck by how alone the mother seemed to feel. Her critical, angry stance dissolved immediately, and she began to cry softly and talk about how overwhelmed and lonely she felt with all of her responsibilities. Fishman encouraged her to express herself. As she did so, the room became quiet, her son stopped being disruptive and her daughter became very solicitous toward her.

After a few minutes, the daughter began to offer comfort to her mother. Fishman's second intervention was to shift the responsibility for comforting the mother from her daughter to her husband. He complimented the girl for her compassion and love for her mother but told her that he thought it was time for her to play while the adults talked. She went back to the play area but remained watchful to see what developed between the adults. It was apparent that the husband's affect had shifted from defensiveness to concern as his wife talked about how difficult her role in the family was.

---

[1] I saw this work on a videotape shown by Braulio Montalvo in a family therapy class I taught at the University of New Mexico. Unfortunately, it is not commercially available.

Seeing this shift, Fishman then asked the husband to offer comfort to his wife. He was wary, saying that he did not think that she would accept his support. Fishman told him to ask her if she would. When the husband asked, she said emphatically that she wanted his support and comfort, which he offered in a hug and with expressions of willingness to be helpful to her, but doubt about whether he could do it in a way that was acceptable to her.

As this conversation continued, the transformation in the children was remarkable. Both children were playing contentedly, without acting to attract attention. Moreover, they were disengaged from the parental concerns as if they now felt that their mother's distress and the conflict between the parents had become manageable.

This is a wonderful example of recognizing what is crucial and acting appropriately on that understanding. I do not know if all of Fishman's interventions are so clearly focused and powerful, and I know for certain that mine are not always so elegant. This level of clarity is something that we can aspire to attain in our clinical work, even though it is unlikely to be continually available to any of us.

Of course, this session was just the beginning of this family's pursuit of two important goods: building a marital alliance between the spouses and helping the stepfather to become a more integral member of the family. The student therapist would have to continue to guide them in these directions, which would come under the heading of "keeping the main thing the main thing." Fishman was able to effect this beginning in a decisive way, with an impressive economy of intervention. My reading of his success is that he saw that the conflictual, chaotic family interaction revolved around the mother's distress and anger about feeling alone and overwhelmed, which resulted from the lack of marital alliance. Fishman could see that the wife's criticism of her husband was a self-defeating attempt to pursue her goal of a marital alliance. His compassionate response to her pain and his move to help the husband respond in a caring and helpful way were guided by his clarity about this goal and his ability to open a pathway for positive change toward it.

Some might point out that existing theoretical perspectives might have guided Fishman's interventions, and they would be correct. It is a truism in family therapy that the marital alliance is central, and when it is disrupted or damaged, the family will manifest difficulties. In addition, the stepfamily literature clarifies that the biological parent is the central figure in the family and is often pulled between his or her biological children and spouse. Stepparents often struggle to be fully involved in the family and are frequently kept at arm's length by children and criticized for their missteps by their partner. Although he was no doubt aware of these theoretical propositions and found some guidance in them, none of these propositions, by themselves, would have given rise to Fishman's specific interventions. He could have entered the session focused on the husband's passivity or on the wife's critical, angry stance. He could have intervened by helping the parents to set limits on their unruly son and distracting daughter. He could have done some educating about normative stepfamily difficulties. Any of these moves would fit the theoretical perspectives that are also compatible with what he did. The fact is that he chose to approach the general difficulties highlighted by theory in a particular way that was highly effective. There are dozens, if not hundreds, of interventions that would have been equally compatible with those theories. It is doubtful if any of them could have had more impact, because they would not have captured the most salient aspects of the session in the way that his reaching out to this mother did. Theory can offer some guidance, but the therapist always has to decide which theoretical ideas are relevant and how they apply in the specific circumstances. Gifted therapists have the ability to consistently strike the chord that is most resonant at the moment.

Another way to think about identifying what is most important in a session is to consider what is at stake for the client. Therapists can often profitably ask themselves what important good the client is afraid of losing or what good the client is trying to protect with his or her problematic behavior. This is a particularly useful question for therapists to ask themselves when clients are acting in ways that are disruptive to the therapy or otherwise self-defeating.

Threats and Vulnerabilities

In one memorable session with a couple, Ana and Mitch, who had been working with me for some weeks following the discovery of his infidelity, I found myself at sea in a vehement confrontation between them that quickly escalated to credible mutual threats of divorce. This was particularly disconcerting to me, because this conflict arose after a series of sessions in which they were making very good progress and their relationship had been improving. Both spouses were strong-willed and fiercely proud individuals who intensely disliked being vulnerable, so they would both take the offensive in their disputes. This pattern of mutual escalation of threats and angry accusations predated the infidelity and had almost never had a positive outcome. In their argument in this session, their anger and threats had escalated so fast that I was initially unclear on how I could intervene to help them turn this confrontation to therapeutic benefit.

I began to ask myself what it was that was at stake for each of them in this argument. As I listened to Ana from this point of view, I began to hear what might be behind her accusations, criticism, and threats. The overt message was that she saw Mitch as exploitative and withholding. She said that she could not continue to participate in the relationship, because it looked like a losing proposition and she needed to think about her future. By thinking about what was at stake for her, it became clear that Ana believed she had been giving much more to the relationship than Mitch had. I began to see that she feared she was being exploited and that if she did not put a stop to it, she would find herself abandoned in 5 or 10 years after giving all that she could to make their relationship work. In other words, she sought the goods of appreciation, recognition, and security. As I explored this with her and helped her to express her fears and doubts, her affect softened and she was able to focus on the specific things she needed from Mitch rather than condemning him in global terms.

Mitch was taken aback by Ana's fury right at the beginning of the session and he reacted defensively, berating her for "tattling" in session. If she was so concerned about this, why didn't she bring it up sooner? He said that her complaints were groundless, because he had been giving a lot to the relationship. Wasn't he here in therapy to try to mend it? Didn't he keep coming even though he got "beaten up" over and over again? He accused her of wanting him to become a lapdog that would jump at her slightest whim and exclaimed that that just wasn't going to happen and she had better look elsewhere for someone to play that role, and so on. Some reflection on his counteraccusations suggested that he truly was taken aback by the unexpectedness and vehemence of her demands and that he feared he would be unable to satisfy them. He seemed to feel that he had no recourse but to defensively criticize and reject the demands to which he did not feel equal. As we talked about this, he agreed that he felt ambushed and that he could respond only by capitulating or by distancing, and his pride would not allow surrender. As his anger cooled, he also expressed feeling hurt that Ana did not give him credit for the efforts he had been making and expressed doubts about being able to do more. In other words, he was seeking the goods of self-respect, recognition, and forgiveness.

Mitch was now beginning to admit to himself that he was unable to give Ana what she needed not just because she wanted too much, but because he was so involved in self-protection that he was not attending to her needs. Seeing her vulnerability in her fear of being exploited and her sense of being alone in trying to improve the relationship helped to shift Mitch's focus to how he had hurt her and how hard it was for him to make amends for that. In a dramatic shift in the therapy, he tearfully acknowledged how much she had endured and expressed his gratitude that she had stuck with him after his infidelity came to light. He told Ana that he knew he did not really deserve her love and perseverance at that time but that he hoped to earn it in the future. For the first time, he fully acknowledged his responsibility for his infidelity and told her categorically that she deserved better from him and that he wanted to give that to her.

Such admissions of culpability, vulnerability, and fallibility were wholly uncharacteristic of Mitch before this session. Generally speaking, he would rather walk on his tongue than admit he was wrong or weak in any way. Of course, one of the goals of the couple therapy was for him to acknowledge frankly the ways that he had hurt Ana and to take full responsibility for it. Another goal had been for her to be able to own her anger and hurt and to express it directly rather than in critical tirades. His responsibility taking and her direct expression of her pain were necessary for them to attain the important goods of forgiveness and reconciliation that they both wanted. We had devoted a good deal of effort toward those goals in previous meetings and this work began to bear fruit in this session. This session was so productive partly because of that previous work, but if I had been unable to recognize the goods that were at stake for these two individuals at the time, it would have been impossible to turn their furious recriminations to fruitful work. Their dispute might have escalated to the point of an open breach in the therapy session that could have suggested to them that their relationship was beyond repair.

Just as we saw in the family with whom Charles Fishman worked, there are several theoretical and technical precepts that helped me to understand and make use of the material this couple presented. Family systems theory provides an understanding of mutual escalation in terms of a positive feedback cycle that requires interruption to prevent extremely negative outcomes. An understanding of the clinical wisdom regarding the treatment of infidelity helped me to recognize the importance of Ana's self-expression and the validity of her concerns that Mitch was not fully doing his part to repair the relationship. Successful therapy also requires the betraying spouse to take responsibility unequivocally, to acknowledge the harm of the infidelity, and to express remorse and to make a demonstrable commitment to fidelity. Helping clients to shift from "hard" emotions like anger and defensiveness to "soft" emotions like fear and hurt is called softening and is an important technique that has been influentially developed in *Emotion Focused Therapy for Couples* (Greenberg & Johnson, 1988).

All of this general knowledge is available to therapists, but it only helps if practitioners can perceive what is important and match the knowledge appropriately to the situation. A therapist has to be able to recognize when there is a positive feedback cycle occurring, when a betrayed partner is ready to express anger or hurt directly, when the betraying spouse is able to begin to take responsibility, and so forth. Softening only works if the clinician can recognize the softer emotions accurately. If the therapist gets the softer emotion wrong, there will be no shift from a hard emotion, because the intervention will lack emotional resonance for the client. In Sherman's (1989) terms, the situation does not come "pre-labeled" as one kind of incident or another. The therapist has to see the essential elements of the occasion to intervene productively. In this case, what helped me to see what was crucial for Ana and Mitch was to ask myself what was at stake for each of them.

Storytelling

I want to relate one more common situation to show how moral perception can help therapists. In my supervision of novice therapists, the situation frequently arises in which a client will tell excruciatingly long stories in session. In many cases, clients will relate one story after another in monologue fashion. The unfortunate students are caught between boredom, confusion, and their belief that they need to be able to follow all the details of these stories and make some sense of them. A seasoned therapist with an inclination to do so might be able to interpret the content of these stories meaningfully and beneficially, but very few therapists would see constant storytelling as the best use of the therapy time. One of the most important aspects of therapy is helping clients to learn how to participate productively in it.

I recommend a relatively simple intervention when clients are inclined to tell long stories. I have the students ask the client to help them understand what was most important in the story. This question conveys an interest in understanding what the client is saying, but tries to help the client learn to clarify what is important to him or her. Sometimes clients are unsure what was important about the story and the question serves to help them recognize their discursive or tangential tendencies, which are forms of avoidance that require therapeutic attention. Over time, the attention to sorting out what is central and what is peripheral in these stories helps clients to reduce their storytelling as they become more capable of focusing their attention on the issues and goods that are important to them. In other words, clients benefit greatly by learning to see more clearly what is most important in their lives so that they can devote their energies to the significant rather than trivial aspects of their world (i.e., clients can learn practical wisdom in their therapy).

By definition, the ability to see what is essential in a situation cannot be stated in abstract terms. For this reason, textbooks, treatment manuals, instructors, and supervisors cannot simply tell us to do x whenever we encounter situation y. For one thing, one has to be able to recognize when one is facing an instance of y, and this requires the ability to see what is essential in the moment. In addition, for any set of situations y there are a virtually infinite number of variations that will require adjustments in x to make the response fitting for the particularities of a specific y. None of this can be specified definitively in advance. Therapists have to be able to work with a great variety of situations that have a family resemblance but are not precisely the same. Recognizing the general pattern is only half of the perceptual task. The other half is understanding how a particular instance differs from the general pattern and how one can adjust to those differences. We develop the capacity to attend to the central aspects of particular situations through reflective experience, as I outline later in this chapter.

Deliberation in Psychotherapy

There are many therapeutic situations in which therapists do not need to pause to deliberate about what the best action would be. Much of the time, it will be immediately apparent how we can be helpful to our clients, and our responses will follow well-practiced patterns. Even very expert therapists experience the need to reflect on their work with some clients from time to time to clarify the best response, however. For less experienced therapists, such deliberation is more frequently necessary. One way to understand supervision is as a joint reflection on what a trainee is doing and on whether there are better ways to proceed. Deliberation is a key component of good therapy in many ways, but because of space limitations I can focus on just a few illustrations here.

Goal Setting

The first place in which deliberation is important is in setting goals with clients. The standard understanding of goal setting is that clients bring their goals to therapy and therapists provide the means to reach those self-determined aims. Some clients oblige therapists by having clearly formulated, achievable goals that therapists can support. There are many clients whose goals are far less clear or achievable, and clinicians often have to assist them in translating their problems into goals. Frequently, the problem-into-goals translation involves significant discussion of what is and is not desirable as well as what is and is not possible. Therapists would be unwilling to help a client with a subtle or not so subtle bid for help in dominating others or in becoming involved in meaningful and rewarding relationships without taking any personal risks. In other words, therapists are unlikely to help clients to pursue impractical or dubious goods.

Goal setting in psychotherapy is often a joint deliberation between therapist and client, shaped primarily by the client's wishes but guided by the therapist's understanding of what is possible and of what he or she is willing to endorse (Woolfolk, 1998). Emily, an attractive, 43-year-old woman presented to a colleague with a set of difficult situations in her life. She was a full-time employee of the state and had two children. Some of her difficulties revolved around the very real challenges of being a single mother with minimal support from her ex-husband and working in the high-pressure environment of child protection services in an underfunded and heavily scrutinized agency. Emily experienced a significant degree of anxiety and felt that she did not have very much control over her life. Although there were some areas in which she truly did not have very much control (her ex-husband's neglect of the children and the stressful conditions of her job), the therapist could see that Emily was actually very well organized and managed her demanding, hectic schedule rather well.

An exploration of Emily's situation and her anxiety revealed that she was troubled by a set of issues with which she had not been able to make any headway. She would worry about one problem when it arose or when her thoughts would wander to it, but all she could do was to fret over how badly it was going and think about how powerless she felt. Then her attention would automatically switch to the next problem and she would repeat the same kinds of thoughts. This sequence would go on until she could not tolerate it any longer and then she would distract herself with TV, her children's homework, or sleep. The therapist pointed out this pattern, which she immediately acknowledged. Ironically, Emily then added her tendency to skip around from topic to topic without resolving anything to her revolving list of worries. She did agree with the therapist in principle that increasing her ability to focus on one problem at a time was necessary to work toward change, but she found it very difficult. Over several weeks, she gradually learned to sustain attention to one problem at a time. She and the therapist then became primarily focused on her desperate fear of being alone and her willingness to remain in a very unsatisfactory romantic relationship rather than risk confronting her partner, seeking a new relationship, or simply becoming unattached.

This example highlights several features of deliberation in psychotherapy. First, it illustrates the fact that therapy clients often are not in a position to specify their goals at the outset. Emily's difficulty with focusing on one problem at a time and taking steps to resolve it is not uncommon. She did not recognize this thought process as a key difficulty, however, because she was caught up in it and in the many details of her worries. Identifying the goal of learning to attend to a single problem long enough to formulate steps to resolve it was a joint achievement with her therapist that grew out of her pain and the therapist's ability to see how she was stymied. Second, it was necessary to learn to focus on one problem at a time to have any chance of reaching Emily's higher-order goal of gaining a greater sense of control in her life, which reflects the general good of living a reasonably ordered and integrated life. Joint deliberation by Emily and her therapist about what was preventing her from feeling more in control revealed that she needed to decrease her tendency to skip from problem to problem. Third, this formulation of her difficulty did not require formal psychotherapy theory, nor is it found in psychotherapy research. Rather, it became apparent to the therapist as a matter of practical reasoning about what prevented Emily from reaching her goal. In other words, this formulation was the outcome of the therapist's use of practical wisdom. One way to look at this therapy is that Emily gained a measure of practical wisdom as well by learning how to deliberate about her difficulties in a more focused and productive manner.

Identifying Intervention Opportunities

After the goals are set, one of the key roles that therapists play is to recognize and make use of the opportunities that present themselves to work on those goals. For example, therapists need to recognize the creeping sense of helplessness that we sometimes feel when working with depressed clients. The clinician must consider whether this feeling arises from the therapist's own circumstances or whether it is a reflection of the client's helplessness. Very often, a client's sense of helplessness becomes palpable in the session, in verbalizations, sighs, and gestures. When therapists become caught up in trying to empower their clients, they often feel defeated by this helplessness and incapable of making any difference. It is natural for them to feel powerless in this situation, but deliberative reflection can clarify that this is an opportunity to help their clients confront their helplessness directly. This kind of deliberation shows how the ability to see the client's and therapist's experience as related to the goal of improving the client's mood makes it possible to use this experiential material in pursuit of the goal. One of the key deliberative elements of psychotherapy is being able to see how to respond to one's situation in a way that facilitates the accomplishment of one's aims. The general question for therapists is: What can I do here and now with the material in this session that will help my client to get closer to his or her goals?

Emily's situation provides another example of how therapists must recognize and act on opportunities to link session content and goals. Although Emily had agreed with the therapist in principle that it was important for her to sustain her attention on one problem at a time, she was unable to do this in session for some weeks. She continued to skip from topic to topic in sessions and was relatively unaware that she was doing so until her therapist pointed it out. There were several interventions that helped Emily come to grips with this topic-skipping. One was to interpret it for her. But the bread-and-butter intervention was to call her attention to her topic switching as it occurred. As Emily became clearer about this problem, the therapist began to ask her which problem seemed more important so they could focus on it. Although this sounds simple in the abstract, it requires close attention to recognize topic switching by individuals who have good conversational skills. There is usually some reasonable connection between

one subject and another, and many clients tell these anecdotes in an absorb-
ing or entertaining way. They are as good at distracting therapists as they
are at distracting themselves. The ability to see opportunities for intervention
depends on the therapist's clarity about the goods the client is pursuing and
on being able to recognize the obstacles to reaching those goals.

Supervision and Consultation as Joint Deliberation

One of the most important and common ways that therapists deliberate
is by discussing clients in supervision or in consultation with peers. These
discussions allow therapists to verbalize their thoughts and experiences with
other professionals and to examine more closely their ways of seeing and
intervening with their clients. Such joint deliberation is crucial in training
therapists, because they are unprepared to work with the concrete details
and confusing circumstances that clients present, no matter how much
academic training about general principles they receive prior to meeting
real people with real problems. This kind of general knowledge is only worth
having, however, if the trainee can learn how to apply it. For this reason,
the most valuable thing that supervisors teach is how to apply general
knowledge by being able to recognize what is important in session and in
the course of therapy, and how to frame and name clients' difficulties and
interaction patterns productively. These abilities must be taught on a case-
by-case basis, because they come to life only in the concrete situations that
therapists face.

Consultation with peers plays a similarly important role for more
accomplished therapists because even the most experienced clinicians get
caught up in their clients' difficulties from time to time or find themselves
stuck in their own characteristic ways. The opportunity to verbalize and
explore difficulties that therapists have with their clients in a trusting and
supportive environment with other professionals is essential to being able
to function well. This joint deliberation helps practitioners to recognize the
pitfalls that ensnare them and to develop ways to overcome these difficulties.
Case consultation is an excellent example of the social dimension of deliberation in which peers discuss the client's circumstances in view of the goals
of therapy and in search of what is possible and best to do to pursue
those goals.

Reasoned Choice in Psychotherapy

"Reasoned choice" is one translation of Aristotle's term *prohairesis*,
which can also be rendered as "choosing over" or "choosing before." When
therapists decide how to conceptualize our clients' difficulties and which
interventions will be best at a particular time, we select from among a set

of alternatives. There are many factors that guide our choice of one viewpoint or intervention over another, and it is not possible to give an exhaustive list of these factors. I want to describe three illustrative considerations that are particularly important in reasoned choice, however. They include a keen sense of the possible, foresight, and self-reflective practice.

Seeing What Is Possible

One of the key characteristics of good therapists is having a keen sense of the possible. So far in this chapter, I have been emphasizing the positive recognition of opportunities to help clients make changes in their cognitive and behavioral patterns. Excellent therapists will see more of these opportunities than average therapists. Cultivating the vision to see the positive possibilities for clients amid their distress can significantly improve one's ability to help clients pursue important goods. I like to think of this as identifying the path of hope. This is the genius in the influential solution-focused approach to therapy. Although it is too much of a one-note song to stand alone theoretically, I have learned a lot from its emphasis on client strengths and success experiences.

Let me give a simple example of one way I make use of positive opportunities in my work with couples. Partners often express their complaints in the form of rhetorical questions such as "I don't understand why you can't just . . ." They don't expect much of a response, and they seldom get a helpful answer. I have made it a habit to use these questions as an opportunity to explore disappointments or frustrations that seem important by telling the questioner that it seems like a really great question, and suggesting that they ask it in a way that allows their partner to give them a good answer. There are two typical outcomes. The other partner either has a very good reason for noncompliance, which contributes to mutual understanding and efforts to find alternatives to the current disappointment, or there really isn't a good reason for the noncompliance, and an open discussion of the reasons that the request is important makes it possible to eliminate this source of disappointment.

It is also important to recognize the constraints that limit what is possible. For example, there are times when standard interventions designed to shift a depressed client's focus away from negative emotions or experiences may be inappropriate. If a client experiences a real loss or a genuine setback such as losing a job, there will likely be a period of time during which there is an emotional crisis that requires empathy and compassion rather than more active confrontation and change. For many clients, bibliotherapy is a useful adjunct to talk therapy for depression. Lower educational achievement, a low level of literacy, or a disinclination to read obviously constrains the possibilities for bibliotherapy. Of course, it is possible to allow oneself to be more constrained than necessary, so the ability to decide which apparent limitations have to be granted and which ones can be overcome is a matter of therapeutic judgment.

Foresight

Foresight is another important aspect of reasoned choice. As therapists consider various options for intervention, they think about how their actions will play out in the conversation with their clients. Good therapists are able to anticipate the likely results of their interventions and plan them accordingly. Of course, no one can stop to consider the likely outcome of everything he or she does, and fortunately, this is not necessary because much of what we do clinically follows a general logic of psychotherapy. When we confront a more complex, difficult, highly charged, or high-stakes situation, we do stop to consider how our actions will play out. In these circumstances, foresight is an essential element of making wise choices.

Therapeutic foresight is obviously fallible, and there will always be surprises in working with clients. For this reason, it is necessary to be flexible enough to modify one's interventions in view of a client's responses to them. In the ongoing give and take of therapy, wise therapists will adapt their conceptualizations and interventions to fit the information and feedback that they receive. As the therapy unfolds, therapists need to monitor the ever-changing situation and assess how they can work toward their clients' goals in the best way.

Foresight also involves the important question of timing. Even when we have a useful understanding of a client's situation and have an appropriate intervention, the intervention will be helpful only if it comes at the right time. As Strupp (1981) pointed out, "unless the timing is right, interpretations have no more effect upon producing a dynamic reorganization of a cognitive-affective structure than reading a menu satisfies a starving person" (p. 230). Novice therapists tend to intervene after the moment has passed because they may not recognize it or they are nervous about seizing the moment. As therapists gain more experience, they struggle with intervening too early, because they see where they want to go before the client is ready to take steps in that direction. This problem of timing is another way that we can see that judgment is critical in good therapeutic practice and underlies the success of any intervention.

Self-Reflective Practice

Therapists learn foresight and the ability to modify interventions in response to clients' actions through reflecting on their work. Self-reflection is an essential aspect of reasoned choice because it provides the opportunity to learn from experience. The mere accrual of experience is insufficient to guarantee excellence or even competence in any endeavor. Good judgment does not magically arise from spending time with clients any more than writing ability arises from spending time in front of a keyboard. This is borne out in the inconsistent effects that researchers find for clinicians' level of experience on therapy outcome (see Beutler et al., 2004, and Christensen & Jacobson, 1994, for reviews). The development of good judgment requires instruction, feedback, and informed practice, not just time with clients.

Experience is useful only when we can mine it for knowledge about what worked well and what did not. Reflective clinicians can recognize patterns of response to their interventions and identify which interventions seem most helpful with which clients, at which particular times. Therapists who can reflect on their work are in a better position to modify their approach as they receive feedback on it in their interactions with clients. To be useful, self-reflection requires the ability to admit mistakes. Therapists must recognize their own fallibility and their responsibility for the outcomes of their interventions. At the same time, one can go wrong by questioning oneself too frequently or by being overly critical of one's efforts. Successful therapists develop a balance between an honest assessment of their errors and a recognition of what they do well.

Therapists learn self-reflection on their practice in supervision, where they review their activities with a more experienced mentor. It is not necessarily easy to present one's work for scrutiny with a balance between self-criticism and self-protection. This is often one of the most important areas of training in supervision. I remember struggling to learn how to use supervision as a trainee. I wanted to learn as much as possible, but I feared the exquisite vulnerability of that kind of scrutiny and evaluation. I had many wonderful supervisors who were more or less patient with me, and they showed me that defensiveness impeded my learning. From these supervisors I learned how to avoid overt defensiveness, but I learned how to use supervision well from Greg Bauer. His gentle and humane feedback made it relatively easy to review my work openly with him. The critical moment in my learning to be a good supervisee was when he made the process of collaborative learning explicit. He talked with me about my excessive expectations of myself that made it hard to talk about my mistakes. I tended to lurch back and forth between being overly self-critical and being defensive. He made it clear that he was on my side and interested in helping me to make the most of my abilities. He reminded me again and again that all therapists are human and prone to making mistakes. His humanity made it possible for me to make better use of his expertise and to grow tremendously as a therapist and eventually as a supervisor.

To be consistently successful with clients, therapists must acquire the ability to recognize mistakes or oversights through self-reflection and attention to the often subtle feedback that clients give about whether one is on target or not. At the same time, therapists have to be confident and willing to take risks to help their clients confront the issues with which they are reluctant to grapple. This means that effective therapists will be able to work within the tension between "conviction and uncertainty" as Downing (2000) put it. He emphasized that "if we are truly to serve the welfare of the client, then nothing could be more important than recognizing the intellectual and moral vulnerabilities which we face daily as practitioners, despite the personal and professional unease this recognition may engender" (p. 5). It is a matter of judgment how confident one should be about a particular understanding of a client's difficulties or a specific intervention, and balanced judgment allows us to proceed confidently without losing sight of our fallibility.

SUMMARY

Practical wisdom seems to me to be central to good psychotherapy. Practical wisdom shows up in the ability to see what is most important, to be able to deliberate about how to address those matters, and to choose an intervention strategy wisely. For some of us, this wisdom comes naturally and is often called *intuition* or *art*. These expressions suggest that practical wisdom is a gift that may not be trainable. I believe that it can be cultivated in trainees and in experienced therapists, and that teaching practical wisdom is an essential part of clinical training.

One approach that has helped me see my clients' situations more clearly and to make good choices about how to intervene is to ask myself questions from time to time during and between sessions with them. I have listed some of these questions here, but this list is obviously suggestive, rather than exhaustive:

- What are this client's goals?
- What can I do here and now to help my client get closer to his or her goals?
- What is at stake for this client right now?
- What are the most important things on which I should focus right now?
- How do the events in this session relate to our overall goals?
- Which real possibilities have been foreclosed unnecessarily here?
- Is this the right time for the intervention I am considering?
- How will this intervention play out with this client?
- Why did this session (course of therapy) go well (poorly)?

These questions help to highlight what is central and what is peripheral, and they allow me to deliberate productively and intervene with confidence.

7

ASKING THE BEST QUESTIONS AND INTERPRETING WISELY IN RESEARCH

For when the thing is indefinite the rule also is indefinite . . .
—Aristotle, *Nicomachean Ethics*

Psychologists have avidly pursued a natural scientific model of research in which we have sought to investigate timeless and universal phenomena to discover the underlying laws that govern the operations of psychological phenomena. Psychologists have traditionally seen this pursuit of knowledge as a disinterested truth seeking that is disengaged from personal and political biases and values, and independent of the scientist's character. Given the success and prestige of the natural sciences, it is no wonder that psychologists have attempted to emulate them. The epistemic goals and methods of a natural scientific approach have been under attack from many quarters, which I touched on in chapter 1. In this chapter I continue to examine the appropriateness of a natural scientific model by contrasting it with a phronetic approach to inquiry, which highlights researchers' judgment and the goods that they seek.

In his short, insightful book, Flyvbjerg (2001) examined the contrast between a natural science model and a phronetic model and suggested two key questions for identifying an appropriate philosophy of social science. The first question is, to what degree do social scientists study temporally and universally invariant laws of behavior versus historically and culturally variable origins of action? The second question is, is it possible to study human behavior from an ethically neutral position or are social scientists inescapably involved in ethical questions? A standard natural science approach assumes temporally and culturally invariant laws of behavior and the ethical neutrality of the investigator, whereas a phronetic approach allows for temporal and cultural variation in explanations and an ethically engaged observer. I suggest that the phronetic approach is more appropriate for a subject matter that has strong context dependency and is concerned with understanding humans as beings whose choices and actions are guided by what they see as worthwhile and good. Moreover, I argue that the investigator's character, particularly the capacity for practical wisdom, plays a crucial role in the conduct of science. I argue that *phronesis* plays a role in both our philosophy of science and our practice of science.

EPISTEME OR PHRONESIS?

Throughout much of this book, I have been contrasting Aristotle's knowledge concepts of *techne* and *phronesis*. He also discussed a third kind of knowledge, which he called *episteme*, and this term is usually translated as scientific knowledge. According to Aristotle,

> What scientific knowledge is, if we are to speak exactly and not follow mere similarities, is plain from what follows. We all suppose that what we know is not even capable of being otherwise; of things capable of being otherwise we do not know. . . . Therefore the object of scientific knowledge is [sic] of necessity. Therefore, it is eternal. . . . (p. 140)

In other words, scientific knowledge deals with what is necessarily and timelessly the case. Aristotle's claim here is the same one that contemporary psychologists often make for their research. Scientific knowledge is about universal and timeless laws of behavior rather than appearances that change across time and culture. *Episteme* is also concerned with things that are as they must be rather than with objects and events that we have the power to change in ways we believe are best.

It follows, in the traditional understanding of psychological science, that we as investigators must study these invariant underlying laws objectively by separating our methods from our values, interests, and desires. Charles Sanders Pierce articulated this position well over a century ago:

> To satisfy our doubts, . . . it is necessary that a method should be found by which our beliefs may be determined by nothing human, but by some external permanency—by something on which our thinking has no effect. . . . Such is the method of science. Its fundamental hypothesis . . . is this: There are real things, whose characters are entirely independent of our opinions of them. (Buchler, 1955, p. 18)

Pierce's statement is consonant with the dominant natural science approach to psychology, which asserts that we can study human psychology and behavior as objects that are what they are independent of how we as actors or observers interpret them. Thus, *episteme* corresponds to our frequently idealized version of science as pertaining to what is universal, invariable, and independent of the values and aims of the investigator.

I begin this chapter by considering the propositions that psychological science is characterized by knowledge about invariant and timeless phenomena that are investigated through entirely dispassionate inquiry. Clarifying the status of the discipline with respect to these two propositions will help us to understand whether it is best to subscribe to an investigative rationality based on *episteme* or on *phronesis*.

Invariant or Variant Phenomena

It is important to note at the outset that psychology comprises at least two broad disciplines. There are areas of psychological investigation that may be best served by straightforwardly natural scientific methods, such as neuropsychology or basic sensory psychology, in which psychology shades into human physiology and anatomy. There is every reason to believe, short of evolutionary change, that the laws governing basic phenomena in these domains are likely to remain invariant across time and culture. This universality is less clear in areas in which the full range of human variability is evident, such as in social or clinical psychology. Disciplinary boundaries have been traditionally drawn in such a way that both the physical and the social aspects of humans are included under the rubric of psychology. Therefore, I acknowledge that the natural science model may be fitting for studies of the physical infrastructure of human action, even as I question its appropriateness for investigating the full range of human activity.

Two additional caveats are in order before I proceed. First, I have chosen to illustrate the temporal and cultural variation in psychological phenomena rather than make an in principle argument against invariance. Such an argument is very involved and is more philosophically demanding than most readers will find useful. I encourage readers interested in this argument to pursue it elsewhere (Richardson & Fowers, 1998; Richardson et al., 1999; Taylor, 1985).

Second, an obvious counterargument to temporal invariance is evolution. It is a common practice in psychology to speculate about the evolutionary origins of contemporary behavior. This practice has its uses, and it suggests a sensitivity to historical change in human behavior. This is more apparent than real, however, because evolutionary change occurs on a geologic time scale. For all practical purposes, evolutionary *change* is not occurring in any way relevant to the contemporaneous pursuit of psychological science. Because of the time scale problem, evolutionary change in humans can be studied only in retrospect and is, by nature, post hoc in form. For all the fervor of evolutionary psychologists, their theories remain highly speculative and their results are far from universally accepted. Although there is little scientific doubt about human evolution, and the general mechanisms of evolution are fairly well understood, evolutionary theory does not help to explain the kinds of cultural and short-term temporal variation in human behavior that casts doubt on the natural science model in psychology.

Temporal Invariance

The idea that there are atemporal laws of human behavior is a longstanding, but wholly unsubstantiated assumption in psychology. Temporal invariance is held dear because it is essential to the *episteme* approach to psychological inquiry, but the stability of human behavior across significant stretches of time simply has not been established empirically. This is partly due to the youth of the discipline. Our theories and methods have evolved so much in the short history of our discipline that there are few, if any, topics that are studied today in anything resembling the way they were studied at a temporal distance of even a few decades. It is therefore impossible to separate instances of apparent temporal variation in behavior from changes in scholarly theory and methods for studying them within the last century. It is possible that temporal stability in psychological phenomena will be established at some time in the future, but at present, it is an article of faith rather than a demonstrable fact. Unless the future of our discipline is much less variable than its past, there is little likelihood of the kind of constancy over long periods that would allow the assumption of temporal invariance to be tested.

Shifts in psychological research over time cannot always be attributed to the salutary effects of theoretical or methodological improvement, however. The content of psychological inquiry has been subject to dramatic fluctuations that seem to reflect the social, political, and funding environment more than any clear scientific priorities. For example, the historian of psychology Kurt Danziger (1990) found that extraversion was studied in 39% of the articles in the *Journal of Abnormal and Social Psychology* between 1920 and 1935, but in only 6% of the articles in the period 1940–1955. Danziger found a similar drop in the investigation of ascendance and a doubling of interest in "emotionality" during these periods. As we know, extraversion has made a significant comeback in recent years in the five-factor model of personality. Danziger concluded,

> There appear to be no grounds intrinsic to the subject matter for this constantly shifting empirical basis of trait psychology. It is much more likely that these changes represent the coming and going of research fads, but in this case the fads are directly related to events in the social

environment of the discipline. Thus, the strong attention paid to the polar categories of "ascendance" and "submission" during the early period of American personality research appears to reflect its practical roots in personnel and officer selection. (p. 163)

Other authors who have investigated documentary evidence related to the stability of behavioral patterns across historical time have reached similar conclusions. Because there was no formal discipline of psychology in earlier centuries, these authors have relied on historical, personal, and literary documents. Baumeister (1987) reviewed historical and literary sources for shifts in the concept of self from the 11th century to the present. He identified dramatic shifts in self-knowledge, self-definition, self-fulfillment, and the relationship between the individual and society. For example, the evidence suggests that there was a very strong pattern of defining oneself in terms of one's group affiliations such as rank, kin, and gender in the medieval period as contrasted with the primary contemporary sources of identity such as personality, personal choices, and one's "inner nature." His review suggests that a construct as central to psychology as the self has undergone significant transformations over the centuries in the Western world, raising serious questions about the temporal invariance of such psychological constructs.

Stroebe, Gergen, Gergen, and Stroebe (1992) discussed variations and similarities in the grieving process over time and across cultures. Of particular interest here, they reviewed historical materials and contrasted descriptions of and prescriptions for grief. They identified a contemporary emphasis on severing bonds with deceased loved ones and "moving on" in contemporary popular and professional literatures. Contemporary theorists and therapists focus on the "necessity" of relinquishing ties to the deceased and developing a new identity and a new life. Letting go is seen as essential today, because the individual's "successful" functioning is dependent on being able to redirect resources to ongoing activities and achievements. A pattern of brief grieving is prescribed to facilitate the return to a "useful" and "functional" life. According to this view, a prolonged sadness or preoccupation with the lost loved one is seen as pathological and given pejorative labels such as separation anxiety and chronic grief syndrome. In contrast, the more Romantic view of grief that predominated a century ago emphasized the deep bonds between the survivor and the deceased. Ongoing remembrance is, according to this viewpoint, a hallmark of the depth of the relationship and of the genuineness of the survivor's love. Prolonged grief is a sign of the importance of the relationship and of the richness of the survivor's inner life. Romantic patterns of thought and experience have not entirely disappeared, but they have been shouldered aside by the more instrumental emphasis on a relatively quick return to normal functioning.

I could provide many more examples of the temporal variation in psychological phenomena, but that would quickly become tedious. No matter how many instances of variation I present, advocates of an *episteme* philosophy of social science could retort that this variation is due to specifiable variables that control the observed differences, and that social norms operate as causal determinants rather than as collective expressions of meaning and value. There is a consistency in this argument, and it has been persuasive for many. Yet it is a weak argument because it begs the question. One cannot make a reasonable argument for temporal invariance by claiming that undocumented, atemporal factors caused observed temporal variation. Moreover, this argument is based on a faith in the unseen rather than on the hard-headed empiricism it claims to represent. At this point, the available data favor the view that human behavior has changed qualitatively through history.

Of course, it is possible that, in the distant future, psychologists will have the kind of data that can demonstrate conclusively that historical change is due to nothing more than shifts in underlying atemporal causal forces. The question is, do we want to place our faith in this unseen and uncertain future possibility or in the more plausible, if more complex, possibility that human actions are shaped by shared understandings of meaning and intelligibility that change in response to circumstances and ongoing cultural dialogue? Given our uncertainty, a phronetic understanding allows us to respond to evident historical change in a way that takes it seriously until a convincing demonstration of temporal invariance is forthcoming.

Cultural Invariance

A second traditional assumption of the natural scientific approach to psychology is that cultural patterns are relatively superficial expressions of variation in underlying universal laws of behavior. Foremost among the universal claims in mainstream psychology is the assumption that humans act primarily to further their individual interest, as discussed earlier in this book. One of the most basic metaphors in psychology is economic exchange in a broad sense in which theorists suggest that individuals behave primarily for the sake of some socially mediated payoff. I cited the anthropologist Alan Fiske's (1991) contention that this individualism is culturally relative rather than universal in chapter 3. I discuss his evidence for this contention here as a way to indicate the cultural relativity of this central premise in psychological theory and research.

Fiske did his fieldwork in West Africa with the Moose (pronounced MOH-say) of Burkina Faso. He suggested that his findings are not limited to this tribe but also apply to the Tallensi of Ghana, the Bambara and Dogon of Mali, and other rural peoples of Africa.

The Moose's collective orientation is evident in many ways and contrasts sharply with the individualistic and instrumental assumptions prevalent in American psychology. In spite of a severe shortage of arable land, the agrarian Moose people freely give land to anyone who requests it if it is not already in use. Land is never rented or sold, and borrowers of land may retain it for generations. This tribe treats all land as commonly held. Water is even scarcer but is also treated as common property. Herds of sheep and goats are also pooled, and village children take turns tending the animals.

The Moose never work in their villages for wages. Rather, they cultivate crops "in communal groups of close kin, working together without keeping track of the input of any individual" (Fiske, 1991, p. 191). When there is too much work for the kin group, they invite friends, neighbors, and in-laws to help. This assistance is generally reciprocated, but without any formal accounting. When the work is finished, everyone eats, but "the senior men get the first and largest shares," as an overt recognition of authority and status, not work output. The grain is stored in communal granaries overseen by the senior male of the kin group. Food is distributed to members of the group as they need it. If members of another group request food, it is given freely if available. "The only valid excuse one can make for refusing to give others what they need is that one has nothing to give. People expect a certain amount of restraint and moderation in the demands that are made, but they try hard to meet genuine needs" (p. 194).

It is not that Moose are simply ignorant about market exchange principles. When they need money, they sell produce or goods in the market. Many men travel to Ivory Coast to work for wages for long periods and some buy land there to cultivate. They understand that labor, land, and produce *can* be commodities and that they would be better off economically in Ivory Coast, but they strongly prefer their communal arrangements. When they return from wage labor, they distribute much of what they earned as gifts to kin, in-laws, friends, and neighbors.

Even courtship is conducted communally. For the most part, Moose men do not choose their own wives, and women do not choose their own husbands. A man may begin courtship by selecting a senior man in another lineage, whom he visits and bestows with gifts and services. This may go on for a long time with no explicit acknowledgment of the courtship. No amount of giving ever entitles a man to a wife. After a period of time, the elder may give a wife to the courting man, without saying who she is. For some time the courting man continues to give gifts and services, many of which are contributed by his lineage mates. When the wife is given to the courting man, the head of his lineage decides whose wife she will be. The husband will often be the one who did the courting, but not always.

The Moose's arrangements make it clear that much psychological theory and research is culturally relative because it is based on the Western cultural assumption that egoistically based exchange motives are basic to human behavior. This example is only one of dozens that show that universal claims about egoism and altruism, interpersonal attraction and mating, and power and legitimacy are very difficult to sustain. This level of cultural variance undercuts the basic invariance necessary to an *episteme*-oriented psychological science, because the basic premises of behavior appear to be radically different across cultures.[1]

There is a growing psychological literature that documents important cultural differences as well. Kitayama, Markus, and Kurokawa (2000) studied happiness in Japan and the United States and found that it was primarily related to individual control and goal achievement in the United States and more strongly related to social support, the realization of social harmony, and collective achievements in Japan. Triandis (1995) cited a number of studies that contrast individualistic cultures that emphasize independence, self-reliance, competition, and in-group distancing with collectivist cultures that highlight interdependence, sociability, family integrity, and in-group closeness.

Of course, there is a great deal of variation within any culture, but significant differences in key constructs across cultures suggest that a great deal of human action is based on understanding and responding to cultural patterns. Notions of appropriateness, custom, and reciprocity govern much of what humans do, whether the activity is characterized as competitive or cooperative, exchange oriented or communal, inclusive or exclusive of others. Individuals are embedded in a social and historical context that shapes their actions by defining what is possible and fitting, which is expressed in everyday relationships and norms. To the degree that human actions are guided by such social norms and practices, they are more a matter of *phronesis* than of *episteme* because they are contingent rather than necessary, historically and culturally relative rather than invariant, and guided by judgment and a sense of what is appropriate at least as much as by causal forces.

Ethical Neutrality or Engagement?

The second question regarding the epistemic aspirations of psychological science is whether researchers can study human behavior from an ethi-

---

[1] Fiske developed a universal theory of social arrangements that is meant to capture wide variability in cultural forms. His global theory of relational behavior is relatively open-ended regarding both cultural and temporal variation. This theory and its relative merits are beyond the scope of this book, and familiarity with Fiske's theoretical views is not necessary for an appreciation of his cultural observations and how they point to the profound cultural variation that undermines psychological universalism.

cally neutral point of view. There is good reason to believe that human behavior is historically and culturally variable, but if the investigator of this sociohistorical kaleidoscope can remain impartial, there still might be hope of describing this variation objectively without being influenced by personal or cultural agendas.

I have already more than tipped my hand regarding psychology's value commitments by outlining the instrumental and individualistic biases of psychological theory, research, and practice in previous chapters. It is surely no accident that the field of psychology, which has developed predominantly in the United States, is characterized by these particular biases, which are widely seen as characteristic of mainstream U.S. culture (Bellah et al., 1985; Sandel, 1996; Sullivan, 1986; Wolfe, 1989). As discussed in chapter 3, instrumentalism makes it very difficult for most psychologists to recognize the possibility of an internal relationship between activities and goals. It also leads psychologists to take an episodic focus on individual behaviors and to neglect consideration of character and the unity of an integrated life. I suggested in chapter 4 that individualism leads us to exaggerate individual autonomy, to prioritize individual interests over social goods, to marginalize social relationships vis-à-vis personal aims, and to be almost entirely blind to the profound dependence individuals have on their social environments.

All of this strongly suggests that psychologists do not stand outside the flux of history and culture when we theorize, investigate, or practice. To the contrary, we are just as firmly embedded in our time and culture as the people that we study. It is possible to gain some perspective on the cultural commitments that shape us, but any distance we attain will be partial and provisional. It is entirely unclear what an acultural, ahistorical standpoint would be and how one could meaningfully engage in observation of human activity if one had no preconceptions at all (such as the idea that human behavior is worth studying or that it is meaningfully patterned).

Some might see the assertion that our discipline has been strongly influenced by its cultural milieu as an indictment of psychology as a science, but it is only a criticism of the field if one expects complete value neutrality. Although I do not have the space here to defend it, I endorse the hermeneutic argument that having a particular standpoint is necessary for any kind of human activity, including psychological research (Gadamer, 1975; Guignon, 1983; Richardson et al., 1999; Taylor, 1985). This means that we cannot engage in theory, research, or practice unless we have some standpoint or some project we are attempting to complete. The perspective from which we begin and the ends we seek give our work its definition. We cannot eliminate these ethical components from our work through some overlay of "objectivity" that somehow erases the cultural, personal, and political commitments that bring particular research problems to light and animate our investigative endeavors. The ethical engagement of our profession is evident in many ways, and I offer a few examples here by way of illustration.

Perhaps the most significant indication that the discipline is involved in ethical projects is found in the mission statements of the American Psychological Association (APA) and the American Psychological Society (APS), the two largest organized groups of psychologists in the world. The mission of the APA is "to advance psychology as a science and profession and as a means of promoting health, education, and human welfare" (APA, 2003a). Similarly, the mission of the APS is "to promote, protect, and advance the interests of scientifically oriented psychology in research, application, teaching, and the improvement of human welfare" (APS, 2003). Both organizations make their commitment to improving human welfare prominent in their mission statements, and the beneficial outcomes of psychological science and practice are among the most important justifications of the profession in our society.

This interest in promoting human welfare is not simply sloganeering, nor is it limited to applied practice. Psychological science is devoted to improving the quality of life either directly, through applied research, or indirectly through the advancement of knowledge, which is both good in itself and serves to inform applications. There are innumerable examples of research efforts that are directly related to improving human welfare, including decades of research devoted to understanding and reducing unwanted forms of aggression, a voluminous literature on marital quality and divorce prevention, nearly a century of research on human intelligence and learning designed to assist educators, the growing field of behavioral medicine, which is increasingly identifying psychological factors in health promotion, and so on.

Psychology's promotion of human welfare is, in many respects, a deeply ethical project that has not been universally valued or pursued. In fact, the interest in improving life is a historical development particular to the modern West. Taylor (1989) termed it the "affirmation of ordinary life." By ordinary life, Taylor referred to everyday labor, marriage and family life, and leisure pursuits. Classically, these activities were seen as mere infrastructure to support incomparably higher forms of activity such as philosophical contemplation, the religious devotion of the monastic orders, or chivalric exploits. The affirmation of ordinary life began in the Reformation's sacralization of everyday activities. Taylor recounted this viewpoint in the following terms: "The highest life can no longer be defined by an exalted *kind* of activity; it all turns on the *spirit* in which one lives whatever one lives, even the most mundane existence" (p. 224). This repudiation of the premodern division of higher and lower pursuits places everyday activities on the same plane of worthiness as what were previously seen as more exalted callings. This viewpoint gradually transcended Christian thought and became general in the West as Enlightenment thinkers translated it into the language of natural law and human dignity.

Science largely replaced contemplation as the supreme intellectual activity in the Enlightenment period. Yet this premier intellectual activity is not seen as separate from and superior to ordinary life. Taylor highlighted the completion of this historical reversal by noting, "science is not a higher activity which ordinary life should subserve; on the contrary, science should benefit ordinary life" (1989, p. 213). In fact, the legitimacy of contemporary science is seen largely in how it serves ordinary life, and this is particularly true of modern investigations of ordinary human activities such as cognition, learning, and social relationships, which would have been seen as less than weighty concerns in earlier times.

The affirmation of ordinary life also encompasses a powerful imperative to reduce human suffering that is uniquely modern. In our time, it is far more common to see suffering as a problem to be eliminated or reduced than to see it in any redemptive fashion, or as the result of divine justice, or as simply unavoidable. The reduction of suffering drives the psychotherapeutic and self-help industries that express our peculiarly modern preoccupation with a "mentally healthy" and happy population. The impetus to ameliorate the human condition also fuels a great deal of research that is justified by its contribution to reducing aggression, divorce, school failure, and so forth. Putting science and professional practice at the service of enhancing ordinary life is crucial to understanding the trajectory of our discipline. Although there is also undoubtedly an important basic research agenda, a very large segment of the field is devoted to serving the needs of and attempting to solve the problems faced in ordinary life. This deeply ethical project goes a long way in defining psychology as a discipline, from the mission statements of professional organizations to the ongoing scholarly and applied activities of their members.

The commitment to affirming and improving ordinary life helps to constitute the discipline of psychology. Without this affirmation of ordinary life, psychology would not be recognizable to us, if it could exist at all. This means that the cultural and historical commitment Western civilization has made to ordinary life is at least as basic to our discipline as the commitment to objectivity.

The social ethics of the profession are also expressed in another important way. Much of the research in the field, whether basic or applied, is made possible by federal grants. These grants are awarded for projects that fit funding priorities set out by Congress and specified by various federal agencies. These funding priorities represent political goals that are shaped through a long process of negotiation, compromise, and restatement. This means that a large proportion of the best research is guided by political agendas as much as by purely scientific concerns. Of course, investigators propose and carry out their work according to scientific standards, and the actual projects reflect some combination of the research-er's and the agency's priorities. There is no question, however, that federal funding priorities have a dramatic effect on what is and is not studied, and that these priorities reflect a political interest in addressing important social problems.

I am suggesting that psychological inquiry is inseparable from the contemporary ethical concerns of its practitioners. In spite of all the efforts that have been made to objectify psychology philosophically, theoretically, and methodologically, psychological research is inescapably grounded in the basic project of improving human welfare. This project is a historical outgrowth of the Western affirmation of ordinary life that confers value on mundane activities and gives the intellectual activity of science the mission of facilitating and enriching ordinary life. Psychological science is funded by and serves the political structure of its society. These political agendas often have laudable aims, but the firm attachment of the discipline to the political priorities of governments undermines researchers' claims to ethical disengagement. Moreover, psychology is not objective in the sense of being neutral with respect to values because our theories and research reflect the cultural values of individualism and instrumentalism. I have made these points primarily through illustrations to enhance readability. I encourage interested or skeptical readers to pursue more extended, philosophically deeper arguments for this viewpoint elsewhere (Danziger, 1990; Richardson et al., 1999; Taylor, 1985, 1989).

The point of my argument in this chapter is not that psychological science is impossible or impossibly corrupt. Rather, it is that we can understand psychological science much better as a discipline characterized by phronetic inquiry than by trying to cast it as natural science. I am suggesting that most research in psychology is concerned with aspects of human experience that are changeable rather than invariant and that our investigations have inescapable ethical purposes interwoven with the pursuit of knowledge. For these reasons, it is better for us to seek knowledge along the lines of *phronesis* rather than *episteme*. As I point out in this chapter, adopting a phronetic philosophy of social science involves a shift in our understanding of psychological inquiry and also suggests that practical wisdom is an important trait for scientists. The remainder of the chapter is devoted to outlining the contours of a phronetically conceived form of psychological inquiry and showing how the conduct of science is guided by practical wisdom.

PHRONETIC INQUIRY

What does phronetic inquiry look like? Although it sounds esoteric, the outlines of what I present here will be familiar to most social scientists, but they will have a decidedly different tone than the standard conceptions of psychological science. The three facets of practical wisdom I have discussed in the last two chapters are equally fitting for the research domain. The quality of our investigations is dependent on the quality of the questions we ask, and this is largely a matter of moral perception, or the ability to see what is most important in an area of research. Deliberation is also essential to choosing the best questions and the best research methods and to making the most appropriate and cogent interpretations of the results. Reasoned choice shows up clearly in research, because every aspect of an investigation can be approached in many ways, with varying results. Defensibly choosing one approach over others is a definitive aspect of scholarly inquiry.

Moral Perception in Research

Some research questions are crucially important to theory and to a research domain and some are peripheral. How do investigators make wise decisions about which questions are most important? The ability to see what is most important in a field of inquiry appears deceptively simple when I read the published work of excellent researchers. This is partly due to the fact that the best published research begins with a polished account of why the particular study is necessary and how it will contribute to our knowledge and practice. Harriet Zuckerman (1977) quoted C. N. Yang, a Nobel laureate, who emphasized, "The simplicity was the result of careful preparation and deliberate weighing of different alternatives of presentation. The emphasis was always on the essential and practical part of the problem" (p. 129). This description of scientific writing illustrates moral perception and deliberation very well. An apparent simplicity in presentation emerges as a result of carefully deliberating about what is *essential* and *practical*.

Scientists known for their innovation and excellent research highlight the challenges of problem setting in science and see the ability to set problems well as a distinguishing feature of the best scientists (Mackworth, 1965; Merton, 1973; Wertheimer, 1959). In a discussion of scientific originality, Mackworth (1965) asserted that problem finding (or setting) is the hallmark of the best scientists whereas complex problem solving is the domain of the expert technician. He also said that

> good scientists have to be careful conservatives and wild radicals almost
> at the same time. An intellectual framework must first be acquired . . .

then prudently followed. . . . The real test comes when this framework has to be discarded rather quickly because another set of ideas fits the actual events more closely. (p. 55)

In this statement, Mackworth gave several indications of the centrality of practical wisdom, although he did not use the term. The need to balance conservative and radical approaches, and to weigh the alternatives of following or abandoning an intellectual framework, indicates the necessity for making wise choices. In addition, scientists must follow the framework prudently, not slavishly.

The central point that Mackworth wanted to make is that "there is an all-important qualitative difference between problem solving and finding" (p. 57). He considered "problem finding more important than problem solving" (p. 52) because problem finders are scarce, and they are the ones who foster new discoveries and original theories. Problem solvers are those who work out the details within already established theories. Problem finders see the important questions in a way that problem solvers cannot. It is this ability to recognize the big questions and to define the unexpected problem that marks out the original scientist, according to Mackworth. In a similar vein, Wertheimer (1959) averred, "often in great discovery the most important thing is that a certain question is found" (p. 123).

When I teach new doctoral students how to approach their research, I use several examples of well-crafted introductions to show them how this problem-setting reasoning is done. Although they can recognize and appreciate this reasoning, the process of problem setting is very difficult for students to learn. There are many things that I recommend to students. I suggest that they read in their area of interest and that they learn the important theories applicable in their topic area. I also teach them some tips about reading and writing problem-setting narratives. For example, every problem has a context in which it occurs, is defined, and has its history. Identifying and describing this context is crucial to understanding the nature of the problem and the shape of possible solutions. This problem context does not come pre-labeled and the investigator has to make it coherent through a construal. Likewise, the researcher has to render the problem itself in a way that admits of some feasible empirical treatment. Although there are some "tricks of the trade," there are no sure-fire techniques or algorithmic processes that will generate good context and problem statements for research. It is a matter of perceiving what is and what is not important and of seeing what is and is not possible. The ability to recognize what is important is the moral perception I discussed in chapter 5, and this capacity to separate the central from the peripheral is at least as important in science as in other human pursuits.

Robert Merton (1973), a pioneer of the sociology of science, described Nobel laureates' views on the process of finding and setting important problems in science. These individuals have a demonstrable capacity for recognizing and pursuing the most important questions. Merton related that they "uniformly express the strong conviction that what matters most in their work is a developing sense of taste, of judgment, in seizing upon problems that are of fundamental importance" (p. 453). This acknowledgment that one of their most important attributes is a sense of taste or judgment is a remarkable statement from such eminent *natural scientists*. Zuckerman (1977) added, "science has its own esthetic. Among elite scientists . . . deep problems and elegant solutions distinguish excellent science from the merely competent or commonplace" (p. 127). She quoted Michael Polanyi: "Discovery requires in fact something beyond craftsmanship, namely the gift of recognizing a problem ripe for solution by your own powers, large enough to engage your powers to the full and worth the expenditure of effort."

These accomplished scientists also expressed their

> conviction that an important problem will come along in due course and that when it does, their acquired sense of taste will enable them to recognize it and handle it . . . . They like to speak of the big problems and the fundamental ones, the important problems and the beautiful ones. These they distinguish from the pedestrian work in which they engage while waiting for the next big problem to come their way. (Merton, 1973, p. 454)

These scientists often spent years looking for such questions or formulating them in a way that they could answer. It is this ability to focus on what is truly significant that distinguishes excellent from ordinary scientific activity. This capacity to see what really matters, what is truly significant, what is essential is exactly what I mean by moral perception.

In chapter 6, I discussed the necessity of training, exemplars, feedback, and self-assessment in the acquisition of practical wisdom as a therapist. A similar process occurs with scientists. Zuckerman (1977) reported that "the elite masters [teachers of the eventual laureates] evoked superior performance by conveying through their own behavior a sense of how much could be achieved in scientific inquiry and what it was like to do *work of significance*" (p. 125, italics added). The laureates Merton describes also typically report that they acquired their sense for the significant problem during their years of training in evocative environments. Reflecting on his years as a novice in the laboratory of a chemist of the first rank, one laureate reported that his mentor "led me to look for important things, whenever possible, rather than to work on endless detail or to work just to improve accuracy rather than making a basic new contribution." Another laureate commented,

> I acquired a certain expansion of taste. It was a matter of taste and attitude and, to a certain extent, real self-confidence. I learned that it was just as difficult to do an unimportant experiment, often more difficult, than an important one. (p. 453)

Merton went on to describe "certain aspects of their character" that "account for their tendency to focus on significant problems." These character strengths include self-assurance, self-direction, fortitude, frustration tolerance, a capacity for delayed gratification, and having high standards. "They are prepared to tackle important though difficult problems rather than settle for easy and secure ones. . . . Their capacity for delayed gratification coupled with self-assurance, leads to" their ability to recognize important problems and to tackle them with confidence (pp. 453–454). There are surely many traits that set the stage for this level of scientific brilliance, but Merton was highlighting two: the moral perception necessary to recognize significant problems and a set of character strengths that make it possible to pursue those problems productively. This is exactly the combination that virtue ethics suggests.

There is no indication from any of these authors or the Nobel laureates they cite that knowledge of abstract theory and technical expertise are sufficient for fostering high-quality research. In fact, they uniformly identified those who follow existing theory and technique as problem solvers, in contrast to problem finders. Competent problem solving is a necessary part of science, but scientific excellence is most prominent in problem finding. Abstract theory provides a general heuristic for research but does not, by itself, clarify which of the thousands of possible research questions investigators should seek to answer.

In psychology, we have focused tremendous energy on developing statistical, measurement, and experimental design technologies that have improved the mechanics of research. Although this technical sophistication is a matter of some pride for psychologists, these techniques do not, by themselves, guarantee high-quality science. The most sophisticated methods cannot compensate for triviality or lack of focus in the purposes of a study. The identification of significant problems that investigators frame in the best way possible is the domain of moral perception, which cannot be reduced to abstract theory or research technique. If we take to heart the Nobel laureates' description of their approach to science, we will begin to pay as much attention to practical wisdom as we do to statistical technique, which might very well deepen the significance and contribution of psychological science.

Deliberation in Psychological Inquiry

Deliberation is a central feature of scientific inquiry. I quoted Yang's perception that apparent simplicity of presentation is the result of extended deliberation that clarifies what is essential in a research problem. This consideration of how best to frame the problem is a crucial form of deliberation that is present in research from the very beginning. Once the research question comes into focus, investigators must consider which methods they will employ to try to answer the question, which means resolving issues relating to research design, sampling, study procedures, and statistical methods. For any given study, these issues can be resolved in many different ways, and careful deliberation is often necessary to optimize the research. The interpretation and presentation of the results require thoughtful consideration as well.

Deliberation does not end when the manuscript is submitted for publication but continues in the editorial review, in which representatives of the wider scholarly community are included in weighing the meaning and worth of the research. Reviewers frequently suggest changes in the way the problem is framed, in statistical methods, in adding, altering, or deleting research questions, and in the interpretation of the results. These recommendations are often very fruitful. I believe that my education in research continued well after I graduated and became a professor, and journal reviewers were among my most beneficial teachers. This sometimes painful but useful instruction helped me to perceive more clearly and to deliberate more effectively about the research problems I took up. Although there are occasionally less than useful reviews and even a few that are mean-spirited, reviewers seem generally interested in promoting good science.

Deliberation can also be seen at work in one of the most famous examples of scientific originality in history—Einstein's development of the special theory of relativity. This story can be told in many ways to illustrate many points. I want to focus on two simple facts from Wertheimer's (1959) account of the process, which he derived from multiple interviews with Einstein. Einstein began to feel troubled by questions about the relationship between the movement of an observer and the speed of light while he was still a secondary school student. The first fact is that he pondered these questions for 7 years before he was able to formulate his theoretical account of relativity. During much of that time, he was intensely puzzled and could not see his way clear to answering his questions. Questions multiplied and the problem became progressively more massive as he grappled with it. A solution finally crystallized when he began to consider eliminating time as an invariant. He then rebuilt physics with the speed of light as the central invariant. The second fact is that once he had solved the problem, it took him only 5 weeks to write his paper on it even though he had a full-time job in the patent office. He spent 7 years deliberating, reframing, and working out his thoughts about relativity. His long period of deliberation had to precede a final formulation of the problem because the problem kept shifting as he considered it. Once he had formulated the theory, he outlined several experimental procedures that could be used to test it, but testing was the last element in the development of the theory.

Few of us study such monumental problems or attempt to rewrite centuries of well-articulated and well-founded theory, so we generally do not need so much time. In some cases, our deliberation is so brief that we may not even notice its occurrence, but that does not negate its value. The importance of deliberation is also apparent in an experience I had recently with a colleague. She completed a very ambitious and difficult dissertation on the interesting topic of how gay men, lesbians, and heterosexuals differed in their approaches to relationships with ex-lovers. She collected a great deal of data, and the data that were central to her hypotheses supported one of the two theories she was testing. This made for an interesting and useful paper for publication (Harkless & Fowers, in press).

As we were finishing this paper, we were looking at some other data she had collected. We had not included these data in the report, because they were not very informative regarding her hypotheses. These apparently ancillary data were measurements of personality traits often thought to be gender sensitive (nonassertiveness, nurturance, dominance, etc.). As we were musing about why she had collected these data, we recalled that it was in an attempt to shed additional light on the post-breakup relationships of the four groups, but it had not worked out well.

We continued to discuss these data in a hindsight review of the incredible amount of work she had done to complete the study. In the process, it gradually dawned on us that these data represented a remarkable and unrecognized opportunity. She has a strong interest in the degree to which the standard conception of two genders holds up when one considers heterosexuals, gay men, and lesbians. With a simple 2 by 2 design, we could assess whether her results supported traditional beliefs about the gender differences between men and women, and whether there was a relationship between sexual orientation and gender characteristics. The existence of such a relationship would suggest that the standard gender conceptualization must be interpreted in light of sexual orientation rather than as a simple effect of gender.

We conducted the appropriate analyses and found both the traditional differences in the gender-sensitive traits of heterosexual men and women and interactions between gender and sexual orientation. These results confirmed our expectation that such gender effects should not be interpreted independently of sexual orientation. This sample provided an excellent opportunity to test this question because it included sizable groups of gay men and lesbians in addition to heterosexuals. This pattern of results does not show up in most studies of gender because sexual orientation is seldom included as a variable and because gay men and lesbians typically represent a small proportion of most samples. These results have much broader and more far-reaching implications than the results of the primary study, because they suggest that gender theorizing may require substantial revision. If we had not paused to consider whether or not these "extra" data were useful, we would not have hit on this very interesting possibility. This is a kind of deliberation that occurs very frequently in research efforts as investigators reconsider their data, their findings, and their conceptualizations in the face of unexpected or less than impressive findings.

We do not expect to win any prizes for deliberation or practical wisdom in this instance. We are actually chagrined that it took us so long to recognize what we had. In one sense, our recognition of the opportunity at our fingertips was serendipitous, because we had not planned to do these analyses. Yet, my colleague had assessed these particular gender-sensitive personality traits because she was interested in the potential influence of gender and sexual orientation on the ways that individuals orient themselves to relationships. It just took us a while to see that we could look at this question in a more general way than simply in terms of post-breakup relationships.

The investigator's deliberative capacity also guides the use and interpretation of statistics, even though this appears to be one of the more technical aspects of research. The very necessity of making inferences from statistics recalls Aristotle's definition of deliberation: "Deliberation is concerned with things that happen in a certain way for the most part, but in which the event is obscure, and with things in which it is indeterminate" (p. 56). The element of judgment can be obscured by our reliance on rule-based decision procedures (e.g., probability values, parsimony, etc.) and a single-minded focus on technical considerations. Knowledge about technical statistical procedures is important, but it cannot substitute for investigator judgment. Rather, we must deliberate and choose wisely to know which statistical methods to use, how best to apply them, and how to interpret them. The desired outcome is to identify the best approach for a given problem and data set so as to bring out the most illuminating and useful construal of the information. Relating statistically significant results to the topic of interest, more broadly conceived, comes naturally to most investigators and is enshrined in the discussion section of journal articles. These interpretations of the results are generally made with appropriate tentativeness and a listing of caveats related to the shortcomings of the particular study. The interpretations are often debatable, however, and the content of many scientific debates centers on whether the investigators' interpretations are optimal.

Deliberation is a critical component of research from the initial conceptualization of a research problem to the choice of methods, interpretation of findings, and the scientific community's consideration of the meaning and value of the study. The researcher's capacity for productive deliberation is essential to good science, but it can be obscured by the tendency in psychology to emphasize the technical aspects of research over its interpretive dimension. Good research design is dependent on the investigator's careful consideration of the investigative situation and on making wise choices.

Reasoned Choice in Research

The idea of reasoned choice in research is almost too obvious to discuss, but I want to mention it both as a way to solidify my claim that practical wisdom is essential for psychological inquiry and for the sake of symmetry with the other chapters in this section. One of the first hard lessons about research in psychology is that there are no perfect studies. There are always trade-offs, and one has to choose one set of advantages and disadvantages over another, depending on the purposes of the study and on what is at stake. Increases in the internal validity of studies generally come at the cost of decreased external validity, greater measurement precision means that researchers have more severely circumscribed the range of their assessment, qualitative methods open up possibilities for exploring meaning and context but make causal inferences highly problematic, and so forth.

The necessity of choosing one approach to inquiry over another is commonly understood. The point I want to make here is that this choice has to be guided by the investigator's judgment about which approach is most appropriate to the investigative situation. There are many factors that make up the investigative situation, including the purposes of the research, the nature of the research question, the degree of development and precision in the theory under investigation, the state of the literature, the nature of the extrascientific concerns involved, and so forth.

Psychotherapy outcome research offers an instructive example. Following Eysenck's (1952) famous challenge to the efficacy of psychotherapy, researchers endeavored to craft higher-quality studies that would provide good tests of whether psychotherapy had beneficial effects. This led to greater sophistication and control in this area of research, with ever-increasing standards for internal validity. The emphasis on experimental control and precision was essential given the questions raised by Eysenck and the stakes involved for a large number of psychologists who practiced psychotherapy. As is well known, better research methods have conclusively shown that a number of approaches to psychotherapy are efficacious with a variety of client difficulties.

More recently, a new challenge has arisen regarding the value of this tightly controlled research for the everyday practice of psychotherapy. It is one thing to show that psychotherapy is efficacious under relatively controlled conditions with a restricted range of clients, but quite a different thing to show that it is effective in ordinary clinical settings. Consequently, it has become increasingly common to conduct a more ecologically valid form of psychotherapy research in which researchers investigate everyday practices in studies that are focused more on external validity (Lambert & Ogles, 2004). Although the internal validity of these field studies is less optimal, they are more appropriate to answer the question of clinical effectiveness in less controlled conditions. This trade-off is necessary because the real-world value of psychotherapy research is at stake. The change from the initial emphasis on experimental control to the complementary recent focus on ecological validity reflects a shift in what is at stake in the research context and illustrates a reasoned choice of the best methods to address the most important issues.

There is a tendency in psychology to favor a particular approach to research that involves the ability to make causal inferences, a high degree of experimental control, highly developed measurement, observational coding, sophisticated statistical modeling, and so forth. This leaning grew out of the effort to develop psychology as a scientific discipline along the lines of more established natural sciences (Danziger, 1990; Leahey, 2000; Morawski, 1988). This preference is so strong that it can sometimes overshadow the relationship between the investigative situation and the researcher's judgment about which approach to inquiry is best. Psychologists' predilection to value certain investigative and statistical practices over others is enshrined in the overwhelming appearance of such methods in the most prestigious journals. To the degree that this inclination goes unchecked, it amounts to "methodolotry" rather than good science.

The phronetic conception of psychological inquiry I am suggesting provides a necessary counterpoint to the partiality toward particular methods that have attained a normative status regardless of their appropriateness to the topic at hand. A phronetic approach would encourage greater attention to the match between the nature of a research question and the methods used in contrast to attempts to squeeze all questions into a limited range of approaches. Likewise, journal editors and reviewers might become as interested in the importance, novelty, and innovative aspects of studies as they are in the degree to which studies conform to normative standards of methodological rigor. In short, *phronesis* has revolutionary implications.

SUMMARY

This chapter addressed the question of *phronesis* in psychological research in terms of the philosophy of science and the character of the scientist. It began with the question of whether we can pursue psychological inquiry most fittingly with an *episteme* or *phronesis* approach. From a philosophy of science perspective, the two key criteria are the invariance of the subject matter and the ethical neutrality of the investigator. With the exception of the physiological aspects of psychology, the origins of human behavior are neither universal nor timeless. The phenomena that psychologists study vary demonstrably in both dimensions and thereby fall under the category of "things capable of being otherwise." Our discipline differs from sciences such as physics or chemistry in that our subject matter is alive, self-modifying, and guided to a significant degree by purpose, choice, and social practice.

Episteme also appears to be an inappropriate philosophy of psychological inquiry because our research is an inherently ethical endeavor as opposed to disciplines in which investigators can separate themselves entirely from the subject matter. The ethics of our work reveal themselves in many places, including the mission statements of professional organizations and the common attempts to solve vexing human problems in research. The ethical dimension of psychology is pervasively present in the degree to which our discipline is guided by historically developed cultural values such as the affirmation of ordinary life, the reduction of human suffering, and individualism. The vast amount of funding for psychological inquiry that originates in political aims to improve society and thereby shapes some of the most rigorous research also shows that it is very difficult to create a purely factual discipline of psychology that is separate from ethical concerns. Indeed, a phronetic approach to psychology would make attention to the goals and goods of research an important question requiring public deliberation—in descriptions of studies and in the evaluation of that work.

This chapter also outlined the ways that *phronesis* figures in the character of the investigator and the conduct of psychological research. In the practice of phronetic inquiry, the character of the investigator figures prominently, particularly the three aspects of practical wisdom (moral perception, deliberation, and reasoned choice) I emphasized in this chapter. The resourcefulness and responsiveness to the situation that good scientists have comes from the character of the individual and his or her clarity about what is important, essential, and worthwhile. It is worth noting that even if one retains an *episteme*-focused philosophy of science, practical wisdom and character remain essential, because asking important questions, deliberating, and making reasoned choices are characteristic of good science in general. The investigator's practical wisdom takes on added resonance in a *phronesis-*

centered philosophy of science because this viewpoint highlights the assertion that science is an ethical project.

Practical wisdom begins with moral perception (the ability to identify and pursue the most important questions). Sociologists and psychologists of science have found that problem finding and problem setting are central to good science and are not reducible to an algorithmic or abstract theoretical approach. Nobel laureates commonly cite acquired taste, aesthetic sense, and judgment as the sources for their ability to see what is most essential and significant in their fields. In psychology, investigative significance is frequently tied to the promotion of some human good such as the reduction of suffering or the encouragement of excellence.

Deliberation also characterizes good science, particularly in framing research problems. Deliberative capacity is essential to many other facets of research, such as considerations involving research design, statistical modeling, interpretation, and the evaluation of the meaning and value of research. Although the ability to deliberate well is, to some extent, a capacity possessed by individuals, it has a very prominent and necessary social dimension as well. Careful consideration of research problems and approaches occurs in research teams, in discussions among colleagues, in the way that different research teams play off one another's work, in the manuscript review process, and finally in the shared evaluation of the research community regarding the worth and meaning of researchers' work. That worth is generally tied to the ways in which the research helps to further socially valued projects and goods.

That reasoned choice is a natural part of research is well recognized in the field already. What is sometimes left unacknowledged is the extent to which research choices result from a complex reading of a variety of important contingencies. When researchers make decisions about how they will approach a problem, they must rely on their grasp of the nature of the problem, the context for the question, what is at stake in the problem, and which trade-offs provide the best response to that constellation of issues. These choices are ultimately guided by which alternatives have the greatest promise for advancing our worthwhile endeavors.

Accomplished researchers use wisdom naturally, but it is one of the hardest skills to teach to students and to investigators early in their careers. Students and novice researchers need to learn to recognize what is worth studying, to recognize the central themes of a research literature, to formulate a question that captures something that is lacking in the literature, to match the research methods to the question, and to have the self-assurance, courage, and persistence to carry out their projects. The best scientists are motivated to pursue this arduous personal development by a love of truth and knowledge.

8

PRACTICAL WISDOM AS THE HEART OF PROFESSIONAL ETHICS

Matters concerned with conduct and questions of what is good for us
have no fixity . . . the agents themselves must in each case consider
what is appropriate to the occasion.
—Aristotle, *Nicomachean Ethics*

During the 20th century, psychology made a convincing case for the
value of its scientific and applied contributions to society. As a result,
psychologists have been granted professional status, legal standing and privileges, and financial support for our research and clinical activities. Having
received these social grants of trust, power, prestige, and financial support,
psychologists recognized the need for some oversight of the use of these
privileges. It is difficult for outsiders to evaluate knowledge, abilities, and
performance in professions like psychology because of the specialized nature
of these capacities. This makes the ongoing self-regulation of its members
an essential element in the development and maintenance of a profession.
The development of an ethics code, as an expression of professionals' special
responsibilities to the public that provides guidance and enforceable rules,
is one of the defining features of a profession (Bersoff, 2003; Kitchener,
2000). The American Psychological Association (APA, 2002) has devoted
tremendous effort to developing and promulgating its Ethics Code. In the
last half century, the code has been revised eight times, with the most recent
revision taking effect in 2002.

Almost all psychologists (including me) agree that ethics standards in
some form are necessary, but few feel that the Ethics Code is sufficient to
guide ethical practice. The authors of the code and experts on professional
ethics recognize that it is an incomplete guide for ethical practice. A full

summary of the ways in which the code is insufficient would be rather tedious and take up too much space for my purposes. I have selected what I think are the most cogent and useful critiques by many of the leading lights of ethics in psychology to set the stage for my argument for the centrality of practical wisdom. My intent is to demonstrate the widespread recognition of the insufficiency of the Ethics Code and the need to develop a deeper and more nuanced conception of ethical reasoning than it offers. I am not suggesting that the code is bad, or that it should be abandoned, only that its limitations must be systematically addressed.

Experts in ethics have offered various ethical decision-making models to supplement the shortcomings of the code. My examination of these models for their ability to provide additional guidance indicates that they all, in different ways, fall prey to the same difficulties with abstraction that characterize the ethical guidelines themselves. Following this discussion, I suggest that practical wisdom is the essential but unarticulated core of ethical reasoning. My conclusion mirrors Aristotle's dictum that it is impossible to act well without practical wisdom. Adherence to rules, guidelines, and decision models are inevitably insufficient.

Keep in mind that this section of the book focuses less on specific character strengths necessary for ethical practice than on practical wisdom and how it helps us to pursue our aims and ideals. Other authors (Doherty, 1995; Kitchener, 2000; Meara et al., 1996; Tjeltveit, 1999) have discussed the relevance of the virtues for professional ethics in interesting and useful ways; my purpose here is to explore the value of practical wisdom in practicing psychology well. To the extent that these authors discuss practical wisdom (often termed prudence), they treat it as one virtue among many, which I believe underestimates its importance and centrality.

THE INSUFFICIENCY OF THE ETHICS CODE

I begin by discussing what I take to be the five most important criticisms of the Ethics Code. First, there is a substantial consensus that the extant Ethics Code is insufficient to guide psychologists in unequivocal ways through the great variety of situations that we face. Second, the guidelines are written in highly generalized and abstract language that offers ambiguous guidance in most cases. Third, critics point out that the individual standards come into conflict with one another in many concrete situations, and the code does not provide much guidance for resolving these conflicts. Fourth, some have criticized the extensive use of modifiers such as *appropriate* and *feasible* as weasel words that render the code's guidance even more vague and unenforceable. Finally, I discuss the questionable project of attempting to circumscribe ethical behavior within a list of prescriptions and proscriptions.

The Open-Ended Scope of Ethical Issues

There is an intractable difficulty of scope with any ethical code, but particularly with one that is designed to cover the enormous diversity of practices, settings, and clientele within a discipline like psychology. Psychology is a sprawling profession, with an enormous variety of roles in which ethical considerations come to bear and with an astonishing range of activities including teaching, research, individual and family therapy, behavioral medicine, organizational consultation, human resources, and forensic practice. Within any given role, there is an unlimited variety of circumstances in which psychologists need to act ethically. The enormous breadth of activities and considerations that require coverage in an ethics code for psychology presents an insurmountable difficulty for any attempt to provide detailed, specific guidance about every situation a psychologist is likely to face.

If the present scope of ethical issues were not daunting enough, the roles, settings, and clientele of psychologists continue to change. New practice areas such as behavioral medicine and the emerging area of prescription privileges create novel questions and issues. Shifts in the social, economic, medical, and legal contexts within which psychologists operate also generate new ethical problems to consider (Koocher & Keith-Spiegel, 1998). We have only to think of the advent of AIDS, the increasing demands for ethical accountability in research, the use of electronic record keeping and transfer that led to the Health Insurance Portability and Accountability Act (HIPAA) regulations, and the Tarasoff decision, to mention just a few significant contextual changes that have affected psychology powerfully. For these reasons, Kitchener (2000) wrote, "formal codes of ethics . . . cannot address all of the concerns that psychologists face. New ethical questions will arise more quickly than ethical codes or texts can track them" (p. xi).

This variety and flux mean that the realm of ethics is open-ended, both in its present breadth and in its temporal fluidity. It is impossible to draw a line around the ethical realm in psychology and circumscribe it fully by any finite set of principles, considerations, standards, or ideals. Consequently, psychologists must use their judgment to extrapolate ethical decisions and actions from the baseline provided in the Ethics Code when they confront situations that are not explicitly detailed in it. As Pope and Vasquez (1998) summarized the situation,

> codes can call our attention to important values and mark off some of
> the extreme areas of unacceptable behavior, but they cannot do our

questioning, thinking, feeling, and responding for us. Such codes can never be a substitute for the active process by which the individual therapist or counselor struggles with the sometimes bewildering, always unique constellation of questions, responsibilities, contexts, and competing demands of helping another person. (p. xiii)

Much the same can be said about ethical practice in any role psychologists fulfill.

Generality as Solution and Problem

Recognizing the open-ended scope of ethical issues is not a counsel of despair as long as we face the fact that we cannot codify ethical questions so fully that our decisions are guaranteed to be correct if we follow some set of guidelines or procedures. The authors of the Ethics Code recognized the open-endedness of ethical situations and coped with it partly by writing their ethics standards with a relatively high degree of generality so that psychologists could apply them to a great many situations. In the simplest and most common situations, these guidelines are clear and sufficient. For example, confidentiality and informed consent are usually straightforward and the abstractness of the guidelines does not present a problem. The drawback of this generality, however, is that the application of these broad, abstract guidelines is not always so clear. Bersoff (2003) highlighted the consequences of this generality:

> Although there may be codes, guidelines, laws, and policies that will be helpful in making and evaluating an ethical decision, they are often fraught with ambiguity or written in generalized language that may not explicitly help to resolve an ethical conflict. (p. xxiv)

There are a few areas in which the code offers explicit, categorical directives, such as prohibiting plagiarism and sexual involvement with clients, and specifying the order of authorship on publications resulting from students' dissertations. Aside from such exceptional instances, Kitchener lamented, "even when a specific section of the code is identified that may be relevant in a particular case, it may be difficult to figure out exactly how it applies" (2000, p. 18). Pope and Vasquez (1998) concurred that the degree of ambiguity in the Ethics Code makes it inappropriate to seek definitive answers to ethical questions in it. Because the ethical standards are so general, making good decisions and conducting oneself properly is largely dependent on psychologists' judgments about how these abstractions can be applied.

Conflicts Among Ethics Standards

A third problem with the Ethics Code is that its guidelines, abstract as they are, come into conflict with each other in some circumstances. Ethics writers frequently present a classic scenario of a conflict between competing obligations to confidentiality and to protecting third parties from harm. Because the real level of risk is never a matter of certainty, therapists must pit their judgment of the risk against the value of confidentiality to the client and the potential benefits of an unimpaired therapeutic relationship. Bersoff (2003) generalized this situation beyond this particular conflict: "It is the rule, rather than the exception, that at any point in time more than one principle can be applied or argument made for and against adopting a particular course of action" (p. xxiv). Ethics experts often cite the contradictions in the ethical guidelines as a shortcoming of the various versions of the Ethics Code (Hansen & Goldberg, 1999; Kitchener, 2000; Koocher & Keith-Spiegel, 1998). Because of these conflicts in the application of the code, Bersoff wrote, "ethics educators are moving away from a 'correct answer' approach to resolving ethical dilemmas. It is very difficult to advocate such an approach when there are internal conflicts within ethics codes" (p. 130). The sum total of the guidance that the Ethics Code offers for conflicts between ethics guidelines is "When conflicts occur among psychologists' obligations or concerns, they attempt to resolve these conflicts in a responsible fashion that avoids or minimizes harm" (APA, 2002, Principle A). When guidelines conflict with each other, the code clearly leaves it to the psychologist to deliberate about and decide how to reconcile the competing obligations in the situation at hand.

"Weasel Words" or Fitting Modifiers?

By my count, the APA Ethics Code uses the open-ended modifiers "appropriate," "reasonable," and "feasible" 86 times in 13 pages of text. Some ethics experts have sharply criticized the use of these terms for adding additional ambiguity to an already vague document. In comments about the 1992 code that are equally relevant to the 2002 version, Bersoff (1994) said, "the code is full of such lawyer driven 'weasel words' as *reasonable* and *feasible*" (p. 384). Koocher (1994) concurred, "It is largely reflective of the style of lawyers rather than psychologists and seems more intended to narrow one's liability than to stir one to the highest ethical functioning. . . . The new code is too full of qualifiers such as 'reasonable precautions,' 'whenever feasible,' and 'attempt to'" (p. 361). Other authors take a similarly dim view of the frequent use of qualifying language (Dana, 1994; Keith-Spiegel, 1994; Perrin & Sales, 1994; Sieber, 1994; Vasquez, 1994).

The authors of the 2002 code addressed the issue of modifiers in their introduction by explaining that the modifiers are intended to "(1) allow professional judgment . . . (2) eliminate injustice or inequality that would occur without the modifier, (3) ensure applicability across a broad range of activities . . . [and] (4) guard against a set of rigid rules . . ." Although Nagy (2000) admitted that the modifiers "may seem vague, legalistic, or affected" he agreed that they represent a semantic method of broadening the guidelines to make them applicable to "a broad array of circumstances" (p. 5). The authors of the Ethics Code and other authors (Knapp & VandeCreek, 2003; Nagy, 2000) have believed that the flexibility provided by the modifiers is necessary to address the open-ended and multifaceted character of ethical decision making and the breadth of psychological practices.

Authors critical of the modifiers have seen them as problematically ambiguous and as detrimental to the APA's ability to discipline its members. There is certainly some danger that unscrupulous or careless psychologists will make use of these modifiers to defend or rationalize questionable actions, as these authors have warned. At the same time, it seems that their condemnation of such modifiers signifies the pursuit of excessive concreteness and definitiveness in a realm that is too complex and multifaceted for us to capture in a set of rules that provides unambiguous direction and evaluative precision for every conceivable situation. This criticism raises the question of whether some future revision of the Ethics Code should or could provide the kind of unambiguous direction these authors seem to want.

In discussing ethical deliberation in general, Nussbaum (1986) commented that there are two possibilities for how rules can function. One is "that the universal rules are themselves the ultimate authorities against which the correctness of particular decisions is to be assessed" and the particular is "relevant only insofar as it falls under the general form, so the aspiring person of practical wisdom will seek to bring the new case under a rule" (pp. 299–300). The other is "that the rules and universal principles are guidelines or rules of thumb: summaries of particular decisions, useful for purposes of economy and aids in identifying the salient features of the particular case." These "principles are perspicuous descriptive summaries of good judgments, valid only to the extent to which they correctly describe such judgments. They are normative only insofar as they transmit, in economical form" the collected wisdom of the group (p. 299). Her point is that if we want definitive guidance for all situations, we have to become rule-bound by assigning each situation to a particular rule and following the dictates of the rule. In contrast, the modifying terms used in the Ethics Code deny this primacy of rules and invoke the idea that the particulars of the situation will be decisive in our deliberations. Let's call these two options the *episteme* and *phronesis* approaches to ethics. The *episteme* approach is based on universal, comprehensive rules, whereas the *phronesis* approach is based on applying good judgment to identify a response that fits a particular case in light of past experience.

In many ways, it would be comforting to have a set of general principles that we could apply to specific situations in determinant ways, as the *episteme* approach promises. Ethical decision making would be a relatively simple matter of learning the principles and then using the prescribed form of reasoning to arrive at the correct ethical response.

The standard dilemma between maintaining confidentiality and averting harm to a third party can serve as an example for purposes of analyzing the question of primacy of rule or circumstance. There are, of course, clear-cut cases in which there are specific threats to an identified individual, the means to carry out the threat are available, and the client intends to carry it through. On the other side, there are cases where the threat is vague, the means are not readily available, and the client makes credible assurances that he or she has no intention of harming anyone. In such cases, little deliberation is necessary and the appropriate course of action is rather clear.

When one or more of these factors is ambiguous, however, the best option is less clear. Consider a situation in which a client expresses strongly hostile feelings toward an identified individual, is considering buying a gun, and is noncommittal or vague about his or her intention to act. At what point in this layered ambiguity would it be proper to break confidentiality and warn a potential victim? What if the client denies any intention to harm but this denial does not seem entirely believable? This is clearly a matter of judgment when the circumstances deviate from the cut-and-dried scenarios. This judgment has to be based on a detailed assessment of the particulars of the situation and a considered decision about the level of threat. It is impossible to specify all of the possible permutations of threat or ambiguity of intention. I think it is clear that we cannot make such a determination based entirely on any formulated rule. We are faced with a decision in which we use ethical standards as guidelines or as summaries of our profession's collected wisdom, but, in the end, our decision rests on our reading of the particulars.

Ethics codes and principles give us helpful suggestions about the things we should consider in our ethical deliberations, but they are terribly vague and general, leaving us without specific guidance. This guidance emerges through deliberating about the salient features of a situation, not from deductive logic proceeding from general principles. A *phronesis* approach to ethics acknowledges the priority of the particular and is flexible in adapting itself to the nuances of the situation in a way that general principles are hard pressed to do.

In general, rules have authority only to the degree that they match the circumstances. To the degree that the general rule does not fit the circumstances well, we must judge how to supplement the rule and amend it to be correct for the present situation. In this way, we see again that judgment provides greater concreteness and flexibility than general rules can (Nussbaum, 1986). Aristotle emphasized that "when the thing is indefinite, the rule also is indefinite" (p. 133). He illustrated this point with a wonderful metaphor. The individual who tries to make decisions entirely from general principles is like a builder who uses a straight ruler to make the curves of a molding, a strategy that is bound to fail. Instead Aristotle recommended using the lead rule favored by carpenters from Lesbos. This soft metal fit itself to the molding and provided a template for making additional pieces. Our deliberation needs to be similarly responsive to the specifics of the situation we find and deal well with its complexity. This means that the shape of the circumstance provides guidance for our decision making, including whether and how a general rule can be applied.

It is not that rules and principles have no place at all. They are very useful in teaching novices the important things to which they must pay attention in a general way. Rules and principles are also useful in guiding us with respect to picking out the most salient features of a situation. Rules also lend a certain degree of consistency across practitioners and across time that helps us to guard against overly subjective or emotion-based decision making (Nussbaum, 1986).

Beyond the Ethics Code

The language of the Ethics Code focuses on a very narrow domain in which ethics is relevant to our practices only when these practices intersect with circumscribed and enforceable questions such as competence, confidentiality, exploitation, and so forth. This narrowness is in tune with a primary purpose of the code—to make the ethical standards enforceable. In contrast, I have argued throughout this book that all of our activities have an ethical dimension once we recognize that our actions are always in the service of valued goods and ideals. All of our actions are part of our pursuit of what we see as worthwhile or good, which makes them ethical pursuits. This viewpoint stands in sharp contrast to the idea that ethics enters the picture only in extraordinary circumstances that somehow impose duties, dilemmas, and "ethical" decisions on us. Psychotherapy, research, and teaching are human endeavors like any other and are therefore part of our common pursuit of the best kind of life. Practical wisdom is the capacity to pursue those goods intelligently, flexibly, and cumulatively. This line of reasoning suggests that practical wisdom offers a more comprehensive approach to professional ethics than do ethical codes.

Virtue ethics concerns itself with the agent's life as a whole rather than simply with models or principles of ethical decision making that are specially designed for isolated incidents judged to raise "ethical questions." This perspective reminds us that excellence is as much a matter of *how* we go about our ordinary activities as it is a matter of what we accomplish or which abstract principles we uphold. Virtue has to do with the kind of person that we are and with how well our actions promote the goods that we espouse.

The fact that the Ethics Code does not fully cover the ethical domain is apparent in many ways. For example, Kitchener (2000) noted that "issues of truth telling and promise keeping are dealt with in a peripheral manner" (p. 18) in the standards, or addressed only in the nonbinding, aspirational principles. It is also curious that the code mentions only briefly psychologists' responsibility to people whom our professional actions may affect but with whom we do not directly work (e.g., friends or family of clients, students, or research participants), in aspirational Principle A. The code does not hold us responsible for the effects of our actions on third parties. Doherty (1995) forcefully argued that therapists do have a responsibility for the way their actions affect people who are not direct parties to their interventions. Consider spouses or children of clients who may gain or suffer as a result of therapeutic (in)action. Consequential actions such as divorce, infidelity, and child abandonment are frequently discussed in therapy. Can we reasonably wash our hands of the effects that our work with clients may have on others in their lives?

These obvious lacunae in the Ethics Code make it clear that it is insufficient for consideration of many ethical questions. Tjeltveit (1999) reminded us that the Ethics Code is a minimalist standard, hardly one that can provide any more than bare-bones propositions about what psychologists should and should not do. He suggested that professionals "who practice ethically draw upon deeper ethical sources" (p. 266). Because the code is so minimal, it is necessarily insufficient for fully ethical practice. He then cited Kitchener's (1996) recognition that "ultimately, the well-being of those with whom psychologists work will depend on how seriously psychologists take their ethical responsibility to treat others with care." In other words, fully ethical practice will depend more on the character and judgment of the psychologist than on the guidelines found in the Ethics Code.

I have pointed out many of the reasons for the widespread recognition of the limitations of the APA Ethics Code. A number of authors have provided summary comments on these shortcomings and made general suggestions about how to deal with them. For example, Kitchener (2000) believed that the limitations of the code make it important "to provide a foundation for thinking well about ethical issues in psychology" (p. xi). This ability to think ethically is important not just because ethics is complex, but because more is involved in behaving ethically than applying ethical rules or making ethical decisions. Current psychological models of moral behavior (Rest, 1994) suggest that sensitivity to ethical issues, moral motivation, and ego strength are all critical. Principle and rule-bound ethics are incomplete. (p. xii)

Similarly, Bersoff (2003) concluded that because knowledge of the Ethics Code is insufficient, psychologists need to have an understanding of problem solving and decision making.

ETHICAL DECISION-MAKING MODELS

Several experts in the ethics of psychology have gone beyond criticism of the code by proposing decision-making models to help psychologists deal with the ambiguity and conflicts in it. Let's consider some of these models to see how well they address the shortcomings of the Ethics Code and provide guidance where it falters.

A Procedural Model

Koocher and Keith-Spiegel (1998) presented a well-known procedural model of decision making. Their model contains nine sequential steps:

1. Determine whether there is an ethical concern.
2. Consult the available guidelines.
3. Consider the sources that might influence your decision.
4. Consult with a trusted colleague.
5. Evaluate affected parties' rights, responsibilities, and vulnerabilities.
6. Brainstorm alternative resolutions.
7. Assess the consequences of each decision.
8. Choose the best alternative.
9. Implement that decision.

In the hands of a knowledgeable psychologist with good judgment, such a procedure would allow careful evaluations of ethical questions. The authors are clear about the limits of such a model, cautioning that although decision-making models "permit a systematic examination of the situation ... the application of decision-making strategies does not actually *make* a decision" (p. 12, italics in original). For those lacking in knowledge or judgment, the procedure is unlikely to lead to a good decision. In fact, another way to look at this procedure is to see it as a formalization of the three facets of practical wisdom I have been discussing in the previous three chapters of the book. Individuals who are not morally perceptive are unlikely to recognize any but the most obvious ethical issues, and if they do, they will be unlikely to know which ethical standards or commentaries are relevant. The morally insensitive are also unlikely to be able to reflect on how their choices may be influenced in ways that lead to misconduct. Consulting with colleagues, considering participants' rights, responsibilities, and vulnerabilities, and generating alternative actions are part of deliberation. Finally, evaluating consequences of these actions, then choosing and implementing a course of action are part of reasoned choice.

It seems to me that Koocher and Keith-Spiegel (1998) have formalized a version of what a wise person would do to resolve an ethical dilemma. Such an outline can be a helpful tool for teaching trainees about ethical decision making. Yet this model is just as abstract and general as the Ethics Code, with little or no specific guidance. It focuses on procedure rather than the specific content of the situation. There is also ample opportunity for conflicting guidance from the code or from colleagues when using this procedure. The quality of decision making is clearly more dependent on the judgment of the psychologist than on the use of such a procedural model, because the model works only if it is used wisely.

Like all ethics educators, Koocher and Keith-Spiegel (1998) emphasize the importance of consulting others to expand one's wisdom and correct for errors, but the quality of this consultation is dependent on the colleague's wisdom. Wisdom can operate without a procedural decision-making model, but such models cannot function without wisdom. I suspect that these authors are aware of this, but they do not devote *any* explicit attention to psychologists' judgment in their book. If we focus our attention on using or teaching procedures in place of cultivating practical wisdom, we may be missing what is central to ethical action. This model (absent practical wisdom) suffers from the same problems of generality and potential for contradiction that undermine the usefulness of the code it was meant to supplement.

A Hierarchical Decision-Making Model

Kitchener (2000) described a four-level hierarchical model of decision making. She suggested that, in most situations, our ordinary moral sense of what is right and proper is sufficient to guide us in acting appropriately and we have little need of ethical codes or reflection on the ethical course of action. This ordinary moral sense is the first level in her model. If ordinary moral knowledge is insufficient, then practitioners can access more general, abstract forms of ethical reasoning. The most concrete guidance is found in the second level, a professional ethics code. If the ethics code does not provide enough guidance, psychologists can refer to the third level, consisting of foundational ethical principles such as beneficence or autonomy. If further guidance is needed, Kitchener recommended seeking it in ethical theory such as the Golden Rule or utilitarian ethics. Fine and Ulrich (1988) endorsed a similar model, based partly on an earlier formulation by Kitchener (1984), using a hierarchy of increasingly abstract reasoning to resolve dilemmas. This can be called an appellate model of ethical reasoning, because indecision at the more concrete levels of deliberation is to be resolved by appeals to more abstract, formal levels of reasoning. This approach has some plausibility in its similarity to the ordinary response of taking a step back from a situation to get a better perspective on it, and because it is parallel to the structure of the philosophy of ethics.

We must ask ourselves, however, whether appealing to a more abstract level of reasoning will help us to resolve the kinds of dilemmas that render our more concrete grasp of things problematic. The first thing to notice is that the move to a higher level of reasoning is the pivotal feature of this model. We would be inclined to make that move only if we recognized a problem with the level of reasoning we were using. According to this model, we would appeal to the Ethics Code when we saw that our ordinary moral sense was not helping resolve an ethical concern. Similarly, we would appeal to formal ethical principles if the Ethics Code did not address the questions we faced. The model only works to the extent that we are capable of recognizing that some ethical issue is unresolved. This capacity to recognize ethical matters is the function of the ordinary moral sense in Kitchener's model. However, to make the appellate model work, we have to perceive that our ordinary moral sense is incomplete or contradictory, and subsequently that the other levels are insufficient to resolve the issue. The model is entirely inert without this recognition. Therefore, the appellate model is entirely dependent on what I have been calling the *moral perception* of the psychologist. In many cases, this moral perception can be taken for granted, as Kitchener does. But there are clearly psychologists whose moral perception is faulty much of the time, and most trainees need to be sensitized to professional ethical issues before they can reliably recognize them and, even more, be able to perceive when their reasoning needs to be supplemented in some way. The key point is that moral perception is the core of the model, without which the more abstract levels of reasoning do not come into play.

Kitchener did discuss practical wisdom, but it is not clear how she saw it interacting with her decision-making model. The model and her discussion of virtue ethics are placed in separate chapters, with no clarification of how practical wisdom can facilitate the use of her decision model.

The second problem with the appellate model is that it does not resolve the difficulties with generality identified in the Ethics Code. The complaint that the code is too vague to give definitive guidance applies equally well to this model, partly because the code makes up one level of the model but also because reasoning derived from ethical principles or theories of ethics is even more abstract and may contribute even more ambiguity. Ethical principles and theories are typically very broad and generally do not offer clear-cut formulations for how to deal with a particular situation.

Third, ethical principles and theories are at least as prone to contradictory recommendations as the standards in the Ethics Code. This is most obvious when we consider the possibility of consulting ethical theories for guidance. Even if we concentrate our deliberation in one kind of ethical theory, we will confront various interpretations. Kitchener recommended utilitarianism, among other theories, but there are several forms of utilitarianism that offer different perspectives on how to act. The problem of contradictory recommendations is much more acute, of course, if we consult more than one theory. Utilitarians, Kantians, and virtue ethicists offer famously different guidance on ethical questions. The bottom line is that there is no single supreme court at the top of the appellate model of reasoning. Instead there is 2,500 years of recorded debate about dozens of different ethical theories with no prospect of consensus. Just as the recognition of difficulties rests on the moral perception of the psychologist, the ability to think through the relevant considerations adequately is dependent on the psychologist's ability to deliberate well. This ethical decision-making model, like ethics codes, principles, and theories, is only as good as the deliberative capacity of the user. None of them offer guidance instantaneously or automatically, nor do they purport to.

A Multidimensional Model

Hansen and Goldberg (1999) pointed out that procedural models treat ethical decisions in a somewhat one-dimensional manner, focusing only on some form of moral reasoning derived from ethical standards, principles, or theories. Instead, they provided a "matrix of considerations" that includes seven dimensions: moral principles and personal values, clinical and cultural factors, professional codes of ethics, agency or employer policies, statutes, rules and regulations, and case law. These authors briefly describe each dimension and recommend considering ethical questions from all of these perspectives before committing oneself to a course of action. They illustrate how the dimensions of the matrix bear on two interesting case studies and show that its multiple considerations are necessary for good decision making. They assert,

> in order to master the complexity of contemporary ethical-legal decision making, professional psychologists need to understand and know how to evaluate these different considerations, especially when they are overlapping or conflicting. Without these skills, such dilemmas cannot be resolved in a systematic or prudent manner. (p. 496)

These authors' contribution is to call attention to the multidimensionality of ethical decision making, arguing that it goes beyond ethical standards, principles, and theories to include culture, statutory and case law, and organizational context. Yet they clearly understood that their model cannot be a substitute for personal judgment and character in acting ethically.

Their model, like the others discussed here, is suggestive and can offer a map of the ethical terrain, but it also has a high degree of generality and is subject to conflicting demands. In the end, this matrix is really a list of seven general considerations, and Hansen and Goldberg recognized that it is not possible to offer explicit, general guidance on such systematic and prudent ethical decisions because "no model, however elaborate, can adequately capture the complexity of ethical-legal dilemmas and decision making. Resolution of such quandaries cannot be neatly placed in decision trees" (p. 501). They contented themselves with elucidating the complexity "and the variety of available choices" in the hope that making them explicit would improve understanding and decision making. The project of identifying the important considerations in acting ethically is an important one, and Hansen and Goldberg's contribution is useful in this endeavor. They conceded, just as other authors have, that "clinical perception and judgment are central in identifying the salient variables and issues" (p. 496) and indispensable when it comes to resolving them.

An Issue-Oriented Model

Gottlieb (1993) proposed a model of decision making that differs in two ways from other models. He focused only on avoiding exploitive dual relationships, and his model consists of two specific content dimensions along which clinicians can assess whether a dual relationship should be avoided: the duration of the relationship and the degree of power exercised by the psychologist. The longer the duration of the relationship and the greater the power a psychologist has with an individual, the more problematic entering into a dual relationship can be and the more inadvisable it becomes. He presents a two-way table, with descriptions of low, midrange, and high power on one axis and descriptions of brief, intermediate, and long duration on the other. The focus on these two dimensions can be very helpful in deliberating about whether to enter into a dual relationship, because they are two generally important considerations that can guide one's reflections.

In spite of its specificity, this model requires judgment as well, because the assessment of the degree of power one holds in a relationship requires perceptiveness. In addition, the model offers clear guidance at the extremes, but when a situation falls in the midrange of the dimensions, the clarity of guidance also diminishes. It is in these gray areas that we need guidance the most, and we are left with a judgment call here. Although power and relationship duration are two important considerations, we may need to consider other factors such as possible role and boundary confusion or effects on third parties in some dual relationship situations. Finally, the gains in the clarity and issue definition this model provides derive from its narrowness of focus on one kind of ethical situation, which Gottlieb was circumspect in acknowledging. The problem with generalizing this approach is that we would need a similar model for each commonly encountered ethical issue, and the proliferation of issue-focused models would quickly become unwieldy and burdensome. This model does point the way toward a different general approach, however. It suggests that one of the keys to good ethical decision making is to identify the important issues in the situation, which I discuss below as moral perception.

Episteme or *Phronesis*?

This discussion of the insufficiencies of the Ethics Code and the decision-making models designed to compensate for the code's lack of guidance makes it clear that ethical decision making cannot be reduced to the formula or decision tree that an *episteme* approach seeks. Psychologists' judgment and maturity are the keys to every aspect of the application of these conceptions and to a great deal that they leave out. From a virtue perspective, the guidelines and models are best seen as earnest, but quixotic attempts to formalize practical wisdom. The efforts of the standard-writing committees and experts do have considerable value in providing frameworks for teaching professional ethics and suggestive (or at times prescriptive) guidelines. This is essential for educational purposes, to assist psychologists who are struggling with quandaries, to communicate the values and commitments of the discipline to the public, and for enforcement of minimum standards of practice.

Virtually every author on professional ethics notes the importance of the psychologist's judgment in ethical decision making, and this judgment is particularly emphasized in the *phronesis* approach. Bersoff (2003) concluded his discussion of the difficulties of applying ethical codes by suggesting that psychologists need to have "a clear conception of the philosophical principles . . . that underlie the formal code of ethics; and a basically sound character that leads one to respond with maturity, judgment, discretion, wisdom, and prudence" (p. 125). I take the repetition of four near-synonyms to be a particularly strong way to emphasize the importance of wisdom. Similarly, Hansen and Goldberg (1999) stated, "Clinical perception and judgment are central in identifying the salient variables and issues involved in any ethical-legal quandary" (p. 496). References to the need for judgment are generally cited at the point where the ethical standards, models, principles, or theories exhaust their guidance. This widespread acknowledgment that the psychologist's judgment is at the heart of ethical matters is paired with a curious silence in the literature about what that judgment is and how it is attained. I will now discuss practical wisdom as a description of professional judgment. I am suggesting that practical wisdom is more a description of what our best practices already are rather than proposing it as a new alternative. The advantages of reconceptualizing our ethical judgment in this way are that we can be clearer about how we already function ethically, and we will be in a better position to teach this critical component rather than neglecting it in favor of formal proscriptions, prescriptions, and procedural models. The better we understand wisdom, the better we can practice it.

PRACTICAL WISDOM IN ETHICS

Although some authors have criticized the frequent reference to terms such as appropriateness and reasonableness, the code writers' recognition of the necessity of such qualifiers points to the key role that practical wisdom has in professional ethical deliberations. Despite concern that such terms represent "weasel words," our ability to apply the standards in ways that are fitting for a variety of work settings, roles, and situations requires this flexibility. This is one of the strengths of a phronetic understanding of ethics—it acknowledges that we often face a significant degree of uncertainty in how best to carry out our professional work. *Phronesis* also encompasses the multidimensional character of our decisions, which go beyond the ethical standards in many ways, as noted by Hansen and Goldberg (1999).

The *phronesis* approach to ethical decision making normalizes the complexity and disorderliness of many of the situations we face and helps us to focus more on acting well than on doing *the* right thing. There are often multiple and countervailing considerations in our real-life circumstances. Aristotle's perspective clarifies how we actually do make ethical decisions and affirms that there is no need to sanitize and abstract ethics from the messiness of life. Professional work, like life, is often untidy, and no set of guidelines or formal models can remove this disorder. This understanding can help us to dispense with the wishful desire for a formal ethical decision-making procedure that will automatically produce the right answer through the application of abstract ethical or decision rules. Instead, we see that we are immersed in a very imperfect world and that our decisions ultimately emerge from the more or less cultivated quality of our humanity, judgment, and maturity. This recognition inspires us to cultivate character strength, both in ourselves and our students, that promotes good practical reasoning. Seeing ethical decision making as an outcome of character development stands in contrast to attempts to develop tidy algorithms that spit out the right answer to ethical questions if we follow the correct formal procedures. A reliance on intellectually grasped principles, no matter how well developed, can never substitute for character and practical wisdom.

This emphasis on ethical decision making as, in large part, an expression of the character of the decision maker is central to virtue ethics. Making good ethical choices is partly a matter of intelligence, training, and experience, of course. But it is even more an expression of character, ethical sensitivity, deliberative capacity, moral motivation, and clarity about what is good. Being able to absorb training in ethics and to become more ethically capable through experience is a function of the kind of person one is. Those who are incontinent, vicious, defensive, or otherwise impaired in their character will not profit very much from training or experience unless they correct their character flaws. Those who are already inclined to act well will willingly absorb the training and experience as a way to improve themselves and do excellent work. We cannot override or alter character by promulgating guidelines, teaching ethics, requiring continuing education, and threatening punishment. We can, however, address character issues in our admissions and student evaluation procedures, in our professional training, and in the ways that we discuss ethics (Handelsman, Knapp, & Gottlieb, 2002).

It is helpful to remember that from the perspective of virtue ethics, ethical practice is not limited to a subset of our activities or to special or unusual circumstances. Rather, there is an ethical dimension to everything we do. Virtue ethics clarifies that morality is coextensive with human life rather than a subject we study to prepare ourselves for occasional incidents that somehow impose duties, dilemmas, and "ethical" decisions on us. This perspective jolts us out of the complacent viewpoint that morality is limited to extraordinary rather than ordinary circumstances and that our theories and practices are separate from the ethical domain except where they intersect with individual ends, rights, and autonomy. This means that there is no realm of ethical rules and behaviors separate from our ordinary living. All of our actions express the moral stance we have taken, reveal the nature of our characters, and point to the goods we believe are worth pursuing. The mind-set that ethical situations are limited to unusual, sensational, or punishable actions is misleading and suggests that psychologists need to somehow switch into an alternate "ethical" mode to deal with them. In contrast, the phronetic approach to ethics suggests that practical wisdom is involved in all of our activities. If we recognize that we are, to a greater or lesser degree, always acting in an ethically relevant way, then we do not have to demarcate and monitor a separate ethical realm from the therapeutic, research, teaching, and consulting work we do. Furthermore, psychologists with good character will want to go beyond the minimum prescribed by the Ethics Code to incorporate their sense of what is worthwhile in their work in an appropriate way.

A phronetic approach to ethics does not dispense with ethical codes and principles, but it does focus primarily on the particulars of the situation to shape our perceptions, deliberations, and choices. As Nussbaum (1986) articulated, getting it right with respect to the specifics of the case takes priority over correctness according to general ethical statements. This priority shows in that we begin with the specifics of the situation and work to appreciate the salient features. Our appreciation of the particulars suggests to us which ethical considerations are pertinent and guides us toward specific standards or principles in choosing a course of action. The ethical standards, models, principles, and theories aid us in our deliberations about the concrete situation to the extent that they shed light on those particulars. Finally we choose the best of the available courses of action, and that choice has to fit the circumstances well to be appropriate. This choice will conform to formal ethical and legal standards (barring extraordinary cases where these standards are ill-fitting), but the only ones that are relevant are those that the occasion calls for. I describe the process of ethical reasoning below in terms of the three interrelated aspects of practical wisdom: moral perception, deliberation, and reasoned choice.

Moral Perception

Ethical considerations must begin, by definition, with the recognition that something of moral importance is at stake. In outlining the "skills and attributes" necessary for sound moral judgment and ethical behavior, Bersoff (2003) stated, "The psychologist must first be sensitive to and appreciate the fact that the situation does indeed raise an ethical and moral issue" (pp. xxiii–xxiv). To some extent, it is almost too obvious to say that we must recognize the ethical aspects of situations before we can respond well to them, but there are several reasons to emphasize this point. For one thing, psychologists and trainees will vary in their ability to perceive the ethical dimension of their work, ranging from those who are highly sensitive to those who are ethically oblivious or even outright vicious (exploitive, deceptive, or avaricious). Ethical concerns often come unannounced, and if a psychologist is not morally perceptive, an ethical issue can quickly mushroom into a serious problem. A lack of ethical vision can lead to serious harm to those with whom one works, to one's reputation, and to the profession. Handelsman et al. (2002) suggested that ethical sensitivity "refers to interpreting a situation as having moral or ethical aspects and implications, even when no explicit dilemma exists" (p. 736). This is because ethical insensitivity can undermine our pursuit of our cherished goals of improving human welfare and increasing our knowledge, as I indicate in the next section.

This responsiveness to ethical questions is central to the ordinary moral sense highlighted by several authors (Beauchamp & Childress, 2001; Hare, 1981; Kitchener, 2000; Rest, 1983). Human beings learn about what is worthwhile or worthless, appropriate or ill-fitting, admirable or deplorable in our socialization. When all goes well, we learn this moral perception and it becomes more developed, subtle, and complex as we mature. This learning is implicit at least as much as it is explicit, because we absorb it in our cultural milieu. The ordinary moral sense is often a prereflective response to the situations we encounter, one that in general is fairly reliable in orienting us to ethical action (Kitchener, 2000). As Tjeltveit (1999) pointed out, because much of the ethical character of our professional activity is of a "mundane, unself-conscious" nature, we need an understanding of our work that accounts for the habitual tendency to act ethically without much thought. This unself-conscious action grows out of the habituation of a moral sense developed by being a member of a particular society. In the *Nicomachean Ethics*, Aristotle noted that his teachings are understandable and useful only to those who already have this moral sense. This moral sense is, of course, quite fallible, but it provides a basic orientation to what is most important and fitting in our daily lives.

One of the key aspects of moral perceptiveness is the ability to construe an occasion in the best way, to clearly recognize its central aspects and classify the situation in an appropriate way. This allows us, for example, to recognize that this particular occasion raises questions about informed consent, publication credit, competence, or justice. Practical wisdom begins in the capacity to discern which features of a situation are most important and which are less vital. The better we can recognize what is central, the better we will be able to sort through the relevant questions and choose the best response.

As Kitchener noted, this implicit ordinary moral sense may not always offer adequate guidance. In such situations, we have to see that there is something amiss, incomplete, or problematic about our initial responses that needs correction. One of the key aspects of moral perception is attention to one's feelings and intuitions. A nagging feeling or disquiet is often a sign that our ordinary moral sense has led us astray or neglected some important question. When we experience this, it is necessary to review the facts of the situation and sort through what it is that we have misconstrued or missed. This is often a point at which consulting with a colleague is helpful, because simply articulating our unease will often help us to identify what is amiss. Our colleagues can also see things that may be in our personal blind spots or help us to disentangle ourselves from our emotional responses or the inappropriately persuasive "special pleading" of clients or students (Hare, 1981).

Moral perception is illuminated by our pursuit of what we see as good. Virtue ethics portrays all of our activities as directed toward some end that is worth having, and these goods are central to living well, which is the aim of the ethical life. The relationship between ethical behavior and the worthwhile goals psychologists seek is also apparent in the Ethics Code, even though it is not generally made explicit. For example, we see the support of our clients', students', and research participants' autonomy, dignity, and privacy as general goods we should pursue in all cases. We have standards requiring informed consent because we see autonomy as a vital good. We have standards regarding discrimination, harassment, and exploitive relationships because we value individual dignity and justice. Confidentiality follows from recognizing privacy and trust as goods. Each of the standards is related to one or more goods, and pursuing those goods requires behavior that is conducive to them. Our moral perception is properly guided by such key ethical commitments because these commitments highlight what is important for us in a situation.

One of the most vital aspects of professional training is to foster ethical sensitivity in our students. Some students come to us with exquisite moral perception and others are less capable of seeing what is at stake ethically in their work. There are many tools that we can use to teach this sensitivity, including the Ethics Code, the ethical principles that underlie the code, and philosophical ethics. The single most important way we teach ethics is in the way that we convey to students and to one another, through all of our actions, what is important and what is trivial. We do this through what we do or do not do, what we attend to or neglect, what we emphasize or marginalize. For example, the good of individual autonomy is featured constantly in psychology, as is the good of relatively unbiased knowledge. We are constantly teaching ethics, sometimes explicitly, but much more of the time implicitly.

It is important for us to emphasize the cultivation and enactment of ethical sensitivity in ourselves and our students because there are so many factors that militate against it, including a one-sided emphasis on clinical technique or research procedures, as well as financial considerations, inducements of fame or prestige, working in a routinized fashion, burnout, and fatigue. The best way to prevent these powerful and sometimes insidious factors from undermining our endeavors and ethics is to cultivate an active sensitivity to ethical concerns that grows out of good character and a strong commitment to the internal goods at the heart of psychology: knowledge and human welfare. The stakes are obviously very high for the research community and the public, but they are for the scientist as well. Aristotle (trans. 1996) emphasized that someone who acts unethically "can never recover by any success, however great, what he has already lost in departing from excellence" (p. 171).

Psychologists can get confused about the priority of internal and external goods and put income or status above the internal goods of the autonomy or dignity of those with whom they work. We can become too invested in obtaining impressive research results to notice that we present only favorable results or perform statistical gymnastics and lose sight of the internal good of knowledge. We can become too invested in a particular point of view and fail to teach our students to see its shortcomings or fully appreciate the alternatives, thereby undermining our internal goal of helping our students to understand and evaluate knowledge claims without excessive bias. A well-cultivated sense of what is most important, along with clarity about the distinction between internal and external goods, can help us to maintain a clear sense of the priority of internal goods.

Deliberation

As a consequence of the generality, vagueness, and incompleteness of the Ethics Code, deliberation is central to good ethical decision making. As Kitchener (2000) put it, "ethical questions are often ambiguous, requiring a great deal of thought about how ethics codes or the advice in ethics texts apply" (p. xi). Once we, as psychologists, have perceived the unresolved ethical concerns in a situation and identified them, the work of applying the available general ethical considerations to the occasion begins. When we deliberate, there are three primary considerations: (a) addressing our specific circumstances, (b) in a way that allows us to pursue our overall aims, and (c) doing so in such a manner that these goals continue to be worth pursuing. Deliberation is the process of moving back and forth between these considerations to arrive at a resolution that deals adequately with the particular case and enhances or at least detracts as little as possible from the therapeutic, educational, research, or consultative goals of our activity.

Of course, there are some ethical questions that require little or no deliberation. In some cases, our ordinary sense of what is best is sufficient. In our day-to-day work,

> some ethical decisions are made routine in such a way that there is no need to probe more deeply because the analysis has been done for similar dilemmas in the past. Maintaining confidentiality, for example, by not revealing that an individual is receiving psychotherapy unless that person grants permission to do so, should become a habit and should not require careful analysis for each client. (Fine & Ulrich, 1988, p. 543)

Many circumstances are ambiguous in their ethical implications, such as determining what constitutes an adverse reaction to study procedures or when investigators' biases inappropriately affect the interpretation of results. Psychologists frequently find themselves in circumstances in which it is unclear which of many ethical principles or guidelines are applicable. Moreover, we must confront difficult questions about precisely how we should apply the ethical precepts that do seem relevant. In ambiguous or ethically conflicted situations, it is important for us to review our overall goals as a way to clarify which aspects of the situation are most important and most relevant to the key aims we are pursuing. This kind of deliberation helps us to decide questions such as when the potential benefits of a study outweigh the negatives of using deception in research, for example.

One of the key acknowledgments of a *phronesis* approach to ethics is that this ambiguity and conflict in goals or concerns cannot be formulated away. This viewpoint does not seek to provide simple or hard and fast decision rules. Rather, it suggests that we must rely on our deliberative capacity to successfully resolve the ethical questions we face. One of the best ways to teach this kind of reflection is through case studies, a common device in texts on ethics because it allows the writer to elucidate specifics of the circumstances and the reasoning behind the ultimate decision about how to proceed. Some aspects of case studies can be generalized, but their contribution is chiefly one of illustrating how deliberation itself proceeds.

A frequent refrain in any discussion of ethics is the importance of consulting with colleagues. Although this is often presented as a risk management device, deliberating with others has the more important purpose of helping us to think through the intricacies of our work more carefully and thoroughly so that we can act in the best way. This joint deliberation is an important acknowledgment of the complexity and significance of the work that we as psychologists do, and of the inevitable blind spots and confusion we sometimes experience. It is a recognition that we are fallible and dependent on one another in significant ways. As we articulate our concerns and respond to others' questions, we can better appreciate what is at stake and which considerations take priority. Consultation leads naturally to making reasoned choices.

Reasoned Choice

Our individual and joint reflection on our circumstances helps us to generate a set of possible actions to address them. You will recall from chapter 5 that reasoned choice is a matter of choosing the best from among the available possibilities. To choose the best alternative, we need to make an assessment of the likely outcomes of the various potential courses of action. We play the possibilities out in our minds or in conversation with colleagues to evaluate the advisability of proceeding in one way or another. In some cases, one alternative will be clearly the best, and in others we will be left with several options, none of which is ideal or even clearly superior to the others. In the latter case, we need to focus on which alternative best addresses what is most crucial in the situation.

For example, a second-year female student in an applied doctoral program had become a source of concern as reports accumulated that she was not completing assigned work in her graduate assistantship and in the required research group, that she had made offensive comments about gay men and lesbians and other individuals who did not share her conservative views, that she had had several angry outbursts toward male coworkers, that she had been deceptive with several faculty members about her work, and that her attitude toward the faculty and her learning was dismissive and recalcitrant. The faculty decided that some intervention was necessary. There were calls by the faculty members and by the other students she had most offended for her immediate dismissal from the program, and one faculty member recommended firing her as a graduate assistant.

As the faculty deliberated, they found that she had an A-minus academic average and that her practicum work was adequate, if on the minimal side. The faculty considered mandating personal therapy but questioned the extent to which a therapist would focus on the training goals they thought were important. The faculty also recognized that this student had a right to her conservative beliefs, but that she needed to learn a more mature and respectful way of expressing them. The faculty decided that there were insufficient grounds for dismissal, and that even if the grounds had been sufficient they would have needed to give the student the opportunity to improve her performance prior to dismissal. In the end, they chose to focus on behaviors and outcomes that were central to their training program and ones that they could determine, observe, and evaluate themselves.

The director of training (DoT) met with the student and focused primarily on giving her feedback about her disrespectful interpersonal behavior toward faculty members and other students and her inadequate performance in the assistantship. The DoT informed her that she had to improve her work performance or risk the loss of the assistantship and that she had to demonstrate respect for others or risk dismissal from the program, which emphasized cultural sensitivity and interpersonal respect. She was given a very low research practicum grade to reflect her poor performance in her research group. The DoT also pointed out that she had offended many students and faculty and lost their trust through deceptiveness. This feedback was important in helping her to improve her performance in these areas, which was essential in her future work with people who might be alienated or harmed in similar ways. The DoT suggested that she not only refrain from further offense or deception but actually work assiduously to repair these relationships. The DoT also suggested that she might find personal therapy helpful in addressing these difficulties, although the faculty did not require it. The DoT informed her that she was on probation for the next year and that the two of them would meet at the end of the semester to assess her progress.

The faculty made a reasoned choice that this response was best because it put them in a position to determine directly whether her behavior matched program expectations, and it gave her a chance to improve in response to feedback before imposing any drastic consequences. It also linked the ethical lapses in her behavior to specific consequences and suggested concrete things she could do to improve. They were very happy to see that following a brief period of defensiveness, this student took the feedback to heart and made clear and demonstrable improvements in all of these areas. Unfortunately, this outcome is not always forthcoming, and recalcitrant students can create very difficult decisions for faculty.

When we have a reasonably clear sense of what is at stake in a situation and we have deliberated sufficiently to make a reasoned choice, we are much more likely to be able to implement our plans and stick to them. The exercise of practical wisdom gives us confidence that we have decided well and that we believe our actions are the best ones under the circumstances and for our goals. As we progress in a course of action, we will sometimes need to revisit our initial impressions of what was important and reconsider our reasoning and choices, and this represents the ongoing use of practical wisdom.

Because practical wisdom is so closely tied to the specifics of each situation, and those specifics are given a high priority in deciding which responses are most fitting, it can seem to be a species of situational ethics. Situational ethics implies an ad hoc or expedient approach to decision making that is determined either entirely by the particularity of the situation, by the instrumental aims of the decision maker, or by some combination of the two. Practical wisdom has significantly more ethical heft than a purely situational approach because our choices are concerned with character and with pursuing what is good overall. Aristotle emphasized, "It is not possible to be good in the strict sense without practical wisdom, or practically wise without moral virtue" (p. 158). This means that individuals who choose wisely have good character. They are committed to seeking what is good in a characteristic way and they embody the character strengths that make that pursuit possible. In other words, the practically wise individual is someone who is able to take full account of the salient features of a situation, choose a course of action that will facilitate the pursuit of what is good, and carry out that choice with the appropriate mix of virtues (e.g., friendship, courage, temperance, generosity, or justice). Our pursuit of worthwhile goals is a long-term endeavor that guides our actions with consistency and purpose. Far from being merely expedient or arbitrary, practical wisdom relates to ongoing ethical concerns that transcend the situation and the whims or immediate desires of the moral reasoner. It is the pursuit of these overall goods within the particularity of the situation that constitutes the exercise of practical wisdom.

SUMMARY

I have argued that the Ethics Code is a useful but insufficient guide for ethical practice, and that the decision-making models developed to compensate for the limits of the code provide some guidance but ultimately rely on the good judgment and character of the psychologist. The recognition of an ethical issue, the ability to apply general ethical standards or decision-making models to the specific situation, and the ability to choose the best course of action are completely dependent on practical wisdom, which I am suggesting is the heart of professional ethics. Moreover, the Ethics Code does not work without good judgment, but the exercise of practical wisdom, with an understanding of the goods we seek, would result in ethical behavior with or without the code.

I am not arguing that we should abandon the Ethics Code or the contributions of ethics educators, because they have substantial pedagogical value and serve as a common reference point. I am suggesting that practical wisdom provides a broader framework for ethical action in psychology and that we should study and teach it avidly as a core aspect of our profession. Practical wisdom provides this broad framework because it is useful not just within the narrow confines of the Ethics Code but also in guiding our decision making in general, including our response to questions typically designated as therapeutic, scientific, or educational rather than ethical. This breadth grows out of the virtue ethics perspective that all human activities have an inherently ethical dimension.

Emphasizing practical wisdom in our ethical deliberations has the additional benefit of encouraging psychologists to go beyond the minimal standards contained in the Ethics Code. Cultivating wisdom involves becoming a person of good character, and making good choices is largely about how to express that character in pursuit of what is worthwhile. Cultivating practical wisdom within the profession would certainly contribute to the laudable goal cited by Handelsman et al. (2002) of "encouraging psychologists to aspire to their highest ethical potential" (p. 731). According to virtue ethics, such an aspiration requires the integration of practical wisdom and virtue, which is a primary topic of the concluding chapter.

III

CONCLUSION

9

A VIRTUE-INFORMED
PSYCHOLOGY

With the presence of the one quality, practical wisdom, will be given
all the virtues.

—Aristotle, *Nicomachean Ethics*

In Part I of this book, I discussed virtue as it is defined by the pursuit
of what is good, and in Part II I explored practical wisdom and its role in
seeking worthwhile ends. Although this division is artificial, I pursued these
topics separately as a way to explore each in depth. This final chapter brings
the two parts of the book together with a discussion of the inseparability
of virtue and practical wisdom. Following this discussion, I outline how
virtue ethics provides an illuminating perspective on some of our professional
roles and conclude with some recommendations for our profession.

VIRTUE AND PRACTICAL WISDOM

It is worth repeating Aristotle's summation of the relationship between
virtue and practical wisdom to emphasize their interdependence. He said,
"It is not possible to be good in the strict sense without practical wisdom,
or practically wise without moral virtue" (p. 158). In the next sections, I
examine how character strengths and wisdom mutually entail one another.

Practical Wisdom Requires Virtue

As I argued in chapter 5, a concept of wisdom must include some
understanding of what is good and of good character. It would be absurd

to consider someone wise who did not have a firm sense of what is worthwhile or good. One would not consider individuals wise who devote themselves to trivial or derivative concerns in life or are distracted and dispersed in their activities. Wisdom is, above all, an appreciation of what it is to flourish as a human being, to make the most of one's life. Virtue ethics suggests that a clear apprehension of what is good will give rise to a genuine desire to pursue that good through actions, leading to a focused, enduring pursuit of worthwhile aims.

Practical Wisdom and Character

Practical wisdom is the capacity to recognize the best way to act in a given situation and to carry out that action in a way that helps the individual to pursue what is good. To pursue worthwhile aims consistently, an individual must embody various character strengths, as I argued in chapter 2. Recall that virtues are the traits that make it possible to seek what is good. Someone who lacks courage, justice, temperance, or any other virtue would be unable to act well consistently. The virtues are the character traits that make the fruitful pursuit of what is good possible.

It is common to see practical wisdom as guiding individuals in acting well, and this is how I explicated it in Part II. Yet virtue ethics also maintains that wisdom arises from acting well. No one is born wise, and cultivating wisdom is a long developmental process that occurs as one learns how to act virtuously. As one develops one's character, it becomes more and more natural to recognize what is best and most important in the situations one confronts, and it becomes clearer what would constitute the best way to act. As I have noted, one forms one's character one action at a time. This accretion of character creates a habitual way of seeing and responding to one's world that becomes second nature. I described the ability to see what is most important and to recognize how to pursue what is good as moral perception, a central aspect of practical wisdom. The ability to perceive what is important grows out of an individual's sensitivity to questions of worth and significance—that is the individual's character. In other words, practical wisdom arises only from a well-formed character.

One way to see the relationship between good character and practical wisdom is to contrast good character with the other three types of character I described in chapter 3. A vicious individual provides the strongest contrast, because the definition of a vicious person is one who has a wholly distorted perception of what is worthwhile. Vicious individuals are those whose lives are devoted solely to pursuing individual, external goods such as wealth, power over others, notoriety, or slavish appetite indulgence, and they do so through deception, exploitation, domination, and so forth. Vicious individuals cannot act wisely because they are mistaken about what is good and their ends are limited to individual, external goods. They do not recognize shared goods, because their understanding of what is worthwhile is entirely self-serving. They scoff at internal goods as self-deceptive and paltry because there is no tangible payoff for such activity. Thus, the highest goods, those that are internal and shared, are ruled out by vice.

Some vicious individuals can and do act cleverly, however, obtaining their ends through careful planning and stratagems. Yet the quality of their ends makes it clear that they are not wise. Vicious individuals seek external ends for their own sake and this pursuit is actually a kind of slavery. Tyrants seek power for its own sake but must constantly defend and expand their power or they will lose it. Profligates seek pleasure, but pleasure sought for its own sake is short-lived and requires continual renewal. The greedy chase money as though having more is better, regardless of how wealthy they become. The avid desire for external ends is insatiable, and those who pursue them without any sense of internal ends are enslaved to the perpetual pursuit of gratification. This thralldom cannot count as wisdom, even if there is cleverness or even ingenuity in the way the vicious individual approaches the activity. Moreover, it seems obvious that tyrants, profligates, and the greedy do not bring out what is highest and best in themselves or others.

The other two character types, the continent and incontinent, also have limited capacity for wisdom. Continent individuals understand what is good and pursue it in spite of their desires to act in a less worthy manner, for less noble ends. They are frequently ambivalent and torn about how they ought to act. Indeed, these individuals act on the basis of "shoulds," or rules that countermand less worthy desires. This tendency to follow rules or conventions with mixed feelings is not compatible with the clarity and focus characteristic of practical wisdom. The more attention and energy an individual has devoted to inner conflict, the less that person will be able to see the situation clearly and respond resolutely.

The incontinent individual is one who has some grasp of what is good but cannot manage to act consistently with that good. Individuals with an incontinent character combine the inner conflict of the continent with the inability to live up to what they recognize as the best kind of life. This is the pattern of life of the wastrel, not the wise person.

Another way to clarify the centrality of character for practical wisdom is by recognizing what kind of knowledge is necessary for practical wisdom (Dunne, 1993). We generally think of knowledge as knowing about something. This is a detached form of knowing that does not involve the character of the knower. The significance of such knowledge consists in its content. Knowledge about geographic facts or the laws of physical motion is of this type.

Research on therapist factors in psychotherapy outcome presents an interesting example of the limits of content knowledge. This literature suggests that when clients perceive their therapists as warm and genuine, they tend to have better outcomes. This knowledge can be, in an important sense, third-person because simply knowing these facts has no necessary relationship to whether I am a warm or genuine person. As a researcher or public policy maker, such detached knowledge may be valuable. As a therapist, a strictly third-person approach to this knowledge may be less valuable. Such detached knowing may prompt me to pretend to be warm and genuine, which I might do for the sake of improving the effectiveness of my therapeutic work. (Although fake genuineness is, of course, oxymoronic, it is nonetheless a common enough ploy among those seeking to manipulate others.) This would be an attempt to apply general knowledge (*episteme*) to a specific situation in an instrumental manner. That is, warmth and genuineness are treated as techniques that are detached from the kind of person I am. If I am a convincing actor, I may actually improve my therapeutic efficacy with such an approach. From a virtue ethics perspective, any success I might have in this pretense would be due more to cleverness than to wisdom, because treating warmth and genuineness as strategies separates them from the kind of person I am. It seems obvious that it may be clever to pretend to have attributes that one does not have, but it can hardly be called wise. Moreover, attempts to use this kind of information in a strategic manner are subject to all of the difficulties enumerated with instrumentalism in chapter 3.

In contrast, if I recognize the value of warmth and genuineness, and the way that these attributes contribute to therapeutic success, I will see them as worthwhile characteristics. This will lead me to cultivate or highlight these attributes in myself and to find ways to express them with clients as part of my efforts to help them change their lives for the better. In this way, my affect, behavior, motivation, and goals operate harmoniously because warmth and genuineness are (or become) part of who I am. (If I find the cultivation and expression of warmth and genuineness unreasonably arduous or impossible, then the wise course would be to seek a different line of work.) In other words, the best way to use this knowledge is to seek to embody it, to become warm and genuine rather than to act as if I had those attributes. It is only through the embodiment of warmth and genuineness that I can fully incorporate this knowledge into my work. This first-person knowledge of these attributes makes them available in an infinitely richer way than third-person knowledge does.

Acting wisely as a therapist includes expressing warmth and genuineness, among other things. Indeed, it is difficult to conceive of a cold, insincere therapist as capable of acting wisely with clients. In regard to these aspects of the therapeutic relationship, practical wisdom consists in knowing when and how to express these attributes. The wisdom of a good therapist shows up in expressions of warmth and genuineness that fit the situation and help clients to seek their goals. Good decision making as a therapist involves resourcefully engaging one's character strengths in pursuing client improvement. The perceptiveness, deliberation, and reasoned choices of the practically wise therapist are inseparably tied to the therapist's engagement in the relationship with the client and commitment to the client's goals.

One could reasonably object that my choice of therapist attributes presupposes the necessity of this kind of personal involvement and embodiment on the part of the therapist. This is, in fact, precisely the way in which virtue ethics casts light on the importance of character (i.e., that there are traits that are necessary for pursuing desired ends). Nevertheless, it is important to point out that good therapists embody many character strengths in their work. Doherty (1995) and Nicholas (1994) enumerated some of them, including courage, compassion, honesty, and justice. It would be difficult to consider a therapist wise if he or she acted in cowardly, callous, dishonest, or unjust ways with clients. Indeed, for Aristotle, practical wisdom is the form of reasoning that enables one to act in ways that are appropriately brave, fair, and honest given the situation.

Practical Wisdom and What Is Good

Practical wisdom is not an abstract form of knowledge but the ability to reason about specific circumstances and to decide the best course of action for the situation at hand. Practical wisdom is similar to cleverness or shrewdness in that all of these attributes involve recognizing what is essential, deliberating well about a situation, and choosing a fitting response. The difference between practical wisdom and cleverness is that cleverness is amoral, concerned only with the effectiveness of the chosen action. Sternberg et al. (2000) discussed cleverness as practical intelligence, a characteristic that serves successful agents, whether they are saints or tyrants. In contrast, someone who has practical wisdom is centrally concerned with pursuing what is good, and, as we saw in chapter 3, we can pursue the highest goods only by acting in a manner that is consistent with those goods. Therefore, our ability to discern, deliberate, and decide is elevated to practical wisdom by the pursuit of what is good and by good character (Dunne, 1993). As Aristotle (trans. 1999) expressed it,

> There exists a capacity called "cleverness" which is the power to perform those steps which are conducive to a goal we have set for ourselves and to attain that goal. If the goal is noble, cleverness deserves praise; if the goal is base, cleverness is knavery. (pp. 169–170)

Acting wisely means acting for the sake of what is good. We can act well consistently only when we have cultivated a good character. Therefore, wisdom entails virtue.

This recognition of the necessary connection between wisdom and the ethical concepts of virtue and goodness is an important contribution that virtue ethics can make to contemporary wisdom theory and research. Psychologists studying wisdom consistently neglect both how wisdom requires the virtues and how wisdom is inextricably involved in seeking valuable ends. This leaves a gaping emptiness at the center of this research that threatens a reduction of the concept of wisdom to cleverness.

Virtue Requires Practical Wisdom

The enactment of character strengths is also necessarily dependent on practical wisdom, a relationship that authors in psychology frequently neglect or underappreciate in their accounts of virtue. Acting well begins with a recognition of what is important in a situation and a sense of how one can pursue one's goals in that situation, and these perceptions are defining characteristics of practical wisdom. An accurate reading of the circumstances tells one whether courage, modesty, generosity, or justice is required in a situation. A misreading of an occasion can lead one to emphasize courage where temperate actions or modest tact are called for. If an occasion is best handled through a tactful discussion, then a focus on courageously confronting a problem would be ill-fitting and more likely to be comic or tragic than virtuous. Even if one exhibited bravery and a willingness to endure significant risk in the confrontation, these responses would be virtuous only if they constituted the best way to pursue one's aims under the circumstances. Therefore, it is only through one's capacity to see what is fitting (moral perception) that one can recognize which character strengths are called for in a given situation.

Similarly, an appreciation of how best to pursue one's aims in a given circumstance will indicate what it means to act generously, justly, or loyally in that particular instance. Consider a junior professor, Dr. Early, who has been working closely with a senior colleague, Dr. Established, for some years. They have worked together on submitting and administering research grants and have published together. Established has introduced Early to a number of important professional contacts and supported Early's efforts toward tenure. Early has contributed copiously to their joint endeavors, both in the general tasks of the research and in providing cutting-edge methodological skills that Established did not possess. In short, both participants have benefited greatly from the collaboration.

As Early completes the first draft of a breakthrough paper that she had initiated, Established claims the first-author position on the basis of her seniority in the collaboration. Early has to decide whether to accept or contest this claim. There are many ways to construe the situation, and each construal takes different aspects of the situation as the most crucial elements. Early's judgment about the most appropriate response to Established will depend on how she sees the situation. Early can see it in many ways and her construal can be more or less perspicuous, leading to more or less fitting responses.

Early could see this situation primarily in terms of loyalty, because Established has done so much for her. From this perspective, it would be best to acquiesce to her colleague's claim of first authorship out of loyalty because giving up a first authorship would acknowledge her indebtedness to Established. If, however, the claim of first authorship is part of a pattern of exploitation or the exercise of ill-founded prerogatives, then loyalty would not be an appropriate basis for giving up first authorship.

If Early's perceptions of the situation suggest exploitation, then a sense of injustice could lead her to contest Established's claim to first authorship because Early had initiated the project and completed the first draft. It would be unfair and dishonest to give Established first-author credit. Such a course of action would require courage, because Early is the junior member of the collaboration, untenured, and at risk of losing Established's support for tenure, and the collaboration itself, with its benefits, might also be in jeopardy if they dispute the first authorship. Yet if Early is close to a tenure decision and a conflict with Established would ruin her chances at retaining a professorship she values highly, then it may be rash rather than courageous to challenge Established.

Early might also decide to be second author out of friendship, because that author arrangement would somehow benefit their ongoing collaboration, or because it will bring important benefits to her friend, Established, and she wants the best for her. On reflection, it may be difficult to sort out confidently who had the original idea for the project and who was most responsible for its successful completion because the two professors work together so closely and cooperatively. If their collaboration is based on character friendship in which both want the best for each other and work together to accomplish goals to which both of them are committed, then this would be a fitting alternative. If the relationship is better characterized as providing mutual advantage, then Early may be best served by defending her first-author prerogative.

The purpose of this sketch is to illustrate that there are many different ways in which one can read Early's dilemma, and the most appropriate response will depend, first, on how she interprets the situation. Her perceptions will indicate the degree to which loyalty, friendship, justice, and courage are called for. As she sorts out the important elements of this situation and takes account of what is at stake, she will then need to decide how to shape her response most appropriately for the situation, for the relationship, for the context, and for her overall goals. It is essential that Early recognize how this incident fits in with the aims and projects that she is pursuing. A good decision about how to respond to Established must be made in view of all else that is important to her (tenure, the collaboration, the friendship, the goals of the research program, the collegial environment of the department, and so forth). A good decision and response to this situation will require the wisdom needed to deliberate well regarding all of these considerations. Clearly, an individual of good character would not engage in an impulsive, intemperate, or one-sided reaction but would reflect on the situation and develop a well-considered response. This illustration demonstrates that our ability to enact character strengths is dependent on our ability to discern the central aspects of the situation, deliberate about what is fitting in the circumstances, and decide which character strengths are appropriate in our responses.

VIRTUE ETHICS AND PSYCHOLOGISTS' ROLES

I have suggested that virtue ethics can help to integrate our work as psychologists in many ways. This perspective can help us to see important commonalities among the many roles that psychologists perform. Virtue ethics suggests that there are deep similarities between the activity of a profession such as psychology and the everyday actions that our research is designed to illuminate and our applied work is designed to facilitate. In other words, this perspective suggests that character strengths and practical wisdom are equally relevant in both professional and personal living, thereby integrating these two domains.

Virtue ethics provides an instructive perspective on the roles and activities of psychologists because it reminds us that we act professionally to achieve important goods and worthwhile aims. These aims vary, but the quality of our professional activities is dependent on the degree to which our work helps us to seek valued goals. In addition, the quality of the profession as a whole is dependent on the degree to which it contributes to the pursuit of human flourishing generally. Psychologists pursue many goals that facilitate human flourishing, such as the self-understanding our research can provide, the reduction of clients' suffering and the enhancement of their well-being and goal achievement through therapy, increases in organizational harmony and productivity promoted by consultants, justice in forensic psychology, and health in behavioral medicine, to name a few. Virtue ethics provides a framework for understanding and evaluating our profession in a general way through its contributions to the pursuit of what is good. Even though the goals of the several subdisciplines vary, they are each valuable to the extent that they contribute to human flourishing, both for individuals and for the collective. Each of the subdisciplines can contribute in a different and, to some degree, complementary way to this overall goal.

Another way we can see the integrative benefits of virtue ethics is that practical wisdom is a common element in all of our roles. As I argued in chapters 5 through 8, the success of all of our activities as psychologists depends greatly on the degree to which we approach them wisely. Successful interventions with clients, good research choices, well-founded assessments of individuals or organizations, and ethical practice in general require us to recognize what is important in the situations we face, how we should address them in a way that helps us to pursue our goals, and what specific actions we should take given the circumstances and in view of our aims. Although the specifics of what makes a decision wise across these domains differ, the capacity for choosing well can be described in similar terms. The training, experience, background knowledge, and sensibilities to inform the best perceptions and choices must be acquired in the specific area, but practical wisdom indicates the way in which our various capacities can be put to use in the best ways.

The character strengths that psychologists need to fulfill their various roles successfully differ somewhat across domains but also have clear family resemblances. Honesty provides a good example of such family resemblances. Intellectual honesty is a cornerstone of good research practice, because misleading descriptions of procedures or results undermine the essential purpose of science: the generation of knowledge. To the degree that investigators deviate from reporting the actual methods, the whole statistical story, or the full pattern of results, they actually reduce the amount of knowledge we have through disinformation and confusion. In a perfect world, researchers would disclose their work fully, and there would be no incentives for doing otherwise. Given the imperfections of our world and ourselves, there will be instances of deception, from minor omissions to outright fraud. If we keep in mind that misleading statements are inimical to knowledge and that scientific excellence is not possible without intellectual honesty, we will be much less likely to mislead in our publications and presentations.

Excellence in the therapist role also requires the character strength of honesty, but of a more personal and context-specific kind. Honesty as a therapist has to do with conveying one's qualifications accurately, presenting oneself genuinely, with offering a realistic portrayal of what clients can expect in therapy, and with the appropriate degree of truth telling in therapeutic work. Ethical standards related to competence and informed consent are meaningless without honesty. Confidentiality is a kind of promise that therapists give to keep information about their clients private, and promise keeping is closely related to honesty. Of course, being honest does not mean that one says everything that is on one's mind or blurts out everything that one sees as a therapist. Like all virtues, honesty involves judiciousness, so it is not full transparency that is called for but truthfulness in what one does say and do, and this honesty must always serve what is good for one's clients.

Teaching and supervising require a combination of the intellectual and personal honesty discussed so far. Intellectual honesty is necessary in presenting material accurately and in a balanced manner. It is all too easy to represent one's favored point of view as the only one available, or at least as the only reasonable alternative, rather than acknowledging that there are multiple points of view or serious questions about the theoretical or philosophical outlook one favors. Instructors and supervisors are important role models in students' development. Representing oneself accurately and being interpersonally honest with students play an extremely important role in teaching them about the value of truth in psychology. Giving students and supervisees honest feedback about their performance is important for their development as individuals and future professionals.

Honesty and courage frequently emerge together, for being truthful is easy when there is little at stake or accurate statements are uncontroversial. When it comes to helping clients to confront blind spots, avoidance, dissimulation, or other undesirable or painful aspects of themselves, therapists have to have the courage to enter into difficult conversations. Challenging an established theory, a reigning orthodoxy, or the value of one's previous work requires courage on the part of a scholar. Helping students to deal with difficult conceptual issues, challenging them to confront their biases and ignorance, and holding them accountable for their performance requires courage in teachers. Although there is only a metaphorical resemblance between a battlefield and teacher–student interactions around grading, it does require a degree of fortitude to assign meaningful evaluations to students in this era of grade inflation, educational consumer ideology, and administrative aversion to controversy.

Let me share an illuminating example of honesty and courage that a friend and colleague demonstrates in her work. She conducts workshops with psychologists and other mental health professionals on working with gay and lesbian clients. The information she presents is not only professional but very personal as well, because she presents as a lesbian psychologist. She describes these presentations as interesting and fun in many respects, but she finds it very challenging to be so openly "out" in a group of primarily heterosexual professionals. It is not that audience members are actively hostile or closed to learning. In fact, they are all voluntary participants and interested in learning more about this population and its special issues and struggles. The hard part is that most professionals do not know a great deal about sexual minorities, and our ignorance and awkwardness can be painful to members of these groups. She often feels as if she is in the line of fire for all of the projections and fears that are inevitably part of such a highly charged topic. For this reason, each presentation is a kind of reenactment of her coming out, which evokes considerable angst.

My friend does these presentations because they need to be done. She relates, "Gay people are getting hurt day in and day out in therapy." This harm is generally unintentional and a matter of ignorance, but it is also related to unacknowledged fears, hidden prejudices, and other personal issues. Therapists need to know more about this group of clients, about revisionist and repressive therapies, and about themselves and their own biases and projections. In other words, she sees an area where she can contribute to the goods of greater professional knowledge, mutual understanding between heterosexuals and gays, and therapeutic benefit for gay male and lesbian clients. She endures her anxiety and the personal exposure of these presentations willingly for the sake of these goods. Similarly, those who attend her presentations willingly confront their limitations, anxieties, and biases for the sake of the same goods. In this way, she and her listeners are working toward the common goods of mutual understanding, acceptance, and inclusion. It would be difficult to understand the professional work that my friend is doing and appreciate the dilemmas and difficulties she faces without employing concepts like the common good, courage, and honesty. Her actions and those of other devoted professionals could, of course, be interpreted as self-interested. But the knee-jerk self-interest interpretation distorts and obscures the motives underlying such activity rather than revealing anything enlightening about those motives.

CONCLUSION

I have argued in this book that virtue ethics provides an illuminating and, I hope, inspiring framework for psychology. Virtue is relevant to research topics as diverse as close relationships, prosocial behavior, authority, goal seeking, well-being, and wisdom, and they can be deepened when informed by a virtue framework. Broad areas of psychology, such as psychotherapy, science, and professional ethics can be better understood and pursued by cultivating character strengths and practical wisdom.

Virtue ethics helps us to see some extremely important aspects of human activity that are largely obscured in the objectivistic attempt to make psychology value neutral. Foremost among these elements is the centrality of pursuing what is good in both ordinary and professional activities. All human action is directed toward pursuing some goal that we think is worthwhile. Individuals and societies can be, and have been, misguided in these pursuits, but the purposive character of our actions must be recognized to fully understand behavior. Recognizing that psychologists' professional activities are also devoted to achieving certain goods improves our ability to pursue those goods through greater clarity and through enhancing our motivation to work toward them. Setting aside the threadbare veil of objectivism will allow us to see our work more clearly and to engage in worthwhile pursuits more wholeheartedly. We do need to remain watchful that we do not allow ourselves to become overly self-serving, culturally or individually biased, or one-sided in our work. The best way to maintain this more modest form of objectivity is by being aware of the goods we are seeking, how those goods form a part of human flourishing, and how they fit within our culturally informed pursuits. This awareness puts us in the position of being able to question both those goods and our practices through open dialogue with differing viewpoints rather than submerging moral questions with a presumption of moral detachment that places those questions beyond scrutiny.

When considering what is good, it is important to remember that no single way of life has been proclaimed as the ultimate best, either by Aristotle or by contemporary virtue ethicists. These thinkers have denied that the ethical truth can be stated in once-and-for-all, universal terms (McDowell, 1996). Aristotle did not give any kind of foundational argument for the superiority of classical Athenian mores. Rather, he began his philosophical reflection on how best to live by taking this cultural milieu as his starting point. The stress on a universal ethic or a general account of the good life is characteristic of Enlightenment-inspired ethical theories (e.g., Kantian and utilitarian approaches), and we should not read such claims back onto Aristotle.

It follows that, from a virtue ethics perspective, no one has the last word on the best kind of life. In fact, Aristotle taught that part of what constitutes the best kind of life is the ongoing exploration of what is highest and finest for us as humans. Some of that exploration takes place within the limited range of views and practices in a given historical culture. It is clear, however, that the resources and possibilities for cultural and personal self-reflection can be greatly multiplied if one can compare and contrast one's way of life with other cultural and historical patterns. This kind of dialogue serves the overall aim of seeking human excellence. Aristotle (trans. 1996) engaged in this sort of comparing and contrasting of customs in the *Politics*. No one can predict the directions that this kind of dialogue will take. It is an open-ended endeavor that requires courage and a steadfast commitment to learning.

Virtue ethics also highlights the importance of recognizing internal goods, which are those goods that are inseparably related to the ways that the goods are pursued. The most important goods (e.g., friendship, solidarity, justice, democracy, flourishing) are internal because they can only be achieved by acting in ways that embody those goods. The exclusively instrumental cast of most psychological theory, research, and practice has obscured this vital part of human experience. The concept of internal goods not only offers a corrective to a one-sided instrumentalism, it also makes it clear that most of the goods that human beings seek through instrumental methods are important only because they make our pursuit of higher-order internal goods possible. The external goods (e.g., money, status, living space) that we characteristically seek through instrumental activity are a vital part of human life, but their value derives from the kind of life and pursuits they make possible, rather than from any intrinsic value they have.

Similarly, virtue ethics highlights the importance of goods that can only be shared, which broadens the vision of our profession beyond the goods that individuals can possess independently. The depth of humanity's mutual dependence is a core assumption of virtue ethics and provides a useful corrective for psychology's overweening individualism. As human beings recognize our pervasive dependence on others, we can renew our commitment to shared goods as essential to our humanity and as a necessary prerequisite to individual flourishing. We as psychologists must learn to curb our tendency toward a one-sided individualism because the drumbeat of individualism tends to undermine the pursuit of shared goods and thereby limit human flourishing. Recognizing the centrality of shared goods and mutual interdependence can help us to make contributions to our society that are more balanced. Above all, the concept of shared goods helps us to recognize the importance of the common good: that what is good for all is often good for the individual, and that what is good for the individual often cannot be neatly separated from what is good for all.

Practical wisdom is central to excellence in professional and personal activities. The capacity to make wise choices is the single most important personal strength a psychologist can have. Wisdom guides us to what is most important in our day-to-day affairs, helps us to pursue our cherished aims in the best way, and gives us the confidence in our choices that helps us to follow them through. Practical wisdom is at the heart of virtue ethics because if we pursue what is good, understand our situation with perspicacity, and choose our course of action wisely, we will act virtuously, whether in the role of teacher, researcher, therapist, or consultant.

One of the most important implications of this book is that character and practical wisdom are so important to excellence in psychology that they should become an explicit focus of our admission decisions, training curriculum, hiring, professional honors, and, most importantly, of our own self-development. I believe that we already do this to some extent. Good judgment is already a prized attribute in students and colleagues. Honesty and courage are generally valued, and the quality of justice is becoming increasingly recognized as we have been reminded of its importance by feminists, multiculturalists, and advocates of social justice. Our Ethics Code implicitly calls for these qualities, and some authors (Beauchamp & Childress, 2001; Kitchener, 2000; Meara et al., 1996) have related the aspirational segment of the code (or similar ethical principles) to character. For example, standards regarding competence and informed consent can only be actualized if the psychologist is honest. Beneficence is a key aspirational principle that can also be seen as a character strength.

We can enhance our appreciation of character in ourselves and our trainees by making it an explicit part of our vocabulary and our activities. We can evaluate applicants for our training programs and for jobs in terms of the strength of their character. A great deal of programmatic and organizational turmoil and misery arises when students, faculty, or staff are dishonest, unjust, excessively self-interested, or manipulative. Even worse, individuals with significant character flaws create havoc in the lives of clients or through fraudulent scientific reports. It is in everyone's best interest to bring in students and colleagues who have good character and to encourage one another to actively maintain and develop the virtues that make excellence possible.

I am not suggesting that we adopt a judgmental attitude about character or become preachy about it. By keeping in mind that none of us reach perfection in excellence and virtue and that errors and human limitations are to be expected, we will reduce the likelihood of slipping into being judgmental or preachy. Instead, we can do a great deal to promote good character simply by exemplifying it and highlighting exemplars of excellence. We can make it explicit that certain character traits are essential to our various roles as psychologists. An ongoing focus on the goods that we are seeking in our professional activities will help us to promote the character strengths central to our work. We can, for example, remind ourselves and teach our students that the love of truth is the primary motive for our science and therefore honesty is a necessary characteristic of a good scientist.

There are, of course, no simple and foolproof ways to assess character. Therefore, our ability to make decisions about admissions and hiring will be matters of judgment. This situation is not a new one, nor is it unique to questions of character. We already have to make admissions, hiring, and recognition decisions on the basis of our best judgment about the individuals we are considering. There are tangible indicators of an applicant's intellectual ability and achievement in test scores, previous grades, and achievements. Similarly, there are indicators of a job applicant's abilities in his or her record of publications, successful grant applications, teaching evaluations, professional positions held, committee memberships and chairpersonships, and so on. None of these indicators is foolproof, however. All of us have been fooled by applicants or have simply misread the evidence. Even if applicants have qualifications that are unquestionable, we must still make a judgment about how well they fit within the priorities and goals of our organization.

Although character assessment requires judgment, there are some concrete indicators of character that we can use. We can examine the evidence for honesty, beneficence, justice, good judgment, and the ability to work with others toward shared goals, to name a few. Letters of recommendation frequently address (or significantly leave out) indicators of good character. The provision of volunteer or community service beyond what is required is a good indicator of generosity or beneficence. Interview questions can be directed toward assessing an individual's ability to be honest, appreciation of questions of justice, and capacity for wise decision making. Discussions with those who have worked with the applicant can be very enlightening, particularly when questions about character are addressed. Individuals with significant character flaws tend to leave a trail of anger, disappointment, and anguish behind them, just as individuals with good character inspire admiration, attachment, and accomplishment.

In closing, it is my hope that this book will help us to see psychology in a new light, one in which our personal qualities as psychologists, and the personal qualities of those with whom we work and whom we try to understand, take on a heightened importance. I hope that this book will fuel our aspirations to pursue the goods that our profession is uniquely positioned to provide for our society and thereby help to reimbue psychology with enthusiasm and a sense of mission. Above all, I hope that the virtue ethics perspective will inspire us to strive to become our best selves and to reach toward the highest in ourselves in our personal and professional lives.

REFERENCES

Ackerman, S., Zuroff, D. C., & Moskowitz, D. S. (2000). Generativity in midlife and young adults: Links to agency, communion, and subjective well-being. *International Journal of Aging and Human Development, 50,* 17–41.

Agnew, C. R., Van Lange, P. A. M., Rusbult, C. E., & Langston, C. A. (1998). Cognitive interdependence: Commitment and the mental representation of close relationships. *Journal of Personality and Social Psychology, 74,* 939–954.

Allport, G. W. (1921). Personality and character. *Psychological Bulletin, 18,* 441–455.

Allport, G. W. (1937). *Personality: A psychological interpretation.* New York: Henry Holt.

Allport, G. W., & Vernon, P. E. (1930). The field of personality. *Psychological Bulletin, 27,* 677–730.

American Psychiatric Association. (2000). *Diagnostic and statistical manual of mental disorders* (4th ed., text revision). Washington, DC: Author.

American Psychological Association. (2002). Ethical principles of psychologists and code of conduct. *American Psychologist, 57,* 1060–1073.

American Psychological Association. (2003a). *About APA* [includes mission statement]. Retrieved February 6, 2004, from http://www.apa.org/about/

American Psychological Association. (2003b). Guidelines on multicultural education, training, research, practice, and organizational change for psychologists. *American Psychologist, 58,* 377–402.

American Psychological Society. (2003). *About APS* [includes mission statement]. Retrieved February 6, 2004, from http://www.psychologicalscience.org/about/

Annas, J. (1993). *The morality of happiness.* Oxford, England: Oxford University Press.

Aristotle. (1996). *The politics and the constitution of Athens* (S. Everson, Trans.). Cambridge, England: Cambridge University Press.

Aristotle. (1998). *The Nicomachean ethics* (D. Ross, Trans.). Oxford, England: Oxford University Press.

Aristotle. (1999). *Nicomachean ethics* (M. Ostwald, Trans.). Upper Saddle River, NJ: Prentice Hall.

Aron, A., Aron, E. N., & Smollan, D. (1992). The Inclusion of Other in the Self (IOS) Scale and the structure of interpersonal closeness. *Journal of Personality and Social Psychology, 63,* 596–612.

Aron, A., Aron, E. N., Tudor, M., & Nelson, G. (1991). Close relationships as including other in the self. *Journal of Personality and Social Psychology, 60,* 241–253.

Aron, A., Paris, M., & Aron, E. N. (1995). Falling in love: Prospective studies of self-concept change. *Journal of Personality and Social Psychology, 69,* 1102–1112.

Arons, M., & Richards, R. (2001). Two noble insurgencies: Creativity and humanistic psychology. In K. J. Schneider, J. F. T. Bugental, & J. F. Pierson (Eds.), *The handbook of humanistic psychology* (pp. 127–142). Thousand Oaks, CA: Sage.

Austin, J. T., & Vancouver, J. B. (1996). Goal constructs in psychology: Structure, process, and content. *Psychological Bulletin, 120,* 338–375.

Baltes, P. B., & Smith, J. (1990). Toward a psychology of wisdom and its ontogenesis. In R. J. Sternberg (Ed.), *Wisdom: Its nature, origin, and development* (pp. 87–120). Cambridge, England: Cambridge University Press.

Baltes, P. B., & Staudinger, U. M. (2000). Wisdom: A metaheuristic (pragmatic) to orchestrate mind and virtue toward excellence. *American Psychologist, 55,* 122–136.

Baltes, P. B., Staudinger, U. M., Maercker, A., & Smith, J. (1995). People nominated as wise: A comparative study of wisdom-related knowledge. *Psychology and Aging, 10,* 155–166.

Batson, C. D. (1998). Altruism and prosocial behavior. In D. T. Gilbert, S. T. Fiske, & G. Lindzey (Eds.), *The handbook of social psychology* (pp. 282–316). Boston: McGraw-Hill.

Baucom, D. H., Epstein, N., & LaTaillade, J. J. (2002). Cognitive-behavioral couple therapy. In A. S. Gurman & N. S. Jacobson (Eds.), *Clinical handbook of couple therapy* (pp. 26–58). New York: Guilford Press.

Baumeister, R. F. (1987). How the self became a problem: A psychological review of historical research. *Journal of Personality and Social Psychology, 52,* 163–176.

Baumeister, R. F., & Exline, J. J. (1999). Virtue, personality, and social relations: Self-control as the moral muscle. *Journal of Personality, 67,* 1165–1194.

Baumeister, R. F., & Exline, J. J. (2000). Self-control, morality, and human strength. *Journal of Social and Clinical Psychology, 19,* 29–42.

Baumeister, R. F., & Leary, M. R. (1995). The need to belong: Desire for interpersonal attachments as a fundamental human motivation. *Psychological Bulletin, 117,* 497–529.

Bayley, J. (2000). *Iris and her friends: A memoir of memory and desire.* New York: Norton.

Bayley, J. (2001). *Elegy for Iris.* New York: St. Martin's Press.

Beauchamp, T. L., & Childress, J. F. (2001). *Principles of biomedical ethics.* Oxford, England: Oxford University Press.

Beiner, R. (1992). *What's the matter with liberalism?* Berkeley: University of California Press.

Bell, D. (1978). *The cultural contradictions of capitalism.* New York: Basic Books.

Bellah, R. N., Madsen, R., Sullivan, W. M., Swidler, A., & Tipton, S. M. (1985). *Habits of the heart.* Los Angeles: University of California Press.

Bennett, W. (1993). *The book of virtues: A treasury of great moral stories.* New York: Simon & Schuster.

Bersoff, D. N. (1994). Explicit ambiguity: The 1992 ethics code as an oxymoron. *Professional Psychology: Research and Practice, 25,* 382–387.

Bersoff, D. N. (2003). *Ethical conflicts in psychology* (3rd ed.). Washington, DC: American Psychological Association.

Beutler, L. E., Malik, M., Alimouhamed, S., Harwood, T. M., Talebi, H., Noble, S., & Wong, E. (2004). Therapist variables. In M. J. Lambert (Ed.), *Bergin and Garfield's handbook of psychotherapy and behavior change* (5th ed., pp. 227–306). New York: Wiley.

Blatt, S. J., Sanislow, C. A., Zuroff, D. C., & Pilkonis, P. A. (1996). Characteristics of effective therapists: Further analysis of data from the National Institute of Mental Health treatment of depression collaborative research program. *Journal of Consulting and Clinical Psychology, 64*, 1276–1284.

Broadie, S. (1991). *Ethics with Aristotle.* Oxford, England: Oxford University Press.

Bronfenbrenner, U., McClelland, P., Wethington, E., Moen, P., & Ceci, S. (1996). *The state of Americans: This generation and the next.* New York: Free Press.

Bruner, J. (1990). *Acts of meaning.* Cambridge, MA: Harvard University Press.

Buchler, J. (Ed.). (1955). *Philosophical writings of Pierce.* New York: Dover.

Buehlman, K. T., Gottman, J. M., & Katz, L. F. (1992). How a couple views their past predicts their future: Predicting divorce from an oral history interview. *Journal of Family Psychology, 5*, 295–318.

Burton, R. V. (1963). Generality of honesty reconsidered. *Psychological Review, 70*, 481–499.

Carnevale, P. J. D., & Isen, A. M. (1986). The influence of positive affect and visual access on the discovery of integrative solutions in bilateral negotiation. *Organizational Behavior and Human Decision Processes, 37*, 1–13.

Carrere, S., Buehlman, K. T., Gottman, J. M., Coan, J. A., & Ruckstuhl, L. (2000). Predicting marital stability and divorce in newlywed couples. *Journal of Family Psychology, 14*, 42–58.

Cassandro, V. J., & Simonton, D. K. (2003). Creativity and genius. In C. L. M. Keyes & J. Haidt (Eds.), *Flourishing: Positive psychology and the life well-lived* (pp. 163–183). Washington, DC: American Psychological Association.

Cawley, M. J., III, Martin, J. E., & Johnson, J. A. (2000). A virtues approach to personality. *Personality and Individual Differences, 28*, 997–1013.

Chandler, M. J., & Holliday, S. G. (1990). Wisdom in a postapocalyptic age. In R. J. Sternberg (Ed.), *Wisdom: Its nature, origins, and development* (pp. 121–141). Cambridge, England: Cambridge University Press.

Chang, E. C., & Sanna, L. J. (Eds.). (2003). *Virtue, vice, and personality: The complexity of behavior.* Washington, DC: American Psychological Association.

Christensen, A., & Jacobson, N. S. (1994). Who (or what) can do psychotherapy: The status and challenge of nonprofessional therapies. *Psychological Science, 5*, 8–14.

Cialdini, R. B., Brown, S. L., Lewis, B. P., Luce, C., & Neuberg, S. L. (1997). Reinterpreting the empathy-altruism relationship: When one into one equals oneness. *Journal of Personality and Social Psychology, 73*, 481–494.

Clark, L. A., Watson, D., & Reynolds, S. (1995). Diagnosis and classification of psychopathology: Challenges to the future system and future directions. *Annual Review of Psychology, 46,* 121–153.

Clark, M. S., Mills, J., & Powell, M. C. (1986). Keeping track of needs in communal and exchange relationships. *Journal of Personality and Social Psychology, 51,* 333–338.

Clarken, J. F., & Levy, K. N. (2004). The influence of client variables on psychotherapy. In M. J. Lambert (Ed.), *Bergin and Garfield's handbook of psychotherapy and behavior change* (5th ed., pp. 194–226). New York: Wiley.

Clary, E. G., Snyder, M., Ridge, R. D., Copeland, J., Stukas, A. A., Haugen, J., & Miene, P. (1998). Understanding and assessing the motivations of volunteers: A functional approach. *Journal of Personality and Social Psychology, 74,* 1516–1530.

Clayton, V. P., & Birren, J. E. (1980). The development of wisdom across the life span: A reexamination of an ancient topic. In P. B. Baltes & O. G. Brim Jr. (Eds.), *Lifespan development and behavior* (Vol. 3, pp. 103–135). New York: Academic Press.

Colby, A., & Damon, W. (1995). The development of extraordinary moral commitment. In M. Killen & D. Hart (Eds.), *Morality in everyday life: Developmental perspectives* (pp. 342–370). Cambridge, England: Cambridge University Press.

Costa, P. T., Jr., & McCrae, R. R. (1991). Facet scales for agreeableness and conscientiousness: A revision of the NEO Personality Inventory. *Personality and Individual Differences, 12,* 887–898.

Covey, S. R., Merrill, S. R., & Merrill, R. R. (1996). *First things first: To live, to love, to learn, to leave a legacy.* New York: Free Press.

Crits-Christoph, P., & Mintz, J. (1991). Implications of therapist effects for the design and analysis of comparative studies of psychotherapies. *Journal of Consulting and Clinical Psychology, 59,* 20–26.

Csikszentmihaly, M., & Csikszentmihaly, I. (1994). *Optimal experience: Psychological studies of flow in consciousness.* Cambridge, England: Cambridge University Press.

Cushman, P. (1990). Why the self is empty. *American Psychologist, 45,* 599–611.

Cushman, P. (1995). *Constructing the self, constructing America: A cultural history of psychotherapy.* Reading, MA: Addison-Wesley.

Dana, R. H. (1994). Testing and assessment ethics for all persons: Beginning and agenda. *Professional Psychology: Research and Practice, 25,* 349–354.

Danziger, K. (1990). *Constructing the subject: Historical origins of psychological research.* Cambridge, England: Cambridge University Press.

Darley, J. M., & Batson, C. D. (1973). From Jerusalem to Jericho: A study of situational and dispositional variables in helping behavior. *Journal of Personality and Social Psychology, 27,* 100–108.

Davis, M. H. (1994). *Empathy: A social psychological approach.* Madison, WI: Brown & Benchmark.

Davis, M. H., & Franzoi, S. (1991). Stability and change in adolescent self-consciousness and empathy. *Journal of Research in Personality, 25,* 70–87.

de Tocqueville, A. (1969). *Democracy in America* (J. P. Meyer, Ed., G. Lawrence, Trans.). New York: Doubleday Anchor. (Original work published 1830)

Dehue, F. M., McClintock, C. G., & Liebrand, W. B. (1993). Social value related response latencies: Unobtrusive evidence for individual differences in information processing. *European Journal of Social Psychology, 23,* 273–293.

DeNeve, K. M., & Cooper, H. (1998). The happy personality: A meta-analysis of 137 personality traits and subjective well-being. *Psychological Bulletin, 124,* 197–229.

Diener, E. (2000). Subjective well-being: The science of happiness and a proposal for a national index. *American Psychologist, 55,* 34–43.

Diener, E. Sandvik, E., Seidlitz, L., & Diener, M. (1993). The absolute relationship between income and subjective well-being: Relative or absolute? *Social Indicators Research, 28,* 195–223.

Dixon, R. A., & Baltes, P. B. (1986). Toward life-span research on the functions and pragmatics of intelligence. In R. J. Sternberg & R. K. Wagner (Eds.), *Practical intelligence: Nature and origins of competence in the everyday world* (pp. 203–234). New York: Cambridge University Press.

Doherty, W. J. (1995). *Soul searching: Why psychotherapy must promote moral responsibility.* New York: Basic Books.

Doris, J. M. (2002). *Lack of character: Personality and moral behavior.* Cambridge, England: Cambridge University Press.

Downing, J. N. (2000). *Between conviction and uncertainty: Philosophical guidelines for the practicing psychotherapist.* Albany: State University of New York Press.

Drane, J. F. (1994). Character and the moral life: A virtue approach to biomedical ethics. In E. R. DuBose, R. P. Hamel, & L. J. O'Connell (Eds.), *A matter of principles? Ferment in U.S. bioethics* (pp. 284–309). Valley Forge, PA: Trinity Press International.

Dunne, J. (1993). *Back to the rough ground: Practical judgment and the lure of technique.* Notre Dame, IN: Notre Dame University Press.

Einstein, D., & Lanning, K. (1998). Shame, guilt, ego development, and the five-factor model of personality. *Journal of Personality and Social Psychology, 66,* 555–582.

Eisenberg, N. (2000). Emotion, regulation, and moral development. *Annual Review of Psychology, 51,* 665–697.

Eisenberg, N. (2002). Empathy-related emotional responses, altruism, and their socialization. In R. J. Davidson & A. Harrington (Eds.), *Visions of compassion: Western scientists and Tibetan Buddhists examine human nature* (pp. 131–164). London: Oxford University Press.

Eisenberg, N., Carlo, G., Murphy, B., & Van Court, P. (1995). Prosocial development in late adolescence: A longitudinal study. *Child Development, 66,* 911–936.

Eisenberg, N., Guthrie, I. K., Cumberland, A., Murphy, B. C., Shepard, S. A., Zhou, Q., & Carlo, G. (2002). Prosocial development in early adulthood: A longitudinal study. *Journal of Personality and Social Psychology, 82,* 993–1006.

Eisenberg, N., Guthrie, I. K., Murphy, B. C., Shepard, S. A., Cumberland, A., & Carlo, G. (1999). Consistency and development of prosocial dispositions: A longitudinal study. *Child Development, 70,* 1360–1372.

Eisenberg, N., Miller, P. A., Shell, R., McNalley, S., & Shea, C. (1991). Prosocial development in adolescence: A longitudinal study. *Developmental Psychology, 27,* 849–857.

Eisenberg, N., & Mussen, P. H. (1989). *The roots of prosocial behavior in children.* Cambridge, England: Cambridge University Press.

Eisenberg, N., & Shell, R. (1986). The relation of prosocial moral judgment and behavior in children: The mediating role of cost. *Personality and Social Psychology Bulletin, 12,* 426–433.

Emler, N. (1999). Moral character. In V. J. Derlega & B. A. Winstead (Eds.), *Personality: Contemporary theory and research* (2nd ed., pp. 376–404). Chicago: Nelson-Hall.

Emmons, R. A. (1986). Personal strivings: An approach to personality and subjective well-being. *Journal of Personality and Social Psychology, 51,* 1058–1068.

Emmons, R. A. (1991). Personal strivings, daily life events, and psychological and physical well-being. *Journal of Personality, 59,* 453–472.

Emmons, R. A. (2003). Personal goals, life meaning, and virtue: Wellsprings of a positive life. In C. L. M. Keyes & J. Haidt (Eds.), *Flourishing: Positive psychology and the life well-lived* (pp. 105–128). Washington, DC: American Psychological Association.

Emmons, R. A., & Crumpler, C. A. (2000). Gratitude as a human strength: Appraising the evidence. *Journal of Social and Clinical Psychology, 19,* 56–69.

Emmons, R. A., & King, L. A. (1988). Conflict among personal strivings: Immediate and long-term implications for psychological and physical well-being. *Journal of Personality and Social Psychology, 54,* 1040–1048.

Epstein, S., & O'Brien, E. J. (1985). The person-situation debate in historical and current perspective. *Psychological Bulletin, 98,* 513–537.

Eron, L. D. (1987). The development of aggressive behavior from the perspective of a developing behaviorism. *American Psychologist, 42,* 435–442.

Eron, L., Huesmann, R., Spindler, A., Guerra, N., Henry, D., & Tolan, P. (2002). A cognitive-ecological approach to preventing aggression in urban settings: Initial outcomes for high-risk children. *Journal of Consulting and Clinical Psychology, 70,* 179–194.

Eysenck, H. F. (1952). The effects of psychotherapy: An evaluation. *Journal of Consulting Psychology, 16,* 319–324.

Ferguson, T. J., & Stegge, H. (1998). Measuring guilt in children: A rose by any other name still has thorns. In N. J. Bybee (Ed.), *Guilt in children* (pp. 19–74). San Diego, CA: Academic Press.

Fine, M. A., & Ulrich, L. P. (1988). Integrating psychology and philosophy in teaching a graduate course in ethics. *Professional Psychology: Research and Practice, 19,* 542–546.

Finkel, E. J., Rusbult, C. E., Kumashiro, M., & Hannon, P. A. (2002). Dealing with betrayal in close relationships: Does commitment promote forgiveness? *Journal of Personality and Social Psychology, 82,* 956–974.

Fiske, A. P. (1991). The cultural relativity of selfish individualism: Anthropological evidence that humans are inherently sociable. In M. S. Clark (Ed.), *Prosocial behavior* (pp. 176–214). Thousand Oaks, CA: Sage.

Flanagan, O. (1991). *Varieties of moral personality: Ethics and psychological realism.* Cambridge, MA: Harvard University Press.

Flyvbjerg, B. (2001). *Making social science matter: Why social inquiry fails and how it can succeed again.* Cambridge, England: Cambridge University Press.

Ford, M. E. (1992). *Motivating humans: Goals, emotions, and personal agency beliefs.* Hillsdale, NJ: Erlbaum.

Fowers, B. J. (1998). Psychology and the good marriage: Social theory as practice. *American Behavioral Scientist, 41,* 516–541.

Fowers, B. J. (2000). *Beyond the myth of marital happiness.* San Francisco: Jossey-Bass.

Fowers, B. J. (2001). The limits of a technical concept of a good marriage: Examining the role of virtues in communication skills. *Journal of Marital and Family Therapy, 27,* 327–340.

Fowers, B. J. (2003). Reason and human finitude: In praise of practical wisdom. *American Behavioral Scientist, 47,* 415–426.

Fowers, B. J. (2004). *Generosity.* Unpublished manuscript.

Fowers, B. J. (2005). Psychotherapy, character, and the good life. In B. Slife, J. Reber, & F. C. Richardson (Eds.), *Critical thinking about psychology: Hidden assumptions and plausible alternatives* (pp. 39–59). Washington, DC: American Psychological Association.

Fowers, B. J., Bucker, J., Calbeck, K. B., & Harrigan, P. (2005). *How do psychologists define a good marriage?* Unpublished manuscript.

Fowers, B. J., & Davidov, B. (2005). *The virtue of multiculturalism.* Manuscript in preparation.

Fowers, B. J., Lyons, E. M., & Montel, K. H. (1996). Positive illusions about marriage: Self-enhancement or relationship enhancement? *Journal of Family Psychology, 10,* 192–208.

Fowers, B. J., Lyons, E., Montel, K., & Shaked, N. (2001). Positive illusions about marriage among married and single individuals. *Journal of Family Psychology, 15,* 95–109.

Fowers, B. J., & Richardson, F. C. (1993). Individualism and aggression: A hermeneutic analysis of Huesman and Eron's cognitive theory of aggression. *Theory & Psychology, 3,* 353–377.

Frankena, W. K. (1973). *Ethics* (2nd ed.). Englewood Cliffs, NJ: Prentice-Hall.

Fromm, E. (1965). *Escape from freedom*. New York: Avon. (Original work published 1941)

Fukuyama, F. (1999). *The great disruption: Human nature and the reconstitution of social order*. New York: Free Press.

Gadamer, H. (1975). *Truth and method*. New York: Crossroad Publishing.

Geertz, C. (1973). *The interpretation of cultures*. New York: Basic Books.

Gilligan, C. (1982). *In a different voice: Psychological theory and women's development*. Cambridge, MA: Harvard University Press.

Gollwitzer, P. M., Heckhausen, H., & Steller, B. (1990). Deliberative versus implemental mind-sets: Cognitive tuning toward congruous thoughts and information. *Journal of Personality and Social Psychology, 59,* 1119–1127.

Gollwitzer, P. M., & Kinney, R. F. (1989). Effects of deliberative and implemental mind-sets on illusion of control. *Journal of Personality and Social Psychology, 56,* 531–542.

Gottlieb, M. C. (1993). Avoiding exploitive dual relationships: A decision-making model. *Psychotherapy: Theory, Research, Practice, Training, 30,* 41–48.

Greenberg, L. S., & Johnson, S. M. (1988). *Emotion focused therapy for couples*. New York: Guilford Press.

Grusec, J. E. (1991). The socialization of altruism. In M. S. Clark (Ed.), *Prosocial behavior* (pp. 9–33). Thousand Oaks, CA: Sage.

Guignon, C. B. (1983). *Heidegger and the problem of knowledge*. Indianapolis, IN: Hackett Publishing.

Guignon, C. B. (1993). Authenticity, moral values, and psychotherapy. In C. B. Guignon (Ed.), *Cambridge companion to Heidegger* (pp. 215–239). Cambridge, England: Cambridge University Press.

Guignon, C. B. (2002). Hermeneutics, authenticity, and the aims of psychology. *Journal of Theoretical and Philosophical Psychology, 22,* 83–102.

Haidt, J. (2003). Elevation and the positive psychology of morality. In C. L. M. Keyes & J. Haidt (Eds.), *Flourishing: Positive psychology and the life well-lived* (pp. 275–289). Washington, DC: American Psychological Association.

Handelsman, M. M., Knapp, S., & Gottlieb, M. C. (2002). Positive ethics. In C. R. Snyder & S. J. Lopez (Eds.), *Handbook of positive psychology* (pp. 731–744). Oxford, England: Oxford University Press.

Hansen, N. D., & Goldberg, S. G. (1999). Navigating the nuances: A matrix of considerations for ethical-legal dilemmas. *Professional Psychology: Research and Practice, 30,* 495–503.

Hare, R. (1981). The philosophical basis of psychiatric ethics. In S. Block & P. Chodoff (Eds.), *Psychiatric ethics* (pp. 31–45). Oxford, England: Oxford University Press.

Harkless, L. E., & Fowers, B. J. (in press). Similarities and differences in relational boundaries among heterosexuals, gay men, and lesbians. *Psychology of Women's Quarterly*.

Hart, D., Yates, M., Fegley, S., & Wilson, G. (1995). Moral commitment in inner-city adolescents. In M. Killen & D. Hart (Eds.), *Morality in everyday life: Developmental perspectives* (pp. 317–341). Cambridge, England: Cambridge University Press.

Hartshorne, H., & May, M. A. (1928). *Studies in the nature of character: Vol. 1. Studies in deceit.* New York: Macmillan.

Hartshorne, H., May, M. A., & Maller, J. B. (1929). *Studies in the nature of character: Vol. 2. Studies in service and self-control.* New York: Macmillan.

Hartshorne, H., May, M. A., & Shuttleworth, F. K. (1930). *Studies in the nature of character: Vol. 3. Studies in the organization of character.* New York: Macmillan.

Hawkins, A. J., Fowers, B. J., Carroll, J. S., & Yang, C. (in press). Conceptualizing and measuring marital virtues. In S. Hofferth & L. Casper (Eds.), *Handbook of measurement issues in family research.* Hillsdale, NJ: Erlbaum.

Heidegger, M. (1962). *Being and time* (J. Macquarrie & E. Robinson, Trans.). New York: Harper & Row.

Holliday, S. G., & Chandler, M. J. (1986). *Wisdom: Explorations in adult competence.* Basel, Switzerland: Karger.

Hursthouse, R. (1999). *On virtue ethics.* Oxford, England: Oxford University Press.

Huston, T. L., & Burgess, R. L. (1979). Social exchange in developing relationships: An overview. In R. L. Burgess & T. L. Huston (Eds.), *Social exchange in developing relationships* (pp. 3–28). San Diego, CA: Academic Press.

Isen, A. M., & Levin, P. F. (1972). Effect of feeling good on helping: Cookies and kindness. *Journal of Personality and Social Psychology, 21,* 381–388.

Jensen, J. P., Bergin, A. E., & Greaves, D. W. (1990). The meaning of eclecticism: New survey and analysis of components. *Professional Psychology: Research and Practice, 21,* 124–130.

Kant, I. (1964). *Groundwork of the metaphysics of morals* (H. J. Paton, Trans.). New York: Harper & Row. (Original work published 1785)

Kaplan, M., & Maddux, J. E. (2002). Goals and marital satisfaction: Perceived support for personal goals and collective efficacy for collective goals. *Journal of Social and Clinical Psychology, 21,* 157–164.

Karasu, T. B. (1992). The worst of times, the best of times: Psychotherapy in the 1990s. *Journal of Psychotherapy Practice and Research, 1,* 2–15.

Karoly, P. (1999). A goal systems–self-regulatory perspective on personality, psychopathology, and change. *Review of General Psychology, 3,* 264–291.

Kasser, T., & Ryan, R. M. (1993). A dark side of the American dream: Correlates of financial success as a central life aspiration. *Journal of Personality and Social Psychology, 65,* 410–422.

Kasser, T., & Ryan, R. M. (1996). Further examining the American dream: Differential correlates of intrinsic and extrinsic goals. *Personality and Social Psychology Bulletin, 22,* 280–287.

Kazdin, A. E. (1986). Comparative outcome studies of psychotherapy: Methodological issues and strategies. *Journal of Consulting and Clinical Psychology, 54,* 95–105.

Keith-Spiegel, P. (1994). The 1992 ethics code: Boon or bane. *Professional Psychology: Research and Practice, 25,* 315–316.

Keyes, C. L. M., & Haidt, J. (Eds.). (2003). *Flourishing: Positive psychology and the life well-lived.* Washington, DC: American Psychological Association.

Keyes, C. L. M., & Ryff, C. D. (1998). Generativity in adult lives: Social structural contours and quality of life consequences. In D. P. McAdams & E. de St. Aubin (Eds.), *Generativity and adult development: How and why we care for the next generation* (pp. 227–263). Washington, DC: American Psychological Association.

King, L. A. (1996). Who is regulating what and why? Motivational context of self-regulation. *Psychological Inquiry, 7,* 57–60.

King, L. A., & Napa, C. K. (1998). What makes a life good? *Journal of Personality and Social Psychology, 75,* 156–165.

Kitayama, S., Markus, H. R., & Kurokawa, M. (2000). Culture, emotion, and well-being: Good feelings in Japan and the United States. *Cognition and Emotion, 14,* 93–124.

Kitchener, K. S. (1984). Intuition, critical evaluation and ethics principles: The foundation for ethical decisions in counseling psychology. *The Counseling Psychologist, 12,* 43–55.

Kitchener, K. S. (1986). The reflective judgment model: Characteristics, evidence, and measurement. In R. A. Mines & K. S. Kitchener (Eds.), *Adult cognitive development* (pp. 79–91). New York: Praeger Publishers.

Kitchener, K. S. (1996). Professional codes of ethics and ongoing moral problems in psychology. In W. O'Donohue & R. F. Kitchener (Eds.), *The philosophy of psychology* (pp. 361–370). London: Sage.

Kitchener, K. S. (1999). *The foundations of ethical practice, research, and teaching in psychology.* Mahwah, NJ: Erlbaum.

Kitchener, K. S. (2000). *The foundations of ethical practice in psychology.* Mahwah, NJ: Erlbaum.

Kitchener, K. S., & King, P. M. (1990). The reflective judgment model: Ten years of research. In M. L. Commons, C. Armon, L. Kohlberg, F. A. Richards, T. A. Grotzer, & J. D. Sinnott (Eds.), *Adult development: Vol. 2. Models and methods in the study of adolescent and adult thought* (pp. 63–78). New York: Praeger Publishers.

Kitchener, K. S., King, P. M., Wood, P. K., & Davidson, M. L. (1989). Sequentiality and consistency in the development of reflective judgment: A six-year longitudinal study. *Journal of Applied Developmental Psychology, 10,* 73–95.

Klerman, G. L., & Weissman, M. M. (1989). Increasing rates of depression. *Journal of the American Medical Association, 261,* 2229–2235.

Knapp, S., & VandeCreek, L. (2003). An overview of the major changes in the 2002 APA Ethics Code. *Professional Psychology: Research and Practice, 34,* 301–308.

Kochanska, G., Padavich, D. L., & Koenig, A. L. (1996). Children's narratives about hypothetical moral dilemmas and objective measures of their conscience:

Mutual relations and socialization antecedents. *Child Development, 67,* 1420–1436.

Kohlberg, L. (1994). Stage and sequence: The cognitive-developmental approach to socialization. In B. Puka (Ed.), *Moral development: A compendium* (Vol. 1, pp. 1–134). New York: Garland Publishing.

Koocher, G. P. (1994). The commerce of professional psychology and the new Ethics Code. *Professional Psychology: Research and Practice, 25,* 355–361.

Koocher, G. P., & Keith-Spiegel, P. C. (1998). *Ethics in psychology: Professional standards and cases.* New York: Oxford University Press.

Kramer, D. A. (2000). Wisdom as a classical source of human strength: Conceptualization and empirical inquiry. *Journal of Social and Clinical Psychology, 19,* 83–101.

Lambert, M. J., Bergin, A. E., & Garfield, S. L. (2004). Introduction and historical overview. In M. J. Lambert (Ed.), *Bergin and Garfield's handbook of psychotherapy and behavior change* (5th ed., pp. 3–15). New York: Wiley.

Lambert, M. J., & Ogles, B. M. (2004). The efficacy and effectiveness of psychotherapy. In M. J. Lambert (Ed.), *Bergin and Garfield's handbook of psychotherapy and behavior change* (5th ed., pp. 139–193). New York: Wiley.

Lasch, C. (1978). *The culture of narcissism.* New York: Norton.

Latané, B., & Darley, J. M. (1970). *The unresponsive bystander: Why doesn't he help?* New York: Appleton-Century-Crofts.

Leahey, T. H. (2000). *A history of modern psychology* (3rd ed.). Englewood Cliffs, NJ: Prentice Hall.

Lewinsohn, P. M., Rohde, P., Seeley, J. R., & Fischer, S. A. (1993). Age-cohort changes in the lifetime occurrence of depression and other mental disorders. *Journal of Abnormal Psychology, 102,* 10–120.

Luborsky, L., McClellan, A. T., Woody, G. E., O'Brien, C. P., & Auerbach, A. (1985). Therapist success and its determinants. *Archives of General Psychiatry, 42,* 602–611.

MacIntyre, A. (1981). *After virtue: A study in moral theory.* Notre Dame, IN: University of Notre Dame Press.

MacIntyre, A. (1998, August). *Moral pluralism without moral relativism.* Paper delivered at the Twentieth World Congress of Philosophy, Boston.

MacIntyre, A. (1999). *Dependent rational animals: Why human beings need the virtues.* Chicago: Open Court.

Mackworth, N. H. (1965). Originality. *American Psychologist, 20,* 51–66.

Malik, M. L., & Beutler, L. E. (2002). The emergence of dissatisfaction with the DSM. In L. E. Beutler & M. L. Malik (Eds.), *Rethinking the DSM: A psychological perspective* (pp. 3–15). Washington, DC: American Psychological Association.

Markman, H. J., Resnick, M. J., Floyd, F. J., Stanley, S. M., & Clements, M. (1993). Preventing marital distress through communication and conflict management training: A four- and five-year follow-up. *Journal of Consulting and Clinical Psychology, 61,* 70–77.

Maslow, A. H. (1971). *The farther reaches of human nature*. Oxford, England: Viking.

McAdams, D. P., de St. Aubin, E., & Logan, R. L. (1993). Generativity among young, midlife, and older adults. *Psychology and Aging, 8*, 221–230.

McCrae, R. R., & John, O. P. (1992). An introduction to the five-factor model and its applications. *Journal of Personality, 60*, 175–215.

McCullough, M. E., Emmons, R. A., & Tsang, J.-A. (2002). The grateful disposition: A conceptual and empirical topography. *Journal of Personality and Social Psychology, 82*, 112–127.

McCullough, M. E., Rachal, K. C., Sandage, S. J., Worthington, E. L., Jr., Brown, S. W., & Hight, T. L. (1998). Interpersonal forgiving in close relationships: II. Theoretical elaboration and measurement. *Journal of Personality and Social Psychology, 75*, 1586–1603.

McCullough, M. E., & Snyder, C. R. (2000). Classical sources of human strength: Revisiting an old home and building a new one. *Journal of Social and Clinical Psychology, 19*, 1–10.

McCullough, M. E., & Worthington, E. L., Jr. (1995). Promoting forgiveness: A comparison of two brief psychoeducational interventions with a waiting list control. *Counseling and Values, 40*, 50–68.

McCullough, M. E., Worthington, E. L., Jr., & Rachal, K. C. (1997). Interpersonal forgiving in close relationships. *Journal of Personality and Social Psychology, 73*, 321–336.

McDowell, J. (1996). Deliberation and moral development in Aristotle's ethics. In S. Engstrom & J. Whiting (Eds.), *Aristotle, Kant, and the stoics: Rethinking happiness and duty* (pp. 19–35). Cambridge, England: Cambridge University Press.

McGregor, I., & Little, B. R. (1998). Personal projects, happiness, and meaning: On doing well and being yourself. *Journal of Personality and Social Psychology, 74*, 494–512.

Meara, N. M., & Day, J. D. (2003). Possibilities and challenges for academic psychology: Uncertain science, interpretative conversation, and virtuous community. *American Behavioral Scientist, 47*, 459–478.

Meara, N. M., Schmidt, L. D., & Day, J. D. (1996). Principles and virtues: A foundation for ethical decisions, policies, and character. *The Counseling Psychologist, 24*, 4–77.

Merton, R. K. (1973). *The sociology of science: Theoretical and empirical investigations* (N. W. Storer, Ed.). Chicago: University of Chicago Press.

Milgram, S., Sabini, J., & Silver, M. (1992). *The individual in a social world: Essays and experiments* (2nd ed.). New York: McGraw-Hill.

Mills, J., & Clark, M. S. (2001). Viewing close romantic relationships as communal relationships: Implications for maintenance and enhancement. In J. Harvey & A. Wenzel (Eds.), *Close romantic relationships: Maintenance and enhancement* (pp. 13–25). Mahwah, NJ: Erlbaum.

Morawski, J. G. (1988). *The rise of experimentation in American psychology*. New Haven, CT: Yale University Press.

Murray, S. L., Holmes, J. G., & Griffin, D. W. (1996). The benefits of positive illusions: Idealization and the construction of satisfaction in close relationships. *Journal of Personality and Social Psychology, 70*, 79–98.

Nagy, T. F. (2000). *Ethics in plain English: An illustrative casebook for psychologists*. Washington, DC: American Psychological Association.

Nicholas, M. W. (1994). *The mystery of goodness and the positive moral consequences of psychotherapy*. New York: Norton.

Nicholson, I. A. M. (1998). Gordon Allport, character, and the "culture of personality," 1897–1937. *History of Psychology, 1*, 52–68.

Niedenthal, P. M., Tangney, J. P., & Gavansky, I. (1994). "If only I weren't" versus "If only I hadn't": Distinguishing shame and guilt in counterfactual thinking. *Journal of Personality and Social Psychology, 67*, 584–595.

Norcross, J. C., Karg, R. S., & Prochaska, J. O. (1997). Clinical psychologists in the '90s: Part I. *The Clinical Psychologist, 50*(2), 4–9.

Nucci, L., & Turiel, E. (1993). God's word, religious rules, and their relation to Christian and Jewish children's concepts of morality. *Child Development, 64*, 1475–1491.

Nussbaum, M. C. (1986). *The fragility of goodness: Luck and ethics in Greek tragedy and philosophy*. Cambridge, England: Cambridge University Press.

Oakley, J., & Cocking, D. (2001). *Virtue ethics and professional roles*. Cambridge, England: Cambridge University Press.

Oishi, S., Diener, E., Suh, E., & Lucas, R. E. (1999). Value as a moderator in subjective well-being. *Journal of Personality, 67*, 157–184.

Omoto, A. M., & Snyder, M. (1995). Sustained helping without obligation: Motivation, longevity of service, and perceived attitude change among AIDS volunteers. *Journal of Personality and Social Psychology, 68*, 671–686.

Orlinsky, D. E., & Howard, K. I. (1980). Gender and psychotherapeutic outcome. In A. M. Brodsky & R. T. Hare-Mustin (Eds.), *Women and psychotherapy* (pp. 3–34). New York: Guilford Press.

Penner, L., & Finkelstein, M. A. (1998). Dispositional and structural determinants of volunteerism. *Journal of Personality and Social Psychology, 74*, 525–537.

Perrin, G. I., & Sales, B. D. (1994). Forensic standards in the American Psychological Association's new Ethics Code. *Professional Psychology: Research and Practice, 25*, 376–381.

Peterson, C., & Chang, E. C. (2003). Optimism and flourishing. In C. L. M. Keyes & J. Haidt (Eds.), *Flourishing: Positive psychology and the life well-lived* (pp. 55–79). Washington, DC: American Psychological Association.

Peterson, C., & Seligman, M. E. P. (2004). *Character strengths and virtues: A handbook and classification*. Washington, DC: American Psychological Association.

Pojman, L. P. (1990). *Ethics: Discovering right and wrong*. Belmont, CA: Wadsworth.

Pope, K. S., & Vasquez, M. J. T. (1998). *Ethics in psychotherapy and counseling: A practical guide for psychologists* (2nd ed.). San Francisco: Jossey-Bass.

Powers, W. T. (1973). *Behavior: The control of perception*. Chicago: Aldine.

Prilleltensky, I. (1997). Values, assumptions, and practices: Assessing the moral implications of psychological discourse and action. *American Psychologist, 5,* 517–535.

Privelte, G. (2001). Defining moments of self-actualization: Peak performance and peak experience. In K. J. Schneider, J. F. T. Bugental, & J. F. Pierson (Eds.), *The handbook of humanistic psychology* (pp. 161–180). Thousand Oaks, CA: Sage.

Prochaska, J. O., & Norcross, J. C. (2002). *Systems of psychotherapy: A transtheoretical analysis* (5th ed.). Belmont, CA: Wadsworth/Thomson Learning.

Putnam, R. D. (2000). *Bowling alone: The collapse and revival of American community*. New York: Simon & Schuster.

Rawls, J. (1971). *A theory of justice*. Cambridge, MA: Harvard University Press.

Rest, J. R. (1983). Morality. In J. Flavell & E. Markham (Eds.), *Manual of child psychology: Vol. 4. Cognitive development*. New York: Wiley.

Rest, J. R. (1994). Background: Theory and research. In J. R. Rest & D. Narvaez (Eds.), *Moral development in the professions: Psychology and applied ethics*. Hillsdale, NJ: Erlbaum.

Richardson, F. C. (2003). Virtue ethics, dialogue, and "reverence." *American Behavioral Scientist, 47,* 442–458.

Richardson, F. C., & Fowers, B. J. (1998). Interpretive social science: An overview. *American Behavioral Scientist, 41,* 465–495.

Richardson, F. C., Fowers, B. J., & Guignon, C. (1999). *Re-envisioning psychology: Moral dimensions of theory and practice*. San Francisco: Jossey-Bass.

Rieff, P. (1966). *The triumph of the therapeutic*. New York: Harper & Row.

Ross, L., & Nisbett, R. E. (1991). *The person and the situation*. Philadephia: Temple University Press.

Roth, A., & Fonagy, P. (1996). *What works for whom? A critical review of psychotherapy research*. New York: Guilford Press.

Rusbult, C. E., & Van Lange, P. A. M. (1996). Interdependence processes. In E. T. Higgins & A. W. Kruglanski (Eds.), *Social psychology: Handbook of basic principles* (pp. 564–596). New York: Guilford Press.

Rusbult, C. E., Verette, J., Whitney, G. A., Slovik, L. F., & Lipkus, I. (1991). Accommodation processes in close relationships: Theory and preliminary empirical evidence. *Journal of Personality and Social Psychology, 60,* 53–78.

Rushton, J.-P. (1984). The altruistic personality. In E. Straub, D. BarTal, J. Karylowski, & J. Reykowski (Eds.), *Development and maintenance of prosocial behavior* (pp. 271–290). New York: Praeger Publishers.

Ryan, R. M., Chirkov, V. I., Little, T. D, Sheldon, K. M., Timoshina, E., & Deci, E. L. (1999). The American dream in Russia: Extrinsic aspirations and well-being in two cultures. *Personality and Social Psychology Bulletin, 25,* 1509–1524.

Ryan, R. M., & Deci, E. L. (2000). Self-determination theory and the facilitation of intrinsic motivation, social development, and well-being. *American Psychologist, 55,* 68–78.

Sampson, E. E. (1977). Psychology and the American ideal. *Journal of Personality and Social Psychology, 35,* 767–782.

Sampson, E. E. (1985). The decentralization of identity: Toward a revised concept of personal and social order. *American Psychologist, 40,* 1203–1211.

Sandage, S. J., & Hill, P. C. (2001). The virtues of positive psychology: The rapprochement and challenges of an affirmative postmodern perspective. *Journal for the Theory of Social Behaviour, 31,* 241–260.

Sandel, M. J. (1996). *Democracy's discontent.* Cambridge, MA: Harvard University Press.

Sandel, M. J. (1998). *Liberalism and the limits of justice* (2nd ed.). Cambridge, England: Cambridge University Press.

Sarason, S. B. (1981). *Psychology misdirected.* New York: Free Press.

Sarason, S. B. (1986). And what is the public interest? *American Psychologist, 41,* 899–905.

Schoen, D. A. (1983). *The reflective practitioner: How professionals think in action.* New York: Basic Books.

Seal, D. W., Agostinelli, G., & Hannett, C. A. (1994). Extradyadic romantic involvement: Moderating effects of sociosexuality and gender. *Sex Roles, 31,* 1–22.

Seligman, M. E. P., & Csikszentmihalyi, M. (2000). Positive psychology: An introduction. *American Psychologist, 55,* 5–14.

Selznick, P. (1992). *The moral commonwealth.* Berkeley: University of California Press.

Shah, J. (2003a). Automatic for the people: How representations of significant others implicitly affect goal pursuit. *Journal of Personality and Social Psychology, 84,* 661–681.

Shah, J. (2003b). The motivational looking glass: How significant others implicitly affect goal appraisals. *Journal of Personality and Social Psychology, 85,* 424–439.

Sheldon, K. M., & Kasser, T. (1995). Coherence and congruence: Two aspects of personality integration. *Journal of Personality and Social Psychology, 68,* 531–543.

Sheldon, K. M., & Kasser, T. (1998). Pursuing personal goals: Skills enable progress, but not all progress is beneficial. *Personality and Social Psychology Bulletin, 24,* 1319–1331.

Sheldon, K. M., & King, L. (2001). Why positive psychology is necessary. *American Psychologist, 56,* 216–217.

Sherman, N. (1989). *The fabric of character: Aristotle's theory of virtue.* Oxford, England: Oxford University Press.

Sieber, J. E. (1994). Will the new code help researchers to be more ethical? *Professional Psychology: Research and Practice, 25,* 369–375.

Simpson, J. A., & Gangestad, S. W. (1991). Individual differences in sociosexuality: Evidence for convergent and discriminate validity. *Journal of Personality and Social Psychology, 60,* 870–883.

Simpson, J. A., & Gangestad, S. W. (1992). Sociosexuality and romantic partner choice. *Journal of Personality, 60,* 31–51.

Snyder, C. R. (2000). The past and possible futures of hope. *Journal of Social and Clinical Psychology, 19,* 11–28.

Spence, J. (1985). Achievement American style: The rewards and costs of individualism. *American Psychologist, 40,* 1285–1295.

Stanley, S. M., Blumberg, S. L., & Markman, H. J. (1999). Helping couples fight for their marriages: The PREP approach. In R. Berger & H. M. Therese (Eds.), *Preventive approaches in couples therapy* (pp. 279–303). Philadelphia: Brunner/Mazel.

Stanley, S. M., Lobitz, W. C., & Dickson, F. C. (1999). Using what we know: Commitment and cognitions in marital therapy. In W. Jones & J. Adams (Eds.), *Handbook of interpersonal commitment and relationship stability* (pp. 411–424). New York: Plenum Press.

Staudinger, U. M., & Baltes, P. B. (1996). Interactive minds: A facilitative setting for wisdom-related performance? *Journal of Personality and Social Psychology, 71,* 746–762.

Staudinger, U. M., Lopez, D. F., & Baltes, P. B. (1997). The psychometric location of wisdom-related performance: Intelligence, personality, and more? *Personality and Social Psychology Bulletin, 23,* 1200–1214.

Staudinger, U. M., Maciel, A. G., Smith, J., & Baltes, P. B. (1998). What predicts wisdom-related performance? A first look at personality, intelligence, and facilitative experiential contexts. *European Journal of Personality, 12*(1), 1–17.

Staudinger, U. M., Smith, J., & Baltes, P. B. (1992). Wisdom-related knowledge in a life review task: Age differences and the role of professional specialization. *Psychology and Aging, 7,* 271–281.

Sternberg, R. J. (1985). Implicit theories of intelligence, creativity, and wisdom. *Journal of Personality and Social Psychology, 49,* 607–627.

Sternberg, R. J. (1990). Wisdom and its relations to intelligence and creativity. In R. J. Sternberg (Ed.), *Wisdom: Its nature, origins, and development* (pp. 142–159). Cambridge, England: Cambridge University Press.

Sternberg, R. J. (1998). A balance theory of wisdom. *Review of General Psychology, 2,* 347–365.

Sternberg, R. J., Forsythe, G. B., Hediund, J., Horvath, J. A., Wagner, R. K., Williams, W. M., et al. (2000). *Practical intelligence in everyday life.* Cambridge, England: Cambridge University Press.

Stroebe, M., Gergen, M. M., Gergen, K. J., & Stroebe, W. (1992). Broken hearts or broken bonds: Love and death in historical perspective. *American Psychologist, 47,* 1205–1212.

Stroebe, W., & Stroebe, M. (1996). The social psychology of social support. In E. T. Higgins & A. W. Kruglanski (Eds.), *Social psychology: Handbook of basic principles* (pp. 597–621). New York: Guilford Press.

Strupp, H. H. (1981). Toward refinement of time-limited dynamic psychotherapy. In S. Budman (Ed.), *Forms of brief therapy* (pp. 219–241). New York: Guilford Press.

Strupp, H. H., & Anderson, T. (1997). On the limitations of therapy manuals. *Clinical Psychology: Science and Practice, 4*(1), 76–82.

Sue, D. W., Arredondo, P., & McDavis, R. J. (1992). Multicultural counseling competencies and standards: A call to the profession. *Journal of Counseling and Development, 70,* 477–486.

Sullivan, W. M. (1986). *Restructuring public philosophy.* Berkeley: University of California Press.

Susman, W. I. (1984). *Culture as history.* New York: Pantheon Books.

Tangney, J. P. (1991). Moral affect: The good, the bad, and the ugly. *Journal of Personality and Social Psychology, 61,* 598–607.

Tangney, J. P. (1998). How does guilt differ from shame? In N. J. Bybee (Ed.), *Guilt in children* (pp. 1–17). San Diego, CA: Academic Press.

Tangney, J. P., Miller, R. S., Flicker, L., & Barlow, D. H. (1996). Are shame, guilt, and embarrassment distinct emotions? *Journal of Personality and Social Psychology, 75,* 256–268.

Tangney, J. P., Wagner, P., & Gramzow, R. (1992). Proneness to shame, proneness to guilt, and psychopathology. *Journal of Abnormal Psychology, 101,* 469–478.

Task Force on the Promotion and Dissemination of Psychological Procedures. (1995). Training in and dissemination of empirically validated psychological treatments: Report and recommendations. *The Clinical Psychologist, 48,* 3–23.

Taylor, C. (1985). *Philosophy and the human sciences: Philosophical papers* (Vol. 2). Cambridge, England: Cambridge University Press.

Taylor, C. (1989). *Sources of the self.* Cambridge, MA: Harvard University Press.

Taylor, S. E., & Gollwitzer, P. M. (1995). Effects of mindset on positive illusions. *Journal of Personality and Social Psychology, 69,* 213–226.

Tjeltveit, A. C. (1999). *Ethics and values in psychotherapy.* London: Routledge.

Tjeltveit, A. C. (2003). Implicit virtues, divergent goods, multiple communities: Explicitly addressing virtues in the behavioral sciences. *American Behavioral Scientist, 47,* 395–414.

Triandis, H. C. (1995). *Individualism and collectivism.* Boulder, CO: Westview Press.

Twenge, J. M. (2000). The age of anxiety? Birth cohort change in anxiety and neuroticism, 1952–1993. *Journal of Personality and Social Psychology, 79,* 1007–1021.

Tyler, T. R. (1997). The psychology of legitimacy: A relational perspective on voluntary deference to authorities. *Personality and Social Psychology Review, 1,* 323–345.

Udy, S. H. (1959). *Organization of work: A comparative analysis of production among nonindustrial peoples*. New Haven, CT: Human Relations Area Files Press.

Van Lange, P. A. M., Rusbult, C. E., Drigotas, S. M., Arriaga, X. B., Witcher, B. S., & Cox, C. L. (1997). Willingness to sacrifice in close relationships. *Journal of Personality and Social Psychology, 72*, 1373–1395.

Vasquez, M. J. T. (1994). Implications of the 1992 ethics code for the practice of individual psychotherapy. *Professional Psychology: Research and Practice, 25*, 321–328.

Waite, L. J., & Gallagher, M. (2000). *The case for marriage: Why married people are happier, healthier, and better off financially*. New York: Doubleday.

Walker, L. J., & Pitts, R. C. (1998). Naturalistic conceptions of moral maturity. *Developmental Psychology, 34*, 403–419.

Wertheimer, M. (1959). *Productive thinking, enlarged edition* (M. Wertheimer, Ed.). New York: Harper & Row.

Wiggins, D. (1980). Deliberation and practical reason. In A. O. Rorty (Ed.), *Essays on Aristotle's ethics* (pp. 221–240). Berkeley: University of California Press.

Williamson, G. M., & Clark, M. S. (1989). Providing help and desired relationship type as determinants of changes in moods and self-evaluations. *Journal of Personality and Social Psychology, 56*, 722–734.

Williamson, G. M., & Clark, M. S. (1992). Impact of desired relationship type on affective reactions to choosing and being required to help. *Personality and Social Psychology Bulletin, 18*, 10–18.

Williamson, G. M., Clark, M. S., Pegalis, L. J., & Behan, A. (1996). Affective consequences of refusing to help in communal and exchange relationships. *Personality and Social Psychology Bulletin, 22*, 34–47.

Wink, P., & Helson, R. (1997). Practical and transcendent wisdom: Their nature and some longitudinal findings. *Journal of Adult Development, 4*, 1–15.

Wolfe, A. (1989). *Whose keeper? Social science and moral obligation*. Berkeley: University of California Press.

Wolfe, A. (2001). *Moral freedom: The search for virtue in a world of choice*. New York: Norton.

Woodruff, P. (2001). *Reverence: Renewing a forgotten virtue*. Oxford, England: Oxford University Press.

Woolfolk, R. L. (1998). *The cure of souls: Science, values, and psychotherapy*. San Francisco: Jossey-Bass.

Zaleski, Z. (1988). Close relationships and acting for self-set goals. *European Journal of Social Psychology, 18*, 191–194.

Zeldow, P. B., Daugherty, S. R., & McAdams, D. P. (1988). Intimacy, power, and psychological well-being in medical students. *Journal of Nervous and Mental Disease, 76*, 182–187.

Zuckerman, H. (1977). *Scientific elite: Nobel laureates in the United States*. New York: Free Press.

INDEX

ABOUT THE AUTHOR

Blaine J. Fowers received his PhD from the University of Texas at Austin in 1987. Dr. Fowers is a professor and director of training for the counseling psychology program at the University of Miami. His primary scholarly interest is in the moral dimension of psychology in both research and practice. His current emphasis is on the contributions of virtue ethics to our understanding of psychological practices, including research and clinical work. His empirical work has been devoted to clarifying the role of cultural values in marriage and the family, including positive illusions about marriage and parenting. He is the author of *Beyond the Myth of Marital Happiness* (2000) and a coauthor of *Re-Envisioning Psychology* (1999). Dr. Fowers is a licensed psychologist and maintains a private practice.